Kant and
the Problem of
Metaphysics

Studies in Continental Thought

Martin Heidegger

Kant and
the Problem of
Metaphysics

Fifth Edition, Enlarged

TRANSLATED BY

Richard Taft

Indiana University Press

BLOOMINGTON AND INDIANAPOLIS

Preparation of this book was aided by grants from the Program for Translations of the National Endowment for the Humanities, an independent federal agency, and from Inter Nationes.

Published in German as *Kant und das Problem der Metaphysik,* Fünfte, vermehrte Auflage, 1991 © 1973 by Vittorio Klostermann, Frankfurt am Main.

This book is a publication of

Indiana University Press
601 North Morton Street
Bloomington, Indiana 47404-3797 USA

http://iupress.indiana.edu

Telephone orders 800-842-6796
Fax orders 812-855-7931
Orders by e-mail iuporder@indiana.edu

© 1990, 1997 by Indiana University Press

The paper used in this publication meets the minimum requirements of American National Standard for Information Sciences—Permanence of Paper for Printed Library Materials, ANSI Z39.48-1984.

Manufactured in the United States of America

Library of Congress Cataloging-in-Publication Data

Heidegger, Martin 1889–1976
[Kant und das Problem der Metaphysik. English]
Kant and the problem of metaphysics / Martin Heidegger ; translated by Richard Taft. — 5th ed. enlarged.
    p. cm. — (Studies in Continental thought)
Includes bibliographical references.
ISBN 0-253-33276-1 (alk. paper). —
ISBN 0-253-21067-4 (pbk. : alk. paper)
1. Kant, Immanuel, 1724–1804—Contributions in metaphysics. 2. Metaphysics. I. Title.
II. Series.
B2799.M5F5513   1997
110'.92—dc21   96-48023

3 4 5 6 7 8 08 07 06 05 04

Contents

The Laying of the Ground for Metaphysics in a Retrieval   143–173

A. THE LAYING OF THE GROUND FOR METAPHYSICS IN ANTHROPOLOGY   144

§36. The Previously Laid Ground and the Outcome of the Kantian
      Laying of the Ground for Metaphysics   144
§37. The Idea of a Philosophical Anthropology   146
§38. The Question Concerning the Human Essence and the Authentic
      Result of the Kantian Ground-Laying   150

B. THE PROBLEM OF FINITUDE IN HUMAN BEINGS AND THE
   METAPHYSICS OF DASEIN   153

§39. The Problem of a Possible Determination of Finitude
      in Human Beings   153
§40. The Original Working-Out of the Question of Being as
      the Way to the Problem of Finitude in Human Beings   155
§41. The Understanding of Being and Dasein in Human Beings   158

C. THE METAPHYSICS OF DASEIN AS FUNDAMENTAL ONTOLOGY   162

§42. The Idea of a Fundamental Ontology   162
§43. The Inception and the Course of Fundamental Ontology   164
§44. The Goal of Fundamental Ontology   167
§45. The Idea of Fundamental Ontology and the
      Critique of Pure Reason   170

APPENDICES
I.   NOTES ON THE KANTBOOK   175
II.   ERNST CASSIRER: PHILOSOPHY OF SYMBOLIC FORMS. PART TWO:
      MYTHICAL THOUGHT. BERLIN, 1925   180
III. DAVOS LECTURES: KANT'S CRITIQUE OF PURE REASON AND THE TASK OF
      A LAYING OF THE GROUND FOR METAPHYSICS   191
IV.   DAVOS DISPUTATION BETWEEN ERNST CASSIRER AND MARTIN HEIDEGGER 193
V.   ON ODEBRECHT'S AND CASSIRER'S CRITIQUES OF THE KANTBOOK   208
VI.   ON THE HISTORY OF THE PHILOSOPHICAL CHAIR SINCE 1866   213
REFERENCES FOR APPENDICES   218

                  EDITOR'S AFTERWORD   219
                  TRANSLATOR'S NOTES   223

TRANSLATOR'S INTRODUCTION TO THE FIFTH EDITION

This volume reproduces my previous translation of *Kant and the Problem of Metaphysics* (which was based on the fourth edition of Heidegger's German text), expanded to include the new materials added when the book was published in German as volume 3 of Heidegger's collected works (*Gesamtausgabe*) in 1991, and simultaneously—independently of the collected works—as an expanded fifth edition. As has been customary with the republication in the Gesamtausgabe of each of Heidegger's works that was originally published during his lifetime, the Gesamtausgabe edition (and in this case the identical fifth edition) has been expanded to include marginal notations that Heidegger made in his personal copy of the book. The Afterword by the German editor, which appears at the end of this volume, explains the provenance of these marginalia; they appear in this volume as footnotes designated by letters, just as in the German edition.

In addition to the marginalia, this edition of the Kantbook has been expanded to include four new appendices, three of which appear here in English for the first time. Again, the Afterword by the German editor describes the rationale for including these texts, as well as information about their original German publication.

As the reader might expect, with so many voices at work in a single book (Heidegger's original published text, my translator's notes to that text, Heidegger's subsequent marginal notes, comments or corrections by the German editor, and, finally, comments or corrections by the translator to those new marginalia), the conventions for rendering the various levels of commentary might be a bit confusing. In the interest of clarity, I have adopted the following conventions:

The main body of the text appears substantially as it did in the previous edition of my translation, including Heidegger's text, Heidegger's footnotes to that text designated by numbers, and my Translator's Notes collected at the back of the volume as endnotes, designated by numbers in brackets, [ ]. I have made a few corrections to my original translation where I have found or been notified of mistakes, and I have revised several of my original translator's endnotes to reflect changes made to the German text. These latter revisions are generally indicated as such in the body of the note. In the main body of the text, and in Heidegger's original notes and the marginalia now added, I have kept the earlier convention of putting German words that are difficult to render, or that have multiple shades of meaning, in italics in square brackets immediately following their occurrence in the translation.

In addition, Heidegger's marginalia have been inserted at the foot of the page where they occur, below any footnotes from the original published book. These marginalia are designated by letters within the body of the text. Occasionally, within these marginal notes, the German editor has injected a phrase or comment; these are enclosed in italic brackets, *[ ]*. Any translator's comments I have added to these marginalia are in square brackets, [ ], and are labeled "tr." In addition, the abbreviations WS and SS used in footnotes refer to the Winter Semester and Summer Semester of the academic year, usually to Heidegger's lectures or courses during those semesters. The abbreviation GA refers to the Gesamtausgabe, the collected edition of Heidegger's works being published by Vittorio Klostermann Verlag, Frankfurt am Main. The abbreviation *CPR* refers to Kant's *Critique of Pure Reason*, tr. Norman Kemp Smith (London: Macmillan, 1929; 12th impression, 1973).

I would like to acknowledge Peter Warnek of Vanderbilt University for his assistance in translating Appendix II, Heidegger's review of Ernst Cassirer's *Philosophy of Symbolic Forms*, volume 2: *Mythical Thought*, for this volume. This essay appeared previously in English in *The Piety of Thinking: Essays by Martin Heidegger*, translation, notes, and commentary by J. G. Hart and J. C. Maraldo (Bloomington: Indiana University Press, 1976), pp. 32–45. However, conventions for rendering Heidegger's texts in English have evolved since that time, necessitating a reworking of that translation. My profound thanks to Mr. Warnek for his excellent retranslation of this essay, accomplished in a short time with little advance notice.

The fragmentary style of a number of the marginal notes, as well as of Appendices I and V, reflects the character of the German original.

Richard Taft

TRANSLATOR'S INTRODUCTION TO THE FOURTH EDITION

Martin Heidegger's well-known and controversial book *Kant and the Problem of Metaphysics* was first published in German in 1929 with subsequent editions appearing in 1950, 1965, and 1973. Although the second and third editions are essentially reproductions of the first, in the fourth and final edition Heidegger added some very significant material to the book in addition to making several revisions to the original text. This translation is based on the definitive fourth edition, although it does take account of the variations in the earlier editions as appropriate.

Kant and the Problem of Metaphysics is significant both as a major contribution to twentieth-century Kant scholarship and as a pivotal work in Heidegger's own development in the period following the publication of his major work, *Being and Time*, in 1927. As an interpretation of Kant, Heidegger's book has attracted a great deal of attention as well as scholarly controversy since its original publication in 1929. This particular interpretation of Kant was worked out in the years immediately following the appearance of *Being and Time*, and is grounded as well in a lecture course from 1927/28 (now published as volume 25 of Heidegger's *Gesamtausgabe* and being translated by Parvis Emad and Kenneth Maly for this publisher), in which he attempted to come to terms with a connection that he saw between Kant's chapter on the Schematism and the problem of time.

Two other sources for this book were a lecture delivered in Riga in September 1928 and, most importantly, a series of lectures that Heidegger delivered at the Davos *Hochschule* in March 1929. The Davos lecture series was particularly important because it brought together Heidegger and Ernst Cassirer, a noted authority on Kant and the editor of the modern edition of Kant's collected works. During this course Heidegger and Cassirer delivered a total of seven lectures (four by Cassirer, three by Heidegger), and they debated some of the more controversial aspects of Heidegger's Kant interpretation (e.g., his emphasis on the transcendental power of imagination, or his attempt to link his reading of Kant to the project of a fundamental ontology that he proposed in *Being and Time*). In the preface to the fourth edition of *Kant and the Problem of Metaphysics*, Heidegger points out the importance of this lecture series for writing that book (he began to write it immediately after the Davos course), and he includes as appendices to that edition a summary he had made of his three lectures and a report of his disputation with Cassirer in connection with the lectures each delivered. The fine points of Kant scholarship aired during this disputation form a vital part of the context of this book.

Over the years, *Kant and the Problem of Metaphysics* has emerged as the cornerstone of an important and original (if controversial) direction in Kant interpretation that continues to assert an influence today.

From the standpoint of the development of Heidegger's own thought as well, this book is of pivotal importance because it takes up and extends a number of themes suggested in *Being and Time*, in particular the problem of how Heidegger proposed to enact his "destruction" of the metaphysical tradition and of what role his reading of Kant would play in that project. It is this problematic which accounts for what some have called the "violence" of Heidegger's interpretation. Only within the last few years, however, beginning with the publication in German of Heidegger's early lecture courses, have we really been able to see how thoroughly the problematic of *Kant and the Problem of Metaphysics* was embedded in the development of Heidegger's thought. We can now see, for example, how Heidegger was struggling to distance his thought from the prevailing neo-Kantian tendency in German philosophical circles at this time, and how one aspect of this distancing involved his highly original interpretation of Kant (again, the Davos disputation with Cassirer is illuminating here). This newly enriched context requires that we understand the present book in terms of its intimate relationship to the various lecture courses Heidegger gave in the late 1920s, the most important of which are only now appearing in English for the first time.

Kant and the Problem of Metaphysics was previously translated by James S. Churchill (Indiana University Press, 1962), but that edition has been out of print for over ten years. Because it was done in 1962, before any real body of Heidegger's works in English existed, Churchill's translation occasionally falls into awkward and misleading renderings of the original that make it hard to use today. Additionally, as the date suggests, Churchill based his translation on the second edition of Heidegger's book and hence it contains none of the Davos materials. In spite of its flaws, however, I made frequent references to Churchill's translation in preparing the present volume and I am indebted to it in many places.

The present translation preserves the language and grammatical constructions used by Heidegger to the greatest extent possible. The paragraphing, footnotes, and footnote numbering of the original text have been retained. To facilitate comparison, the pagination of the German edition appears in square brackets in the running heads of this translation.

The technical devices used in the text have been kept to a minimum. Heidegger's footnotes are consecutively numbered throughout the text and appear at the bottom of each page. The translation also includes a set of translator's notes, which appear at the end of the text. For ease of identification, the translator's notes are consecutively numbered within each major section, and note numbers are contained in square brackets. Explanatory interpolations and supplemental information added by the translator to the text and footnotes also appear within brackets. In the few instances where Heidegger himself amended the text, his words or phrases are contained within braces. Any deviations from these conventions are clarified in the notes.

Like any scholarly project, this translation has benefited in many ways from contacts I had with various people during the course of my work. Above all I would like to thank my wife and daughters for their patience, sorely tried at times, during the time it took to finish the translation. I would also particularly like to thank Joseph Fell for his patient and wise counsel with some particularly nagging problems early on and John Sallis for his encouragement and help in my getting involved with this project in the first place. I would also like to thank Charles Sherover, whose detailed and insightful review of the finished manuscript allowed me to correct a number of mistakes. Professor Sherover also has indelibly etched in my mind, and I hope in this translation, the important Kantian distinction between *Gegenstand* and *Objekt*. Finally I would like to thank Professor O. Pöggeler, Professor C. F. Gethmann, and Dr. F. Hogemann for their help in clarifying several points of fact for me.

In spite of all the helpful discussions and comments I have received in the course of doing this translation, I take full responsibility for any mistakes that still remain.

This translation was made possible in part through grants from the National Endowment for the Humanities and Inter Nationes.

Richard Taft

REFERENCES TO WORKS OF KANT AND HEIDEGGER

For most of his references to Kant's writings, Heidegger refers to the standard Cassirer edition, cited in the notes as *Werke*. The full citation is *Immanuel Kants Werke*, ed. Ernst Cassirer with the collaboration of Hermann Cohen, Artur Buchenau, Otto Buck, Albert Görland and B. Kellermann, 11 vols. (Berlin: Bruno Cassirer, 1912; reprinted, 1922; reissued, Hildesheim: Gerstenberg, 1973).

In addition to the Cassirer edition, the following works have been referred to at various points:

Immanuel Kant, *Kritik der reinen Vernunft*, ed. Raymund Schmidt (Hamburg: Felix Meiner, 1926; 2nd revised edition, 1930; with index by Karl Vorländer, 1971; reprinted 1976), Philosophische Bibliothek, vol. 37a. Translation: *Critique of Pure Reason*, tr. Norman Kemp Smith (London: Macmillan, 1929; 12th impression, 1973).

Immanuel Kant, *Kritik der praktischen Vernunft*, ed. Karl Vorländer (Hamburg: Felix Meiner, 1929 [9th edition]; reprinted, 1974), Philosophische Bibliothek, vol. 38. Translation: *Critique of Practical Reason*, tr. Lewis White Beck (Indianapolis: Bobbs-Merrill, 1978).

Immanuel Kant, *Kritik der Urteilskraft*, ed. Karl Vorländer (Hamburg: Felix Meiner, 1924 [6th edition]; reprinted, 1974), Philosophische Bibliothek, vol. 39a. Translation: *Critique of Judgment*, tr. J. H. Bernard (New York: Hafner, 1892; revised and reprinted, 1951).

In addition, the following editions of Heidegger's major work *Sein und Zeit* have been cited at various points in the notes:

Martin Heidegger, *Sein und Zeit* (Tübingen: Niemeyer Verlag, 1927; 13th unaltered edition, 1976). Translation: *Being and Time*, tr. John Macquarrie and Edward Robinson (New York: Harper & Row, 1962).

Martin Heidegger, *Gesamtausgabe,* ed. Friedrich-Wilhelm von Herrmann et al. (Frankfurt am Main: Klostermann, 1975-). As of 1996 approximately 45 volumes had been released, of which *Sein und Zeit* is volume 2. *Kant und das Problem der Metaphysik* was published as volume 3 in 1991.

Kantbuch.

PREFACE TO THE FOURTH EDITION

In Heidegger's personal copy of the first edition of this book there is a note on the title page that, judging by the handwriting, dates from the mid-1930s. The note reads:

Kantbook.
With *Being and Time* alone—; soon
clear that we did not enter into
the real question [see I 3. T[1] and Destruction[2]]
A refuge— underway and
          not new discoveries
          in Kant Philology.—
[Being] Beingness—Objectness
     and "time"
            Schematism
but at the same time: the particular way is obstructed
     and is made susceptible to misinterpretation
See Part IV[3]
Beiträge[4]—Beginning to new beginning—Concept
   of Reflection

The preceding remarks mentioned the decisive motivation for the publication of the Kant book: the misunderstanding of the Question of Being presented in *Being and Time*, which had already become clear in 1929. In preparing the lecture course on "Kant's *Critique of Pure Reason*" that was held in the Winter Semester of 1927/28,[1] my attention was drawn to the chapter on Schematism, and I glimpsed therein a connection between the problem of Categories, that is, the problem of Being in traditional Metaphysics and the phenomenon of time. In this way the manner of questioning from *Being and Time* came into play as an anticipation of my attempted interpretation of Kant. Kant's text became a refuge, as I sought in Kant an advocate for the question of Being which I posed.

---

1. This refers to Part 3 of Division I of *Being and Time*.
2. The destruction of the history of Ontology in Division II of *Being and Time*.
3. The fourth part of the Kant book.
4. *Beiträge zur Philosophie* (GA, vol. 65). [The word order of the last two lines of this transcription has been changed from that of the fourth edition to that of the GA edition. The text of this footnote has also been changed to reflect the publication of the *Beiträge* in the GA in 1989—tr.]

The refuge, moreover, determined in this way, led me to interpret the *Critique of Pure Reason* from within the horizon of the manner of questioning set forth in *Being and Time*. In truth, however, Kant's question is foreign to it, even though it would have given another meaning to the presupposed manner of questioning.[2]

In later writings (see the preliminary note to the third edition, 1965) I attempted to retract the overinterpretation [*Überdeutung*] without at the same time writing a correspondingly new version of the Kant book itself

Hansgeorg Hoppe provides an instructive critical overview of the change in my Kant interpretation, referring to earlier critical comments in the anthology *Durchblicke* (1970), published by Vittorio Klostermann, pp. 284–317.

The discussion of the "Transcendental Power of Imagination" set forth in the Kant book is supplemented by Hermann Mörchen in his Marburg dissertation (1928) entitled, "Die Einbildungskraft bei Kant," *Jahrbuch für Philosophie und phänomenologische Forschung*, volume XI (Saale: Max Niemeyer Halle, 1930). An unaltered edition was published by Max Niemeyer (Tübingen: 1970) as an offprint.

The Kant book, written immediately after the conclusion of the second Davos *Hochschule* course (March 17–April 6, 1929), was based on the preparatory work [for that course] (see the preface to the first edition).

The *appendix* to the present edition contains my summary of my three Davos lectures on "Kant's *Critique of Pure Reason* and the Task of a Laying of the Ground for Metaphysics" (appearing in the *Davoser Revue*, IV, 7, 1929, pp. 194–196).

In addition there is a report on the disputation between Ernst Cassirer and me in connection with the lectures we held. In three lectures, Cassirer spoke about philosophical anthropology, specifically, about the problem of space, of language, and of death.[5]

The Kant book remains an introduction, attempted by means of a questionable digression, to the further questionability which persists concerning the Question of Being set forth in *Being and Time*.

The growing and unacknowledged anxiety in the face of thinking no longer allows insight into the forgetfulness of Being which determines the age.

I would like in particular to thank the publisher, Dr. Vittorio Klostermann, for his longstanding interest in this book. My thanks are also extended to Dr. Hildegard Feick (Wiesbaden) and Dr. Friedrich-Wilhelm von Herrmann (Freiburg im Breisgau) for the careful handling of the corrections.

End of August 1973   M.H.

---

5. The text of the *Davoser Disputation* is a transcript compiled by O. F. Bollnow and J. Ritter, who were participants in the Davos course. According to a communication from O. F. Bollnow, it is not a word-for-word protocol, but is rather a subsequent elaboration based on notes taken at the time. O. F. Bollnow furnished the typed text for the purpose of typesetting, and for that we would thank him here.

PREFACE TO THE FIRST EDITION

The essentials of the following interpretation were first presented in a four-hour lecture during the Winter Semester of 1927/28[3] and later on several occasions in lectures and lecture-series (at the Herder Institute in Riga in September 1928 and in a course at the *Davoser Hochschule* [the Davos Academy] in March of this year [1929]).

This interpretation of the *Critique of Pure Reason* arose in connection with a first working-out of Part Two of *Being and Time*. (See *Being and Time*, first half, in *Jahrbuch für Philosophie und phänomenologische Forschung*, edited by E. Husserl, vol. VIII [1927], p. 23f. The pagination of a second, corrected edition, which has now appeared, corresponds with that of the "*Jahrbuch*.")[4]

In Part Two of *Being and Time*, the theme of the following investigation was treated on the basis of a more comprehensive manner of questioning. By contrast, a progressive interpretation of the *Critique of Pure Reason* was rejected there. The present publication should serve as a fitting supplement to that [book].[5]

At the same time this investigation serves as a "historical" introduction of sorts to clarify the problematic treated in the first half of *Being and Time*.

Another essay of mine, which has also appeared as a monograph, provides further clarification of the guiding manner of questioning: *Vom Wesen des Grundes* (see *Festschrift für E. Husserl*, a supplementary volume to the *Jahrbuch für Philosophie und phänomenologische Forschung*, 1929, pp. 71–110.)[6]

The present work is dedicated to the memory of Max Scheler. Its content was the subject of the last conversation in which the author was allowed once again to feel the unfettered power of his spirit.

Todtnauberg im bad. Schwarzwald
Pentecost 1929

PREFACE TO THE SECOND EDITION

This work, which was published two decades ago and which immediately sold out, appears here unaltered. It retains the form in which it has been both successful and unsuccessful in various ways.

Readers have taken constant offense at the violence of my interpretations. Their allegation of violence can indeed be supported by this text. Philosophicohistorical research is always correctly subject to this charge whenever it is directed against attempts to set in motion a thoughtful dialogue between thinkers. In contrast to the methods of historical philology, which has its own agenda, a thoughtful dialogue is bound by other laws—laws which are more easily violated. In a dialogue the possibility of going astray is more threatening, the shortcomings are more frequent.

The instances in which I have gone astray and the shortcomings of the present endeavor have become so clear to me on the path of thinking during the period referred to above that I therefore refuse to make this work into a patchwork by compensating with supplements, appendices and postscripts.

Thinkers learn from their shortcomings to be more persevering.
Freiburg im Breisgau
June 1950

PRELIMINARY NOTE TO THE THIRD EDITION

The following may serve as a guide for correctly understanding the tide of this work: The problem for Metaphysics, namely, the question concerning beings as such in their totality, is what allows Metaphysics as Metaphysics to become a problem. The expression "The Problem of Metaphysics" has two senses.

To supplement the present work, the reader should refer to the following: *Kants These über das Sein* (Frankfurt a.M.: Verlag Vittorio Klostermann, 1963) and *Die Frage nach dem Ding: Zu Kants Lehre von den transzendentalen Grundsätzen* (Tübingen: Verlag Max Niemeyer, 1962).[7]

Freiburg im Breisgau

Spring 1965

Introduction

The Theme and Structure of the Investigation

The following investigation is devoted to the task of interpreting Kant's *Critique of Pure Reason* as a laying of the ground for metaphysics and thus of placing the problem of metaphysics before us as a fundamental ontology.

Fundamental Ontology means that ontological analytic of the finite essence of human beings which is to prepare the foundation for the metaphysics which "belongs to human nature." Fundamental Ontology is the metaphysics of human Dasein which is required for metaphysics to be made possible. It remains fundamentally different from all anthropology and from the philosophical. The idea of laying out a fundamental ontology means to disclose the characteristic ontological analytic of Dasein as prerequisite and thus to make clear for what purpose and in what way, within which boundaries and with which presuppositions, it puts the concrete question: What is the human being? However, provided that an idea first manifests itself through its power to illuminate, the idea of fundamental ontology will prove itself and present itself in an interpretation of the *Critique of Pure Reason* as a laying of the ground for metaphysics.

To this end, the general meaning of the term "laying the ground" [*Grundlegung*] must first be clarified. The expression's meaning is best illustrated if we consider the building trade. It is true that metaphysics is not a building or structure [*Gebäude*] that is at hand, but is really in all human beings "as a natural construction or arrangement."[1] As a consequence, laying the ground

---

1. *Critique of Pure Reason,* 2d ed., p. 21. The first edition (A) and the second (B) are juxtaposed

1

for metaphysics can mean to lay a foundation [*Fundament*] under this natural metaphysics, or rather to replace one which has already been laid with a new one through a process of substituting. However, it is precisely this representation which we must keep out of the idea of a ground-laying, namely, that it is a matter of the byproduct from the foundation [*Grundlagen*] of an already-constructed building. Ground-laying is rather the projecting of the building plan itself so that it agrees with the direction concerning on what and how the building will be grounded. Laying the ground for metaphysics as the projecting [*Entwerfen*] of the building plan, however, is again no empty producing of a system and its subdivisions. It is rather the architectonic circumscription and delineation of the inner possibility of metaphysics, that is, the concrete determination of its essence. All determination of essence, however, is first achieved in the setting-free of the essential ground.

Laying the ground as the projection of the inner possibility of metaphysics is thus necessarily a matter of letting the supporting power of the already-laid ground become operative. Whether and how this takes place is the criterion of the originality and scope of a ground-laying.

If the following interpretation of the *Critique of Pure Reason* succeeds in bringing to light the originality of the origin of metaphysics, then this originality can only really be understood if it was also already required for the concrete happening of the letting-spring-forth [*Entspringenlassen*], that is to say, if the laying of the ground for metaphysics comes to be retrieved [*wiederholt*].

To the extent that metaphysics belongs to and tactically exists with "human nature," it has already developed in some form. Hence an explicit laying of the ground for metaphysics never appears out of nothing, but rather arises from the strength and weakness of a tradition that sketches out the possibilities of a beginning for itself. With reference to the tradition enclosed in itself, then, every ground-laying is, with reference to what came earlier, a transformation of the same task. Thus, the following interpretation of the *Critique of Pure Reason* must, as a laying of the ground for metaphysics, seek to bring to light a fourfold division:

1. The starting point for the laying of the ground for metaphysics.
2. The carrying-out of the laying of the ground for metaphysics.
3. The laying of the ground for metaphysics in its originality.
4. The laying of the ground for metaphysics in a retrieval.

---

to one another in exemplary fashion in Raymund Schmidt's edition (Meiners Philosophische Bibliothek, 1926). In what follows, this work will always be cited according to both A and B. [These same page references are retained by Kemp Smith in his English translation of the *Critique*—tr.]

Part One

The Starting Point for the Laying of the Ground for Metaphysics

The exposition of the Kantian starting point for laying the ground for metaphysics is equivalent to answering the question: Why for Kant does laying the ground for metaphysics become the *Critique of Pure Reason*? The answer must be developed through a discussion of the following three questions: (1) Which concept of metaphysics is found in Kant? (2) What is the starting point for the laying of the ground for this traditional metaphysics? (3) Why is this ground-laying a critique of pure reason?

§1. The Traditional Concept of Metaphysics

The horizon from within which Kant saw metaphysics and in terms of which his ground-laying must be fixed may be characterized roughly by means of Baumgarten's definition: "*Metaphysica est scientia prima cognitionis humanae principia continens.*"[2] Metaphysics is the science which comprises the first principles of human knowledge.[a] In the concept of the "first principles [*ersten Prinzipien*] of human knowledge" lies a peculiar and at first a necessary ambiguity "*Ad metaphysicam referunter ontologia, cosmologia, psychologia et theologia naturalis.*"[3] The motives and history of the development and consolidation of

---

2. A. G. Baumgarten, *Metaphysica,* 2d ed. (1743), §1. [Literal translation: "Metaphysics is the science that contains the first principles of human knowledge"—tr.]

3. Ibid., §2. [Literal translation: "Ontology, cosmology, psychology, and natural theology refer to metaphysics"—tr.]

a. Metaphysics is the first science in so far as it comprises the decisive grounds for what human knowing represents.

this Scholastic concept of metaphysics are not presented here. A short reference to what is most essential should [suffice to] loosen the problematic content of this concept and prepare us for understanding the fundamental meaning of the Kantian starting point for the ground-laying.[4]

It is known that the initial, purely technical meaning of the expression μετὰ τὰ φυσιχά (the collective term for those of Aristotle's treatises that were arranged [in sequence] after those belonging to the *Physics*) later became a philosophically interpreted characteristic of what is contained in these rearranged treatises. This change of meaning, however, is not as harmless as people ordinarily think. Rather, it channeled the interpretation of these treatises in a specific direction, and thereby the interpretation determined what Aristotle treated as "Metaphysics." Nevertheless, we must ask whether what is brought together in the Aristotelian *Metaphysics* is "metaphysics." Admittedly, Kant himself still wants to assign a substantial meaning directly to the expression: "As far as the name metaphysics is concerned, it is not to be believed that it arose by chance because it fits so exactly with the science: now φύσις is called Nature, but we can arrive at the concept of Nature in no other way than through experience, so that the science which follows from it is called Metaphysics (from μετὰ, *trans*, and *physica*). It is a science that is, so to speak, outside of the field of physics, which lies on the other side of it."[5]

The technical expression itself, which occasioned this fixed, substantial interpretation, sprang forth from a difficulty concerning the unbiased understanding of the writings of the *corpus aristotelicum* ordered in this way. In subsequent Scholastic Philosophy (Logic, Physics, Ethics), there was no discipline or framework in which to insert precisely what Aristotle strove for here as πρώτη φιλοσοφία, as authentic philosophy or philosophy of the highest order. μετὰ τὰ φυσιχά is the title of a fundamental philosophical difficulty.

---

4. Following the precedent of H. Pichler's *Über Christian Wolffs Ontologie* (1920), Kant's relationship to traditional metaphysics has recently come to be more urgently and more comprehensively researched. See above all the investigation by H. Heimsoeth, "Die metaphysischen Motive in der Ausbildung des kritischen Idealismus," in *Kantstudien*, vol. XXIX (1924), pp. 121ff.; and also *Metaphysik und Kritik bei Chr. A. Crusius; Ein Beitrag zur ontologischen Vorgeschichte der Kritik der Reinen Vernunft im 18. Jahrhundert*, in *Schriften der Königsberger Gelehrten Gesellschaft III Jahr*, Geisteswiss. Kl. Hft. 3 (1926). In addition there is the longer work by M. Wundt, *Kant als Metaphysiker: Ein Beitrag zur Geschichte der deutschen Philosophie im achtzehnten Jahrhundert* (1924). R. Kroner's *Von Kant bis Hegel*, 2 vols. (1921 and 1924), presents Kantian philosophy in view of the history of metaphysics after Kant. On the history of metaphysics in German Idealism see also Nicolas Hartmann, *Die Philosophie des deutschen Idealismus*, Part I (1923) and Part II (1929). A critique of this research is not possible here. One thing should be noted, however: from the start, all these works adhere to the interpretation of the *Critique of Pure Reason* as "Theory of Knowledge" or "Epistemology," and, moreover, they also emphasize metaphysics and "metaphysical motives."

5. M. Heinze, *Vorlesungen Kants über Metaphysik aus drei Semestern*. Abhdlg. der K. Sächsisch. Ges. der Wissenschaften. Volume XIV, phil.-hist. Kl. 1894, p. 666. (Sep. S. 186.). See also Kant, *Über die Fortschritte der Metaphysik seit Leibniz und Wolff, Werke*, VIII, p. 301ff.

This difficulty also had its basis [*Grund*] in the lack of clarity concerning the essence of the problem and in the findings [*Erkenntnisse*] discussed in the [various] sections. To the extent that Aristotle himself has anything to say about this, a remarkable doubling [*Doppelung*] appears precisely in the determination of the essence of "First Philosophy." It is both "knowledge of beings as beings"[1] (ὂν ᾗ ὄν) and also knowledge of the most remarkable region of beings (τιμιτώατον γένος) out of which the being as a whole (καθόλου) determines itself.

This dual characterization of the πρώτη φιλοσοφία does not contain two fundamentally different ways of thinking that are independent of one another, nor may one of them be weakened or eliminated in favor of the other, nor is it even possible for the apparent disunity to be hastily reconciled into a unity. It is of much greater value to illuminate the grounds for the apparent disunity and the manner in which both determinations belong together as the leading problem of a "first philosophy" of beings. This task becomes all the more urgent because the above-mentioned doubling does not first occur with Aristotle. Rather, the problem of Being has prevailed since the beginnings of ancient philosophy.

But to remain with the problem of the essential determination of "Metaphysics," we can anticipate what would have been said: Metaphysics is the fundamental knowledge of beings as such and as a whole. This "definition," however, can only have value as an announcement of the problem, that is, of the question: In what does the essence of the knowledge of Being by beings lie? To what extent does this necessarily open up into a knowledge of beings as a whole? Why does this point anew to a knowledge of the knowledge of Being? Thus, "Metaphysics" simply remains the title for the philosophical difficulty.

Western metaphysics after Aristotle owes its development not to the assumption and implementation of a previously existing Aristotelian system, but rather to a lack of understanding concerning the questionable and open nature of the central problems left by Plato and Aristotle. Two themes have determined the development of the above-mentioned Scholastic concept of metaphysics, and at the same time they have increasingly hindered the possibility that the original problematic can be taken up once again.

One theme concerns the division of the content of metaphysics and arises from Christianity's devout interpretation of the world. According to this interpretation, every being that is not divine is created: the *Universum*. In turn, the human being has a special place among the created beings to the extent that everything depends on the salvation of the human soul [*Seelenheil*] and its eternal existence [*Existenz*]. Therefore, according to this world- and Dasein-consciousness [*Welt- und Daseinsbewußtsein*], the totality of beings is divided into God, Nature, and humankind, and to each of these spheres respectively is then allied Theology (the object[2] of which is the *summum ens*), Cosmology, and Psychology. They constitute the discipline of *Metaphysica Specialis*. In contrast, *Metaphysica Generalis* (Ontology) has as its object the being "in general" (*ens commune*).

The other theme that is essential for the development of the Scholastic concept of Metaphysics concerns its type of knowledge and its method. Since its object is the being [*Seiende*] in general and the highest being [*das höchste Seiende*] in which "everyone takes an interest" (Kant), Metaphysics is science of the highest dignity, the "queen of the sciences." Accordingly, the type of knowledge it has must also be the most rigorous and the most binding. This requires that it be assimilated to an appropriate ideal for knowledge, as "mathematical" knowledge is reputed to be. It is rational in the highest sense and a priori because it is independent of chance experiences, i.e., it is pure science of reason. Thus the knowledge of beings in general (*Metaphysica Generalis*) and the knowledge of its principle divisions (*Metaphysica Specialis*) become a "science established on the basis of mere reason."

Now Kant adheres to the purpose of this metaphysics; indeed, he shifts it still further in the direction of *Metaphysica Specialis*, which he calls "authentic metaphysics," "metaphysics in its final end."[6] In view of the constant "miscarriage" of all undertakings in this science, its inconsistency and inefficacy, nevertheless all attempts to extend the pure knowledge of reason must first be held back until the question of the inner possibility of this science is clarified. Thus arises the task of a ground-laying in the sense of an essential determination of metaphysics. How did Kant undertake this essential delimitation of metaphysics?

§2. The Point of Departure for the Laying of the Ground for Traditional Metaphysics

In metaphysics as the pure, rational knowledge of what is "common" to [all] beings,[3] and as knowledge of the specific wholeness of its principle divisions, there transpires from time to time an "overstepping" of what experience can offer of the particulars and of the parts. In overstepping the sensible, this knowledge seeks to grasp supersensible being. "Its procedure," however, has been "up to now merely a random groping and, what is worst of all, a groping among mere concepts."[7] Metaphysics lacks binding proof of the insights it claims. What gives this metaphysics the inner possibility to be what it wants to be?

A laying of the ground for metaphysics in the sense of a delimitation of its

---

6. *Über die Fortschritte*, p. 238.
7. B xv.

inner possibility, however, must now aim above all for the final end of meta-physics, i.e., for an essential determination of *Metaphysica Specialis*. In an exceptional sense, then, this is knowledge of the supersensible being. The question of the inner possibility of such knowledge, however, is presented as thrown back upon the more general question of the inner possibility of a general making-manifest of beings as such. Ground-laying is now elucidation of the essence of a comporting toward beings in which this essence shows itself in itself so that all assertions about it become provable on the basis of it.

But what then does the possibility of such a comporting toward beings entail? Is there an "indication" of what makes such a comporting possible? In actual fact: [it is] the method of the natural scientists. Upon them "a light broke. . . . They realized that reason has insight only into what it produces itself according to its own design [*Entwurf*], that it must not allow itself to cling, as it were, to Nature's apron strings, but must lead the way with principles of its judgments according to permanent laws, and that it must constrain Nature to answer its own questions."[8] In the first place, the "previously projected plan" of one Nature in general determines in advance the constitution of the Being of beings, to which all questions that are investigated should be capable of being related. This preliminary plan of the Being of beings is inscribed within the basic concepts and principles of the Science of Nature to which we already referred. Hence, what makes the comporting toward beings (ontic knowledge) possible is the preliminary understanding of the constitution of Being, ontological knowledge.

Mathematical natural science gives an indication of this fundamental conditional connection between ontic experience and ontological knowledge. However, its function for the laying of the ground for metaphysics exhausts itself therein, for the reference to this conditional connection is not yet the solution to the problem. It is rather only a statement of the direction in which it, to be understood in its more fundamental universality, must first be sought. Whether it can be found only there, and whether it can be found at all, i.e., whether the idea of a *Metaphysica Specialis* in general can be projected in accordance with the concept of positive (scientific) knowledge—precisely this should first be determined.

The projection of the inner possibility of *Metaphysica Specialis* has been led back beyond the question concerning the possibility of ontic knowledge to the question concerning the possibility of that which makes ontic knowledge possible. It is, however, the problem of the essence of the preliminary understanding of Being, i.e., of ontological knowledge in the broadest sense. The problem of the inner possibility of ontology nevertheless includes the question concerning the possibility of *Metaphysica Generalis*. The quest for a laying of the ground for *Metaphysica Specialis* is in itself forced back to the question concerning the essence of *Metaphysica Generalis*.

With the laying of the ground for metaphysics put in this way, however, Kant is brought immediately into the dialogue with Aristotle and Plato. Ontology now becomes a problem for the first time. With that, the first and deepest shock wave strikes the structure of traditional metaphysics. The indeterminacy and obviousness with which *Metaphysica Generalis* hitherto treated the "commonality" of the *ens commune* disappears. For the first time, the question of the ground-laying requires clarity concerning the manner of universalization and the character of the stepping-beyond which lies in the knowledge of the constitution of Being. Whether Kant himself achieves the full clarification of this problem remains a subordinate question. It is enough that he recognized its necessity and, above all, that he presented it. Consequently, it also becomes clear that ontology in no way refers primarily to the laying of the ground for the positive sciences. Its necessity and its role are grounded in a "higher interest" which human reason finds in itself. Now because *Metaphysica Generalis* provides the necessary "preparation"[9] for *Metaphysica Specialis,* however, then in laying the ground for the former, the essential determination of the latter must be transformed.

Laying the ground for metaphysics as a whole means unveiling the inner possibility of ontology. That is the true sense, because it is the metaphysical sense (referring to metaphysics as the only theme) of what has been misinterpreted constantly under the heading of Kant's "Copernican Revolution." "Up to now it has been assumed that all our knowledge must conform to objects. But all attempts to establish something in regard to them a priori by means of concepts through which our knowledge would be extended have come to nothing under this assumption. Hence, we must attempt for once to find out whether we might not progress better in the tasks of metaphysics if we assume that objects must conform to our knowledge. This would agree better with what is desired, namely, the possibility of having a knowledge of objects a priori, of determining something about them before they are given to us."[10]

With this Kant wants to say: not "all knowledge" is ontic, and where there is such knowledge, it is only possible through ontological knowledge. Through the Copernican Revolution, the "old" concept of truth in the sense of the "correspondence" (*adaequatio*) of knowledge to the being is so little shaken that it [the Copernican Revolution] actually presupposes it [the old concept of truth], indeed even grounds it for the first time. Ontic knowledge can only correspond to beings ("objects") if this being as being is already first apparent [*offenbar*], i.e., is already first known in the constitution of its Being. Apparentness of beings (ontic truth) revolves around the unveiledness of the

---

9. *Über die Fortschritte,* p. 302.
10. B xvi.

constitution of the Being of beings (ontological truth); at no time, however, can ontic knowledge itself conform "to" the objects because, without the ontological, it cannot even have a possible "to what."

With this it has become clear that the laying of the ground for traditional metaphysics begins with the question of the inner possibility of ontology as such. But why does this ground-laying become a *"Critique of Pure Reason"*?

§3. The Laying of the Ground for Metaphysics as "Critique of Pure Reason"

Kant reduces the problem of the possibility of ontology to the question: "How are a priori synthetic judgments possible?" The interpretation of this formulation of the problem makes it clear that the laying of the ground for metaphysics is carried out as a critique of pure reason. The question concerning the possibility of ontological knowledge requires its preliminary characterization. In keeping with the tradition, Kant understands knowing in this formula as judging. What kind of knowledge is under consideration in ontological understanding? It is that [knowledge] in which the being is known. What is known there, however, belongs to the being, no matter how it is always experienced and determined. This known what-Being [*Wassein*] of the being is brought forward a priori in ontological knowledge prior to all ontic experience, although it is precisely for this [ontic experience]. Knowledge which brings forth the quiddity [*Wasgehalt*] of the being, i.e., knowledge which unveils the being itself, Kant calls "synthetic." Thus the question concerning the possibility of ontological knowledge becomes the problem of the essence of a priori synthetic judgments.

The instance that grounds the legitimacy of these material judgments [*sachhaltigen Urteile*] concerning the Being of beings cannot lie in experience, for experience of beings is itself always already guided by ontological understanding, which becomes accessible through experience in a more determinative respect. Ontological knowledge is hence a judging according to grounds (principles) which are not brought forth experientially.

But our faculty of knowing a priori according to principles Kant then names pure reason."[11] Pure reason is "that which supplies the principles to know something entirely a priori."[12] Hence, insofar as the principles contained in reason constitute the possibility of a priori knowledge, the unveiling of the possibility of ontological knowledge must become an elucidation of the

---

11. *Kritik der Urteilskraft,* Preface to the First Edition (1790). *Werke,* V, p. 235. [Translation: *Critique of Judgment,* tr. J. H. Bernard.]
12. A 11, B 24.

essence of pure reason. The delimitation of the essence of pure reason, however, is at the same time the differentiating determination of its nonessence
and, with that, the limitation and restriction (critique) of its essential possibilities. Laying the ground for metaphysics as unveiling the essence of ontology is "Critique of Pure Reason."

It is ontological knowledge, i.e., the a priori synthesis, "for the sole sake of
which the whole critique is undertaken."[13] Just by establishing the guiding
problem of this grounding of metaphysics, a more precise determination of
this synthesis becomes all the more pressing. Not only did Kant generally use
this expression in a multitude of senses,[14] but these [many meanings] are even
intertwined within the formula for the problem of the laying of the ground
for metaphysics. The question concerns the possibility of a priori synthetic
judgments. Now every judgment as such is already an "I connect": namely,
subject and predicate. As judgments, "analytic" judgments are also already
synthetic, even if the ground for the univocity of the subject-predicate connection lies merely in the representation of the subject [der Subjektvorstellung].
But the synthetic judgments, then, are "synthetic" in a twofold sense: first, as
judgments in general; and second, insofar as the legitimacy of the "connection"
(synthesis) of the representation is "brought forth" (synthesis) from the being
itself with which the judgment is concerned.

In synthetic a priori judgments, however, which are now the problem before
us, it is a matter of still another type of synthesis. This [other type of synthesis]
should bring forth something about the being which was not derived experientially from it. This bringing-forth of the determination of the Being of the
being is a preliminary self-relating to the being. This pure "relation-to . . ."
(synthesis) forms first and foremost the that-upon-which [das Worauf] and the
horizon within which the being in itself becomes experienceable in the empirical synthesis. It is now a question of elucidating the possibility of this a
priori synthesis. Kant calls an investigation concerning the essence of this
synthesis a transcendental investigation. "I entitle all knowledge transcendental that is occupied in general not so much with objects as with the kind of
knowledge we have of objects, insofar as this is possible a priori."[15] Hence,
transcendental knowledge does not investigate the being itself, but rather the
possibility of the preliminary understanding of Being, i.e., at one and the same
time: the constitution of the Being of the being. It concerns the stepping-over
(transcendence) of pure reason to the being, so that it can first and foremost
be adequate to its possible object.

To make the possibility of ontology into a problem means: to inquire as to
the possibility, i.e., as to the essence of this transcendence which characterizes

---

13. A 14, B 28.
14. See §7 below, p. 26.
15. B 25 (A 11).

the understanding of Being, to philosophize transcendentally. This is why Kant uses the designation "Transcendental Philosophy" for *Metaphysica Generalis (Ontologia)*[16] in order to make the problematic of traditional ontology discernable. Accordingly, when mentioning this traditional ontology, he speaks of the "transcendental philosophy of the ancients."[17]

The *Critique of Pure Reason*, however, gives no "system" of transcendental philosophy, but rather it is "a treatise on method."[18] In this context, however, that does not signify a doctrine concerning the technique for proceeding. It signifies instead the working out of a complete determination of the "whole contour" and the "whole internal, articular structure" of ontology. In this laying of the ground for metaphysics as projection of the inner possibility of ontology, the "complete sketch of a system of metaphysics is drawn."[19]

The intention of the *Critique of Pure Reason*, therefore, remains fundamentally misunderstood, if it is interpreted as a "theory of experience" or even as a theory of the positive sciences. The *Critique of Pure Reason* has nothing to do with a "theory of knowledge."[4] If one generally could allow the interpretation of the *Critique of Pure Reason* as a theory of knowledge, then that would be to say that it is not a theory of ontic knowledge (experience), but rather a theory of ontological knowledge. But even with this conception, already far removed from the prevailing interpretation of the Transcendental Aesthetic and Analytic, we have not encountered what is essential, namely, that ontology as *Metaphysica Generalis*, i.e., as the basic part [*Grundstück*] of metaphysics as a whole, is grounded [*begründet*], and here for the first time it is seen for what it is. With the problem of transcendence, a "theory of knowledge" is not set in place of metaphysics, but rather the inner possibility of ontology is questioned.

If its truth belongs to the essence of knowledge, then the transcendental problem of the inner possibility of a priori synthetic knowledge is the question concerning the essence of the truth of ontological transcendence. It is a matter of determining the essence of "transcendental truth, which precedes all empirical truth and makes it possible."[20] "For no knowledge can contradict it without losing all content at the same time, i.e., all relation to any object and consequently, all truth."[21] Ontic truth necessarily adjusts itself to the ontological. Accordingly, the legitimate interpretation of the sense of the "Copernican Revolution" is renewed. Hence, with this revolution Kant forces the problem of ontology to center stage. Nothing can be presupposed on behalf of the problematic of the possibility for original, ontological truth, least of all the

---

16. A 845f., B 873f.; A 247, B 303; see also *Über die Fortschritte*, pp. 238, 263, 269, 301.
17. B 113.
18. B xxii.
19. B xxiii.
20. A 146, B 185.
21. A 62f., B 87.

factum of the truth of the positive sciences. On the contrary, the ground-laying must pursue the a priori synthesis exclusively in itself, pursue it to the seed [*Keim*] which provides its ground and which allows that synthesis to develop into what it is (allows it to be possible in essence).

From the clear insight into the peculiarity of a laying of the ground for metaphysics, Kant says of the *Critique of Pure Reason:* "This work is difficult and demands a reader resolved to think himself gradually into a system in which nothing yet lies at its ground as given except for reason itself, and [who] thus seeks to develop knowledge from its original seeds without seeking the support of any fact."[22]

Thus, the task then arises of showing how this development of the possibility of ontology from its seeds is to be carried out.

---

22. *Prolegomena zu einer jeden künftigen Metaphysik*, §4, *Werke,* IV, p. 23.

Part Two

Carrying Out the Laying of the
Ground for Metaphysics

In order to project the inner possibility of ontological knowledge, we must first have opened up a view into the dimension of going back [*Dimension des Rückgangs*] to the ground which supports the possibility of what we are seeking in its essential constitution. Now, it is the necessary fate of any real incursion into a hitherto concealed field that at first it is determined "little by little." In the course of the advance itself, the direction of an approach is first consolidated and the feasibility of the path is developed. Hence, if the first incursion from the security and unwavering directive force [*Richtkraft*] of the creative opening-up remains operative, then to begin with we are lacking an explicit, systematic uprooting and marking of the field. Indeed, "Critique requires knowledge of the sources, and Reason must know itself. . . ."[23] And certainly, it is through the Critique that Kant first laboriously extracted this most original self-knowing of Reason.

The following interpretation, on the other hand, must explicitly insure the guiding view in advance and so anticipate the main stages of the inner procession of the whole of the ground-laying, because it [the interpretation] is not yet and no longer in possession of the original directive force of the projecting. Before we allow the carrying-out of the laying of the ground for metaphysics to be performed, we must secure the view of that dimension of the ground-laying which "goes back." This part is thus divided into two sections:

A. The Characterization of the Dimension of Going-Back [needed] for Carrying Out the Laying of the Ground for Metaphysics.

---

23. *Kants handschriftlicher Nachlaß*, vol. V, Metaphysik (*Ges. Schriften*, ed. Preuß. Akad. d. Wissenschaften III. 5.) 1928, Nr. 4892. See B. Erdmann, *Reflexionen Kants zur kritischen Philosophie*, II, 217.

B. The Stages of Carrying Out the Projection of the Inner Possibility of Ontology.

A. THE CHARACTERIZATION OF THE DIMENSION OF GOING-BACK [NEEDED] FOR CARRYING OUT THE LAYING OF THE GROUND FOR METAPHYSICS

The task is the essential determination of ontological knowledge through elucidation of its origin in the seed which makes it possible. To that end, clarity must prevail first and foremost with respect to the essence of knowledge in general, with respect to the place and manner of its field of origin. In the previous interpretation of the *Critique of Pure Reason*, it is precisely the preliminary and sufficient characterization of the original dimension that was unduly neglected or was misinterpreted. Therefore, a productive appropriation [*Aneignung*] of its fundamental tendency through a determination of the intentions of the work, which fluctuate in any case, cannot succeed. Together with the characterization of the field of origin, we must also allow the manner of the unveiling of the origin to be characterized in its peculiarity.

1. THE ESSENTIAL CHARACTERISTICS OF THE FIELD OF ORIGIN

§4. The Essence of Knowledge in General[a]

Kant does not discuss the essential characteristics of the field of origin explicitly or thematically;[b] instead, he takes them for granted in the sense of "self-evident presuppositions." This is all the more reason why the interpre-

---

a. Develop more precisely by proceeding from the difference between knowledge [*Erkenntnis*] as *re-presenting* [*Vor-stellen*] and as *Knowledge* [*Wissen*] —knowledge [*Erkenntnis*] as Knowledge [*Wissen*] of the guiding concept; see WS 1935/36 [*Die Frage nach dem Ding. Zu Kants Lehre von den transzendentalen Grundsätzen*. GA, vol. 41], p. 136ff. [*What Is a Thing*, tr. W. B. Barton and V. Deutsch (South Bend: Gateway, 1967), p. 132ff.—tr.]
b. See p. 18. [The reference is to Heidegger's note "c" on that page—tr.]

tation should not be permitted to overlook the previously worked-out function of these "assumptions." They can be summarized in the thesis:

The ground for the source [*Quellgrund*] for laying the ground for metaphysics is human pure reason, so that it is precisely the humanness of reason, i.e., its finitude, which will be essential for the core of this problematic of groundlaying. Hence, it is worthwhile for the characterization of the field of origin to concentrate on the clarification of the essence of the finitude of human knowledge. This finitude of reason, however, in no way consists only or primarily in the fact that human knowing demonstrates many sorts of deficiencies such as instability, imprecision, and [the potential for making] errors. Rather, this finitude lies in the essential structure of knowledge itself. The tactical limitedness of knowledge is first and foremost a consequence of this essence.

In order to set forth the essence of the finitude of knowledge, a general characterization of the essence of knowing[c] is required. Already in this regard, what Kant says in the first sentence of the thematic discussion in the *Critique of Pure Reason* is usually appraised much too lightly: "In whatever manner and by whatever means a knowing [*eine Erkenntnis*] may relate to objects, *intuition is that through which it relates itself immediately to them*, and upon which all thought as a means is directed."[24][d]

In order to understand the *Critique of Pure Reason* this point must be hammered in, so to speak: knowing is[e] primarily[f] intuiting. From this it at once becomes clear that the new interpretation of knowledge as judging (thinking) violates the decisive sense of the Kantian problem. All thinking is merely in the service of intuition.[g] Thinking is not simply alongside intuition, "also" at hand; but rather, according to its own inherent structure, it serves

---

24. A 19, B 33 (emphasis by Kant himself).

c. human

d. See CPR, B 306; priority of intuition! See [*Über die*] *Fortschritte* (Meiner), p. 157.

e. essentially! See p. 36! See p. 47. [The reference is actually to Heidegger's marginal note "b" on that page—tr.]

f. See p. 17, "properly speaking." [The reference is to Heidegger's marginal note 'l' on that page—tr.]—what does this mean? Intuiting here means the being itself *has been made apparent* qua what has been *taken in* from what is there [hin-*nehmendes*]. Knowing [*Erkennen*] is "primarily," i.e., first and foremost, according to the *ground* of its essence (as finite); thinking belongs, as something *secondary*, to precisely *this essence*, only for that reason is it something primary! But "secondary" is meant here in the sense of the structure of the construction of the essence, not in the popular sense of "fundamentally superfluous." Precisely because knowing is *primarily* intuition, *an intuiting alone* is never for us knowledge! In that regard, see the same relativity with respect to the Transcendental Aesthetic, p. 47.

g. See B 219. *Synthetic* unity in *any* consciousness as "what is *essential* in any knowledge of the *object* of the senses." But "synthesis" there is still servitude, i.e., knowledge here is *essentially finite*. Thinking is only essential because intuition as letting-be-encountered is *fundamentally essential* [*Grundwesentlich*]. To be sure, understanding surpasses intuition—in its finitude and neediness. And the greater *this* priority, all the more unconditional is the dependency upon intuition. All the less [reason] to disconnect them.

that to which intuition is primarily and constantly directed. If thinking is to be essentially relative to intuition, however, then both intuition and thinking must have a certain inherent relationship that allows their unification. This relationship, this descendency from the same class (genus), is expressed in the fact that for both of them "*Representation* in general (*repraesentatio*)" "is the species."[25]

In the first place, "representation" here has the broad, formal sense according to which one thing indicates, announces, presents another. Now this representing can be such that it takes place "with consciousness."[26] There belongs to it a knowledge of the announcing and of the having-been-announced by something (*perceptio*). Now if the representing of something occurs through something other than the representing, so that the represented in this representing is instead represented as such (i.e., "consciously"), then such a representing is a referring to what presents itself as such in the representing. In this sense of "objective perception," knowledge is a representing.

The knowing representing is either intuition or concept (*intuitus vel conceptus*).[h] "The former relates immediately to the object and is single; the latter refers to it mediately by means of a feature which several things can have in common."[27] According to the first sentence of the *Critique of Pure Reason* quoted above, knowing is a thinking intuiting. Thinking, however, is "in general representing," it is in the service only of that particular object or of the concrete being itself in its immediacy, and it is to be made accessible to everyone. "Each of these two {intuition and thinking} is indeed representation, but is not yet knowledge."[28]

From this one could conclude that a reciprocal and indeed fully balanced relationship prevails between intuiting and thinking. As a result, one may say with equal justification: knowing is intuitive thinking, and thus at bottom [*im Grunde*] is certainly judgment.

In contrast to this, however, we must maintain that intuition constitutes the authentic essence of knowledge and that, despite the reciprocity of the relationship between intuiting and thinking, [intuition] does possess authentic importance. This stands out clearly, but not just on the basis of Kant's explanation, quoted above, which emphasizes the word "Intuition." Rather, only with this interpretation of knowledge is it also possible to grasp what is essential in this definition, namely, the finitude of knowledge. That first sentence of the *Critique of Pure Reason* is already no longer a definition of knowing in general,

---

25. A 320, B 376f.
26. Ibid.
27. Ibid.
28. *Über die Fortschritte*, p. 312.

h. See A 271, B 327 comparing Locke and Leibniz; sensibility and understanding [are] "two completely different sources of representations."

but rather is already the determination of the essence of human knowledge. "On the other hand, any knowledge of what concerns man {in distinction from 'God or another higher spirit'} consists of concept and intuition."[29]

The essence of finite human knowledge is illustrated by the contrast between it and the idea of infinite divine knowledge, or *intuitus originarius*.[30] Still, divine knowledge is intuition—not because it is divine but because it is knowledge in general. Now the difference between infinite and finite intuition consists in the fact that the former, in its immediate representation of the individual, i.e., of the unique, singular being as a whole, first brings this being into its Being, helps it to its coming-into-being (*origo*).[i] Absolute intuiting would not be absolute if it depended upon a being already at hand and if the intuitable first became accessible in its "taking the measure" of this being. Divine knowing is representing which, in intuiting, first[j] creates the intuitable being as such.[31] But because it immediately looks at the being as a whole, simply seeing through it in advance, it cannot require thinking.[k] Thinking as such is thus already the mark of finitude. Divine knowing is "intuition (for all its knowledge must be intuition and not *thinking*, which always shows itself to have limits)."[32]

But the decisive element in the difference between infinite and finite knowledge would not be grasped and the essence of finitude would be missed if one were to say that divine knowing is only intuiting while human [knowing] on the other hand is a thinking intuiting. The essential difference between these kinds of knowledge lies instead primarily in intuiting itself, since properly speaking[l] even knowing is intuition. The finitude of human knowledge must first of all be sought in the finitude of its own intuition. That a finite, thinking creature must "also" think is an essential consequence of the finitude of its own intuiting. Only in this way can the essentially subordinate place of "all thinking" be seen in the correct light. In what does the essence of finite intuition lie, then, and with it the finitude of human knowledge in general?

---

29. Ibid.
30. B 72.
31. B 139, 145.
32. B 71.

i. See *Fortschritte* (Vorländer), p. 92.
j. Altogether first; it has already as such allowed its "object" to come forth.
k. It is "free from all sensibility and at the same time from the need for knowing by means of concepts" (ibid.).
l. "primarily"?

§5. The Essence of the Finitude of Knowledge

In the first place, we can say negatively: finite knowledge is noncreative intuition. What has to be presented immediately in its particularity must already have been "at hand" in advance. Finite intuition sees that it is dependent upon the intuitable as a being which exists in its own right. The intuited is derived [*hergeleitet*] from such beings; thus, this intuition is also called *intuitus derivativus*, "deduced" ["*abgeleitete*"], that is, intuition which conduces [*sich herleitende Anschauung*].[33a] Finite intuition of the being cannot give the object from out of itself. It must allow the object to be given. Not every intuition as such, but rather only the finite, is intuition that "takes things in stride." Hence, the character of the finitude of intuition is found in its receptivity. Finite intuition, however, cannot take something in stride unless that which is to be taken in stride announces itself. According to its essence, finite intuition must be solicited or affected by that which is intuitable in it.

Because the essence of knowledge lies primarily in intuition and because the finite essence of man provides the theme[c] for the entire [task of] laying the ground for metaphysics,[b] Kant therefore continues immediately after the first sentence of the *Critique*: "This {intuition} takes place, however, only insofar as the object is given to us; but this, in turn, is only possible, to us human beings at least, insofar as the mind is affected in a certain way."[34] It is true that the phrase "to us human beings at least" was inserted in the second[d] edition, but this only makes it more obvious that in the first edition finite knowledge is the theme from the outset.

Because human intuition as finite "takes in stride" and because the possibility of a "receiving"[e] which takes-in-stride [*eines hinnehmenden "Bekommens"*] requires affection, therefore organs of affection, "the senses," are in fact neces-

---

33. B 72. [This phrase is particularly difficult to render into English because Heidegger is playing two words against each other which have the same root (*leiten*, to lead) and which often serve as synonyms (both can be rendered as "derivative"). He does this by playing with the etymological sense of the prefixes of each word, such that *abgeleitete* is intended to convey the sense of "leading away," while *herleitende* connotes a "leading toward." To preserve these two senses of derivation as well as Heidegger's word play, I have rendered these terms as "deducing" and "conducing" respectively, reflecting the Latin roots *deducere* and *conducere*—tr.]

34. A 19, B 33.

a. But not deduced [*deduziert*] by chance from absolute Intuition; in its structural essence, finite knowing is *that which comes forth from*, i.e., allows itself to be given from elsewhere (instead of creating itself); what is not meant, however, is that finite knowing would be a "derivative" of the absolute. With respect to the question of the ontic origin, this is not treated in any way.

c. [This note comes before 'b' in the translation because of the different word order in the original German—tr.] not the proper theme; indeed, that is *knowledge*, see p. 14 above. [The reference is to Heidegger's marginal note 'b' on that page—tr.]

b. as natural predisposition of men

d. indeed, *precisely* [inserted] in it at that!

e. That which comes near—re-ceive [*Beikommendes—be-kommen*] sary. Human intuition, then, is not "sensible" because its affection takes place through "sense organs," but rather the reverse. Because our Dasein is finite— existing in the midst of beings that already are, beings to which it has been delivered over—therefore it must[f] necessarily take this already-existing being in stride, that is to say, it must offer it the possibility of announcing itself. Organs are necessary for the possible relaying of the announcement. The essence of sensibility exists in the finitude of intuition. The organs that serve affection are thus sense organs because they belong to finite intuition, i.e., sensibility. With this, Kant for the first time attains a concept of sensibility which is ontological rather than sensualistic. Accordingly, if empirically affective intuition of beings does not need to coincide with "sensibility," then the possibility of a nonempirical sensibility remains essentially open.[35]

Knowledge is primarily intuition, i.e., a representing that immediately represents the being itself. However, if finite intuition is now to be knowledge, then it must be able to make the being itself as revealed accessible with respect to both what and how it is for everyone at all times. Finite, intuiting creatures must be able to share in the specific intuition of beings. First of all, however, finite intuition as intuition always remains bound to the specifically intuited particulars. The intuited is only a known being if everyone can make it understandable to oneself and to others and can thereby communicate it. So, for example, this intuited particular—this piece of chalk—must allow itself to be determined as chalk, or rather as a body. In this way, we are able jointly to know this being as the same for all of us. In order to be knowledge, finite intuition always requires such a determination of the intuited as this and that.

In such a determining, what is represented in accord with intuition is further represented with a view to what it is "in general." Such determining, however, does not thematically represent the general as such. It does not make the corporeality of the thing into an object. Instead, the determinative representing of what is intuitively represented indeed takes a look at the general, but only keeps it [the general] in view in order to direct itself to the particular and thus to determine the particular from that viewpoint. This "general" representing, which as such is in service to the intuiting, makes what is represented in the intuition more representable[1][g] in the sense that it grasps

---

35. "Sensible intuition is either pure intuition (space and time) or empirical intuition of what is immediately represented, through sensation, as actual in space and time." B 146f.

f. in order in general to arrive at beings
g. to grasp this better! Representing in general—representing in concepts—thinking—judging makes the intuitively given particular *more representable*.
(1. provided that the concept applies to many individual objects; 2. provided that this universal is accessible to everyone; 3. so *beings* themselves are first more accessible)
is that necessary and why? The representing which takes things in stride *qua* intuiting thus will be *taking*, and so is it first able to have "a being." And because thinking *is so necessary* (why?) and thereby made more representable, therefore subservient! in *intuition* as *repraesentatio* still no beings? indeed—provided that after all we never *just intuit*.

many under one, and on the basis of this comprehensive grasping [*Umgreifens*] it "applies to many." Hence, Kant names this representing in general (*repraesentatio per notas communes*),[2] "representing in concepts." The determinative representing thereby shows itself as the "Representation {concept} of a representation" (intuition).[3]h Determinative representing, however, is in itself an assertion of something about something (predication). "Judgment is therefore the mediate knowledge of an object, that is, the representation of a representation of it."[36] The "faculty of judging," however, is the understanding, and the representing that is proper to it makes the intuition "understandable."i

Insofar as the judging [act] of determination is essentially dependent upon intuition, thinking is always united with it by virtue of its service to intuition. By means of such a union (synthesis), thinking is mediately related to the object. This becomes evident (true) in the unity of a thinking intuition. Accordingly, the synthesis of thinking and intuiting accomplishes the making-evident of the encountered being as object. We will therefore call it the veritative synthesis which makes [something] true ([or] evident).[4] This [synthesis] coincides with the above-mentioned "bringing-forward" of the relevant determinateness of the beings themselves.

Thinking which unites with intuition in the veritative synthesis, however, is now and for its part—namely, as judging—a unifying (synthesis) in another sense. Kant says: "A judgment is the representation of a unity of the consciousness of various representations, or the representation of the relationship between the same, insofar as they constitute a concept."[37] Judgments are "functions of unity," i.e., a representing of the unifying unity of concepts in their character as predicates. This unifying representing we name predicative synthesis.

The predicative synthesis, however, does not coincide with that unifying in which judging presents itself as the joining of subject and predicate. This latter synthesis of subject and predicate we name the apophantic.

Accordingly, in the veritative synthesis, which in general constitutes the essence of finite knowledge, the predicative synthesis and the apophantical synthesis are necessarily joined together into a structural unity of syntheses.

Now, if one maintains that the essence of knowledge according to Kant is "synthesis," then this thesis still says nothing as long as the expression synthesis is allowed to remain in ambiguous indeterminacy.

Finite intuition, as something in need of determination, is dependent upon the understanding, which not only belongs to the finitude of intuition, but is itself still more finite in that it lacks the immediacy of finite intuiting. Its

---

36. A 68, B 93.
37. See I. Kant, *Logik: Ein Handbuch zu Vorlesungen*, ed. G. B. Jäsche, *Werke*, VIII, §17, p. 408.

h. right here, and on the grounds that the critical concept of judgment was introduced
i. 1) The essence of *analytic* and *synthetic* judgments for themselves—2) the essence of this difference; both as the index of the finitude of knowledge and of *thinking*.

representing requires the indirection [*Umweg*] of a reference to a universal by means of and according to which the several particulars become conceptually representable. This circuitousness [*Umwegigkeit*] (discursiveness) which belongs to the essence of understanding is the sharpest index of its finitude.

However, just as the metaphysical essence of finite intuition as receptivity now retains in itself the universal, essential character of intuition in that it is "giving," so too the finitude of the understanding also indicates something more of the essence of absolute knowledge, namely, an "original intuition {an intuition which lets something spring forth}."[5] In and through intuiting, this [original intuition] first brings forth the intuitable being from out of itself. Of course the understanding, related to finite intuition as it is, is no more creative than is [intuition]. It never produces the being, but rather, as distinct from the "taking-in-stride" of an intuiting, it is a type of bringing-forth. Of course, judgment about beings does not simply bring forth the universal in which the intuited comes to be conceptually represented. In terms of its content, the universal is derived from the intuitable. Only the manner in which this content as a comprehensively grasped unity applies to many is the result of the understanding.

In producing the form of the concept, the understanding helps to set forth [*beistellen*] the content of the object. In this sort of "setting" [*Stellens*],[j] the peculiar re-presenting [*Vor-stellen*] of thinking reveals itself.[6] The metaphysical essence of the understanding, which is "productive" in this way, comes to be co-determined through this character of the "from out of itself" (spontaneity), but without getting to the heart of the matter.

The finitude of knowledge has been characterized hitherto as intuition that takes things in stride and that is therefore thinking. This clarification of finitude took place with reference to the structure of knowing. By virtue of the fundamental significance which finitude has for the problematic of the laying of the ground for metaphysics, the essence of finite knowledge should come to be illuminated from still another side, namely, with a view toward what is knowable in such knowledge.

If finite knowledge is intuition that takes things in stride, then the knowable must show itself from itself. What finite knowledge can make manifest from this is essentially the being which shows itself, i.e., the appearing, appearance. The term "appearance" means the being itself as object of finite knowledge. More precisely stated: only for finite knowledge is there anything at all like an object.[k] It alone is delivered over to the being which already is. Infinite

---

j. -together [This notation is keyed to the German word "*Stellens*," which I have translated as "setting," as in "setting forth"; but it is also the "presenting" ("*stellen*") in "re-presenting" ("*vor-stellen*") a few words later on. The German notation is simply the prefix "*Zu-*," which would result in the word "*Zu-stellens*" if attached as indicated. In this context, *Zu-stellens* should be translated as something like the "setting-together"—tr.]

k. *Objectivity* is *Being* [*Seyn*]! in the empirical sense knowledge, however, cannot be opposed by any such being to which it must conform. Such conforming-to . . . would be a dependency-on . . . , and therefore finitude. Infinite knowing is an intuiting which as such allows the being itself to stand forth. Absolute knowing discloses the being [in the act of] letting-stand-forth and possesses it in every case "only" as that which stands forth in the letting-stand-forth, i.e., it is disclosed as a thing which stands forth [als Ent-stand].[7] Insofar as the being is disclosed for absolute intuition, it "is" precisely in its coming-into-Being. It is the being as being in itself, i.e., not as object. Strictly speaking, therefore, we do not really hit upon the essence of infinite knowledge if we say: this intuiting is first produced in the intuiting of the "object."

The being "in the appearance" is the same[l] being as the being in itself, and this alone. As a being, it alone can become an object, although only for a finite [act of] knowledge. Nevertheless, it reveals itself in accordance with the manner and scope of the ability that finite knowledge has at its disposal to take things in stride and to determine them.

Kant uses the expression "appearance" in a narrower and in a wider sense. Appearances in the wider sense (phenomena) are a kind of "object,"[38] namely, the being itself which finite knowing, as thinking intuition that takes things in stride, makes apparent. Appearance in the narrower sense means that which (in appearance in the wider sense) is the exclusive correlate of the affection that is stripped of thinking (determining) and that belongs to finite intuition: the content of empirical intuition. "The undetermined object [Gegenstand] of an empirical intuition is called *appearance*."[39] Appearing means: "to be an Object [Objekt] of empirical intuition."[40][8]

Appearances [Erscheinungen] are not mere illusion [Schein], but are the being itself. And again, this being is not something different from the thing in itself, but rather this [thing in itself] is precisely a being. The being itself can be apparent without the being "in itself" (i.e., as a thing which stands forth) being known. The double characterization of the being as "thing in itself" and as "appearance" corresponds to the twofold manner according to which it [the being] can stand in relationship to infinite and finite knowing: the being in the standing-forth [Entstand] and the same being as object [Gegenstand].[9]

If in fact the finitude of human beings is the basis for the problem[m] of laying the ground for ontology in the *Critique of Pure Reason*, then the "critique" of this difference between finite and infinite knowledge must carry special weight. Thus Kant says of the *Critique of Pure Reason* that "the Object is to be

---

38. A 235 (heading), 249.
39. A 20, B 34.
40. A 89, B 121.

l. not the sameness of the What, but rather the That of the X!
m. not the explicit theme!

taken *in a twofold sense*, namely, as appearance and as thing in itself."[41] Strictly speaking, one should not speak of "Object" ["*Objekt*"],[n] because for absolute knowledge there can be no objects [*es keine Gegen-stände geben*] [in the sense of things which stand against it]. In the *Opus Postumum* Kant says that the thing in itself is not a being different from the appearance, i.e., "the difference between the concept of a thing in itself and the appearance is not objective but merely subjective. The thing in itself is not another Object, but is rather another aspect (*respectus*) of the representation of *the same Object*."[42]

Based on this interpretation of the concepts "appearance" and "thing in itself," which is oriented toward the difference between finite and infinite knowledge, it is now also possible to clarify what the expressions "behind the appearance" and "mere appearance" mean. This "behind" cannot mean that for finite knowledge as such, the thing in itself still stands in opposition to it. Similarly, it cannot mean that the thing in itself does not become "fully" grasped, that its essence is free floating and yet occasionally becomes indirectly visible. Rather, the expression "behind the appearance" expresses the fact that finite knowledge as finite necessarily conceals at the same time, and it conceals in advance so that the "thing in itself" is not only imperfectly accessible, but is absolutely inaccessible to such knowledge by its very essence. What is "behind the appearance" is the same being as the appearance. Because it only gives the being as object, however, this appearance does not permit that same being to be seen fundamentally as a thing which stands forth. "According to the *Critique*, everything in an appearance is itself again appearance."[43]

It is therefore a misunderstanding of what the thing in itself means if we believe that the impossibility of a knowledge of the thing in itself must be proven through positivistic critique. Such attempts at proof suppose the thing in itself to be something which is presumed to be an object within finite knowledge in general, but whose tactical inaccessibility can and must be

---

41. B xxvii.

42. Kant, *Opus Postumum*, presented and commented upon by E. Adickes (1920), p. 653 (C551). Emphasis added by the author.[o]

43. Kant, "Über eine Entdeckung, nach der alle neue Kritik der reinen Vernunft durch eine ältere entbehrlich gemacht werden soll" (1790). *Werke*, VI, p. 27.

n. more precisely: [one should] also not [speak of] "the *being*-which is in certain way" [das so *Seiende*]; for God is in no way a being [*Seiendes*] if "Being" ["*Sein*"] belongs to finitude

o. See C 567. "The concept of a thing in itself [as] its counterpart=X is necessarily set in opposition to the concept of an object as *appearance*, but not as one object (*realiter*) differentiated from others [distinct, given in reality]—rather, simply according to concepts (*logice oppositum*) as something which is given (*dabile*), but from which [something] will be abstracted, and which merely subjectively constitutes a member of the classification as objective noumenon. This noumenon, however, is nothing more than a representation of reason in general, and [with] the question: How is synthetic a priori knowledge possible? [it is] not a particular Object [*Objekt*], which would be what is objective [*das Gegenständliche*] in the phenomenon" (reference by R. Jancke, *Die Kant-Interpretation Martin Heideggers*, Archiv f. systematische Philosophie und Soziologie XXXIV, p. 271).

proven. Accordingly, the "mere" in the phrase "mere appearance" is not a restricting and diminishing of the actuality of the thing, but is rather only the negation of [the assumption] that the being can be infinitely known in human knowledge. ". . . (in the world of sense), however deeply we inquire into its objects, [we have] to do with nothing but appearances."[44]

Finally, the essence of the difference between appearance and thing in itself appears with particular clarity in the double meaning of the expression "outside us."[45] In both meanings, the being itself is always meant. As thing in itself, it is always outside us to the extent that we as finite creatures are excluded from the kind of infinite intuition which pertains to it. If it signifies the appearances, then it is outside us to the extent that we ourselves are indeed not this being, and yet we have a means of access to it. At the same time, however, the discussion of the difference between finite and infinite knowledge with a view to the difference in character between what is known in each respectively now points out that these concepts of appearance and thing-in-itself, which are fundamental for the *Critique*, can only be made understandable and part of the wider problem by basing them more explicitly on the problematic of the finitude of the human creature. These concepts, however, do not refer to two classifications of objects arranged one behind the other within "the" completely indifferent, fixed [field of] knowledge.

With this characterization of the finitude of human knowledge, what is essential to the dimension within which the task of laying the ground of metaphysics takes place is revealed. At the same time there results a clearer indication of the direction which the [process of] going back to the source of the inner possibility of ontology has to take.

§6. The Ground for the Source of the Laying of the Ground for Metaphysics

The interpretation of the essence of knowledge in general and its finitude in particular revealed that finite intuition (sensibility) as such requires determination through the understanding. Conversely, the understanding, which in itself is already finite, is dependent upon intuition: "For we can understand nothing except what one of our words brings with it corresponding to something in intuition."[46] Hence, when Kant says "Neither of these qualities {sensibility and understanding} is to be preferred to the other,"[47] it appears to contradict [the fact that] the fundamental character of knowing is to be found

---

44. A 45, B 62f.
45. A 373.
46. A 277, B 333.
47. A 51, B 75.

in intuition. The necessary way in which sensibility and understanding belong together in the essential unity of finite knowledge, however, does not exclude but rather includes an order of precedence in the structural grounding of thinking in intuition, which exists as the initial representing. Precisely this order of precedence concerning the reflexive belonging-together of sensibility and understanding must not be overlooked, it must not become leveled off to an indifferent correlation of content and form, if we want to come closer to the innermost course [Zuge] of the Kantian problematic.

Nevertheless, for the question of going back to the ground for the source [Quellgrund] of the possibility of finite knowledge, it appears sufficient to hold to the simple and reflexive duality of its elements. And this is all the more necessary as Kant himself expressly fixes the "springing forth" of our knowledge in "two basic sources [Grundquellen] of the mind": "Our knowledge springs forth from two basic sources [Grundquellen] of the mind; the first is the capacity to receive representations (receptivity for impressions), the second is the power to know an object through these representations (spontaneity of concepts)."[48][10] And even more pointedly, Kant says that "other than these two sources of knowledge [Erkenntnisquellen]" (sensibility and understanding), we have "no others."[49]

This duality of sources, however, is no mere juxtaposition. Rather, only in the union of both of them as prescribed by their structure can finite knowledge be what its essence requires. "Only through their union can knowledge spring forth."[50] The unity of their unification is nevertheless not a subsequent result of the collision of these elements. Rather, what unites them, this "synthesis," must let the elements in their belonging-together and their oneness spring forth. If finite knowledge, however, has its essence precisely in the original synthesis of the basic sources [Grundquellen] and if the laying of the ground for metaphysics must push ahead into the essential ground of finite knowledge, then it is inescapable that the naming which indicates the "two basic sources [Grundquellen]" already suggests an allusion to the ground of their source [ihren Quellgrund], i.e., to an original unity.

Thus in both the introduction and the conclusion to the Critique of Pure Reason, Kant gives a remarkable characterization of the two basic sources which goes beyond their mere enumeration: "Only this much appears to be necessary by way of introduction or anticipation, namely, that there are two stems of human knowledge, *sensibility* and *understanding*, which perhaps spring forth from a common, but to us unknown, root. Through the former, objects are given to us; through the latter, they are thought."[51] "We shall

---

48. A 50, B 74.
49. A 294, B 350.
50. A 51, B 75f.
51. A 15, B 29.

content ourselves here with the completion of our task, namely, merely to outline the *architectonic* of all knowledge arising from *pure reason*; and in doing so we shall begin from the point at which the common root of our power of knowledge [*Erkenntniskraft*] divides and throws out two stems, one of which is *reason*. By reason I here understand the whole higher faculty of knowledge and am therefore contrasting the rational with the empirical."[52] The "empirical" here signifies the experiencing taking of things in stride: receptivity, sensibility as such.

Here the "sources" are understood as "stems" which spring forth from a common root. But whereas in the first passage the "common root" was qualified with a "perhaps," in the second the "common root" is reputed to exist. Nonetheless, in both passages this root is only alluded to. Kant not only fails to pursue it further, but even declares that it is "unknown to us." From this, something essential arises for the general character of the Kantian laying of the ground for metaphysics: it leads not to the crystal clear, absolute evidence of a first maxim and principle, but rather goes into and points consciously toward the unknown. It is a philosophizing laying of the ground for Philosophy.

II. THE MANNER OF UNVEILING THE ORIGIN

§7. The Outline of the Stages in the Laying of the Ground for Ontology

The grounding of metaphysics is the projection of the inner possibility of a priori synthesis. Its essence must be determined, and its origin in the ground of its source [*Quellgrund*] must be presented. The explanation of the essence of finite knowledge and the characterization of the basic sources [*Grundquellen*] have circumscribed the dimension of the revealing of the essential origin. In this way, however, the question of the inner possibility of a priori synthetic knowledge has attained more precision and at the same time has become more complex.

The preparatory exposition of the problem of a grounding of metaphysics yields the following:[53] Knowledge of beings is only possible on the grounds of a prior knowledge, free of experience, of the constitution of the Being of

---

52. A 835, B 863.
53. See above, §2, p. 6.

beings. Now finite knowledge (the finitude of which is in question) is essentially an intuition of the being which takes it in stride and which is determinative. If finite knowledge of beings is to be possible, then it must be grounded in a knowing of the Being of beings prior to all receiving. For its own possibility, therefore, the finite knowledge of beings requires a knowing which does not take things in stride (and which is apparently nonfinite), such as a "creative" intuiting.

So the question concerning the possibility of a priori synthesis narrows down to this: How can a finite creature, which as such is delivered over to beings and is directed by the taking-in-stride of these same beings, know, i.e., intuit, prior to all [instances of] taking the being in stride, without being its "creator?" In other words: how must this finite creature be with respect to the constitution of its own Being so that such a bringing-forward of the constitution of the Being of beings which is free from experience, i.e., an ontological synthesis, is possible?

If the question concerning the possibility of a priori synthesis is framed in this way, however, and if all knowledge as finite is bifurcated into the two previously mentioned elements, i.e., if it is itself a synthesis, then a peculiar complication enters into the question concerning the possibility of a priori synthesis. For this synthesis is not identical with the above-named veritative synthesis, which is concerned solely with ontic knowledge.

The ontological synthesis, as knowledge in general, is already synthetic, so that the laying of the ground must begin with a setting forth of the pure elements of pure knowledge (pure intuition and pure thinking). After that, it is of value to clarify the character of the original, essential unity of these pure elements, i.e., the pure veritative synthesis. This should be done in such a way, however, that it also determines pure intuition a priori. The concepts belonging to it—not just to their form, but also to their content—must spring forth prior to all experience. In this case, however, the pure predicative synthesis, which necessarily belongs to the pure veritative synthesis, is of a special sort. Therefore, as with the ontological synthesis, the question concerning the essence of the "ontological predicate" must shift to the center of the problem of the a priori synthesis.

The question of the inner possibility of the essential unity of a pure veritative synthesis, however, pushes us even further back to the clarification of the original ground for the inner possibility of this synthesis. By unveiling the essence of pure synthesis from its ground, then, the insight first arises as to the extent to which ontological knowledge can be the condition for the possibility of ontic knowledge. In this way, the full essence of ontological truth is circumscribed.

Accordingly, laying the ground for ontology runs through five stages as indicated by the following headings: (1) the essential elements of pure knowledge; (2) the essential unity of pure knowledge; (3) the inner possibility of the essential unity of ontological synthesis; (4) the ground for the inner possibility of ontological synthesis; (5) the full determination of the essence of ontological knowledge.

§8. The Method for Revealing the Origin

The provisional characterization of the essential structure [Wesensbaues] of finite knowledge has already revealed a wealth of structures [Strukturen] which belong inherently to synthesis. Now, to the extent that pure veritative synthesis contains the idea of knowledge which in a certain sense appears to be nonfinite, the question of the possibility of ontology for a finite creature becomes more complicated. Finally, the indications concerning the ground for the source of the basic sources of finite knowledge[11] and its possible unity leads to the unknown.

Given the character of the leading problem and the dimension of its possible treatment, it is not surprising that the way in which the origin is disclosed and the manner of going back to the ground of the source remains undetermined for the time being. Their certainty and determinacy first grow, as it were, during the advance into the hitherto concealed region and from the confrontation with what shows itself there. Indeed, the region of the unveiling of the origin is none other than the human "mind" (mens sive animus). Opening up this [region] is [usually] assigned to "Psychology." However, to the extent that this concerns an interpretation of "knowledge," the essence of which commonly has to do with judging (logos), "Logic" must also be a partner to this opening up of the mind. When considered superficially, "Psychology" and "Logic" divide this task or, in other words, struggle for preeminence and in this way extend and transform themselves.

But if on the one hand one considers the originality and uniqueness of what Kant sought and if on the other hand one sees the questionable character of what has been handed down, namely, that neither "Logic" nor "Psychology" is at all suitable for such a problematic, then it proves to be hopeless to want to get hold of what is essential in the Kantian laying of the ground for metaphysics by means of a manual [showing a] "logical" or "psychological" way of questioning or by means of a completely superficial connecting of the two. However, the fact that "Transcendental Psychology" merely expresses a perplexity becomes clear as soon as one has grasped the fundamental and methodological difficulties that are involved in the determination of the finite human essence.

Just this, then, remains: to leave open the method for unveiling the origin, and not to press it hastily into a handed-down or newly devised discipline. With this leaving open of the character of the method, we must, of course, remember the explanation which Kant himself offered concerning the *Critique of Pure Reason* immediately after its completion: "This sort of inquiry will always remain difficult."[54]

All the same, a general indication of the fundamental character of the procedure for this laying of the ground for metaphysics is required. The type of investigation can be understood as "analytic" in the broadest sense. It concerns finite pure reason with a view to how, on the grounds of its essence, it makes something like ontological synthesis possible. That is why Kant describes the *Critique* as a "study of our inner nature."[55] This revealing of the essence of human Dasein is "to the philosophers, however, even a duty."[a]

For all that, however, "analytic" does not mean an unknotting and breaking up of finite pure reason into its elements, but rather the reverse: an "unknotting" as a freeing[b] which loosens the seeds [*Keime*] of ontology. It unveils those conditions from which an ontology as a whole is allowed to sprout [*aufkeimen*] according to its inner possibility. In Kant's own words, such an analytic is a bringing of "itself to light through reason," it is "what reason brings forth entirely from out of itself."[56][c] Analytic thus becomes a letting-be-seen [*Sehenlassen*] of the genesis of the essence of finite pure reason from its proper ground.

In such an analytic, therefore, lies the projecting anticipation of the entire inner essence of finite pure reason. Only in the thorough development of this essence does the essential structure of ontology become visible. As thus unveiled, this structure at the same time determines the construction of the substructures [*Fundamente*] necessary to it. This projecting freeing of the whole, which an ontology essentially makes possible, brings metaphysics to the ground and soil [*Grund und Boden*] in which it is rooted as a "haunting"[57] of human nature.

---

54. Letter to M. Herz, 1781. *Werke*, IX, p. 198. [Translation is in *Kant: Philosophical Correspondence 1759-99*, ed. and tr. A. Zweig (Chicago: University of Chicago Press, 1967), p. 95. The full sentence by Kant reads, "This sort of investigation will always remain difficult, for it includes the *metaphysics of metaphysics*"—tr.]

55. A 703, B 731.

56. A xx.

57. B xv. [The German *Heimsuchung* is translated by Kemp Smith as "visitation," but the term also connotes a haunting or an obsession. I render it "haunting" to show the sense in which the questions Kant asks are an inescapable and lingering part of human nature. We should at the same time be attuned to the literal sense of the word, which suggests the seeking of a home—tr.]

a. See Transcendental Reflection as the *Critique*'s method, A 262f., B 319.

b. Making fluid, bringing into flux! Origin

c. Dis-articulating [*Zer-gliedern*], bringing the *unity* of the *articulation* [*Gliederung*] to light.

B. THE STAGES OF CARRYING OUT THE PROJECTION OF THE INNER POSSIBILITY OF ONTOLOGY

At this point, the interpretation of the *Critique* must be revived and the leading problem must be affirmed more precisely. What is at issue is the essential possibility of ontological synthesis. When unfolded, the question reads: How can finite human Dasein pass beyond (transcend) the being in advance when this being is not only something it did not create itself, but something at which it must be directed in order to exist as Dasein? The problem of the possibility of Ontology is accordingly the question of the essence and essential ground of the transcendence of the preliminary understanding of Being. The problem of the transcendental, i.e., of the synthesis which constitutes transcendence, thus can also be put in this way: How must the finite being that we call "human being" be according to its innermost essence so that in general it can be open to a being that it itself is not and that therefore must be able to show itself from itself?

The stages to answer this question have already been sketched out above.[58] It is now worth reviewing them individually, although with a disclaimer concerning one interpretation that would exhaustively treat all of them in the same way. We thereby follow the inner movement of the Kantian ground-laying, but without holding to his particular arrangement and the formulation therein. It is worth going back behind these in order to be able to assess the appropriateness, the validity, and the limits of the external architectonic of the *Critique of Pure Reason* based on the most original understanding of the inner course of the ground-laying.

THE FIRST STAGE IN THE GROUND-LAYING: THE ESSENTIAL ELEMENTS OF PURE KNOWLEDGE

If the essence of a priori synthetic knowledge is to be brought to light, then a clarification is first required of the standing of its necessary elements. As knowing, the transcendental synthesis must be an intuition and, as a priori knowing, it must be a pure intuition. As pure knowing which belongs to human finitude, pure intuition must necessarily be determined through a pure thinking.

---

58. See §7 above, p. 27f.

A) Pure Intuition in Finite Knowing[a]

§9. The Elucidation of Space and Time as Pure Intuitions

Can such a thing as a pure intuiting be found in the finite knowing of beings?[b] What is sought is an immediate, although experience-free, allowing of an individual to be encountered. It is true that, as finite, pure intuiting is a representing which takes things in stride. However, what should now be taken in stride, where it concerns the knowing of Being and not beings, cannot be a being which is at hand and which presents itself. On the contrary, the pure representing which takes things in stride must give itself something[c] capable of being represented. Pure intuition, therefore, must in a certain sense be "creative."

What is represented in pure intuition is no being (no object [Gegenstand], i.e., no appearing being), but at the same time it is plainly not nothing. It is worth emphasizing all the more urgently what comes to be represented in, and only in, pure intuition and how, corresponding to what is represented, the manner of the representing is to be delimited.

Kant posits space and time as pure intuitions. It is worthwhile, first of all with reference to space, to show how it manifests itself in the finite knowledge of beings and, accordingly, to show that alone in which its essence is presentable.

Kant lays out the unveiling of the essence of space and time in such a way that he [first gives] a negative characterization of the phenomenon, from which he then lets the appropriate positive characterization follow.

It is no accident that the essential characterization begins negatively. It starts with the precautionary statement that space and time are this and not that since the positive [aspect] of what is apprehended is already known—and known essentially—in advance, even though it is not yet recognized but rather is misunderstood in a certain way. Space, i.e., the relations of beside-, above-, and behind-one-another,[d] are not found anywhere "here" or "there." Space is

---

a. See p. 101, and §28 generally.

b. See *Fortschritte*, p. 91f., regarding the projection of the idea of an a priori intuition.

c. its own [Heidegger has marked the German word "*ein*" (translated as "something") and the note simply says "*sein*," which in this context is a possessive pronoun, indicating that the "something" that is capable of being represented in fact belongs to or is part of the pure representing that takes things in stride—tr.]

d. here clearly the differences among the places

not a thing at hand among other beings,ᵉ it is no "empirical representation,"ᶠ
i.e., it is not the represented in such a representing. In orderᵍ for what is at
hand to be able to appear as extended in accordance with definite spatial
relations, space must already be apparent prior to any taking in of what is at
hand in a way that takes in stride. It [space] must be represented as that
"within which" what is at hand can first be encountered: Space is [something]
represented which is necessary, and necessary in advance, in finite human
knowing; i.e., it is a pureʰ represented [*rein Vorgestelltes*].ⁱ

Now if, however, this represented "applies to every" particular spatial relation, then it appears to be a representation which "applies to many," i.e., a
concept. In turn, the essential analysis of what is represented as space provides
information about the representing which belongs to this represented. Space
is, as Kant says (again speaking negatively), no "discursive" representation.
The unity of space is not with respect to more and particular spatial relations
held together and assembled from a comparative consideration of them.ʲ The
unity of space is not that of a concept, but rather the unity of something which
in itself is a unique one [*ein einzig Eines*]. The many spacesᵏ are only limitations
of the one, unique space. This [unique space], however, is not only limitable
from time to time; rather, even the limiting limits themselves are their essence,
i.e., they are spatial. The unified, unique space is wholly itself in each of its
parts. Representing of space is hence immediate representing of a unified
particular, i.e., intuition, provided that the essence of intuition must be determined as *repraesentatio singularis*. And indeed, according to what has already been said, space is what is intuited in a pure intuition.

Pure intuition as intuition, however, must not onlyˡ give what is intuited
immediately, but must give it immediately as a whole. And indeed, this pure
intuiting is no mere taking of a part in stride; with the reduction it also looks
especially at the whole. "Space is represented as an infinite given magnitude."⁵⁹
To say that space is a magnitude [*eine Größe*] does not mean that it is of such
and such an extent [*ein soundso Großes*], nor does infinite magnitude [*un-
endliche Größe*] mean an "endless" extent [*ein "endlos" Großes*]. Instead, "magnitude" ["*Größe*"] here means extensiveness [*Großheit*], which first makes such

---

59. A 25 (B 39).

e. "external"—*aside from me* and *aside from another*
f. Space is not simply what can be stripped off—*Abstractum* from many different things.
g. In order, therefore, for
h. which makes the appearing possible
i. The second argument does not follow from this; necessity; nothing from the determination
which depends upon the appearing, but rather the reverse.
j. to no. 1? no! there the *empirical* negates the *representation*.
k. individual [as in, "The individual spaces . . ."—tr.]
l. as something individual, but immediately this, i.e., representing as a whole, i.e., *giving*; this
individual has the particularity of uniqueness [*dieses Einzelne hat die Einzelheit der Einzigkeit*], i.e.,
the characteristic individual—"*this*"

and such an extent ("quantities") possible. "The quantum, wherein alone all quantity can be determined, is indeterminate and continuous with respect to the number of parts: space and time."[60]

To say that this extensiveness is "infinite," then, means that as compared with the determinate, particular parts space is not something different from the degree and richness of the compound. Instead it is infinitely,[m] i.e., essentially, different. It precedes all the parts as the limitable, unified whole. It does not have the multitude of particulars "under itself," as is the case with the universality of concepts; rather, as what is already co-intuited "in itself," so it is that this pure intuition of the whole can yield the "parts" at any time. The representing of such an "infinite" extensiveness as given is hence a giving intuiting. Provided that the unified whole was given especially, this representing allows what is representable in it to spring forth, and in this sense it is called an "original"[n] representing.[61]

Pure intuition, then, very much has its 'something intuited,' and indeed has it to the degree that it gives this intuited only in and through the intuiting itself. The intuited is, of course, neither a being which is at hand, nor is it thematically grasped in the pure intuiting itself. In being busy with the things and in perceiving them, their spatial relationships are indeed "intuited,"[o] but for the most part they are not thought of as such.[p] In a preliminary glimpse, what is intuited in pure intuition stands without reference to a particular object and is unthematic as well. Nevertheless, in this way what is glimpsed in the unified whole makes possible the ordering according to [which things can be] beside-, under-, and in back of one another. What is intuited in this "way of intuiting" is not simply nothing.

From the above it is already possible to conclude that the further explication of the "original representing" in pure intuition will only be possible when it has been successful in bringing to light with more urgency the sense in which pure intuition is "original," i.e., how it allows what is intuited in it to spring forth.[q]

---

60. *Kants handschriftlicher Nachlaß*, vol. V, no. 5846. See Erdmann, *Reflexionen II*, 1038.
61. A 32, B 48; see also B 40.

m. transcendental concept of the infinite
Observation on the Thesis of the First Antinomy; see A n. 5. [The observation to the Thesis of the First Antinomy can be found in KPR A 430, B 458ff. —tr.]
n. See p. 99 below. [The reference is to Heidegger's marginal note 'b' to §28—tr.]
o. pure
p. *Fortschritte*, p. 92 Z. 14, p. 103 Z. 10
q. §28, p. 100ff.

§10. Time as the Universal Pure Intuition[a]

Pure intuition is required as the one essential element of ontological knowledge in which the experience of beings is grounded. But as pure intuition, space gives in advance merely the totality of those relations according to which what is encountered in the external senses would be ordered. At the same time, however, we find givens of the "inner sense" which indicate no spatial shape and no spatial references. Instead, they show themselves as a succession of states of our mind (representations, drives, moods). What we look at in advance in the experience of these appearances, although unobjective and unthematic, is pure succession. Therefore, time is "the form of inner sense, i.e., of the intuiting of ourselves and our inner state."[62] Time determines "the relation of representations in our inner state."[63] ". . . time cannot be a determination of outer appearances; it has to do with neither shape nor position, etc."[64]

In this way both pure intuitions, space and time, are allotted to two [different] regions of experience, and at first it appears to be impossible to find a pure intuition which constitutes every instance of knowledge of the Being of experienceable beings and which, therefore, permits the problem of ontological knowledge to be formulated universally. Now to be sure, in addition to the association of both pure intuitions with the two regions of appearances, Kant states this thesis: "Time is the formal a priori condition of all appearances whatsoever."[65] Hence, time has a preeminence over space. As universal, pure intuition, it [time] must for this reason become the guiding and supporting essential element of pure knowledge, of the transcendence which forms knowledge.

The following interpretation shows how time shifts more and more to the forefront in the course of the individual stages of the laying of the ground for metaphysics, and hereby first reveals its own particular essence in a more original way than the provisional characterization in the Transcendental Aesthetic permits.

How does Kant now ground this priority of time as universal, pure intuition? At first it may strike us that Kant denies the external appearances of the determination of time, especially when it is in the everyday experience of

---

62. A 33, B 49.
63. A 33, B 50. [Heidegger's page citation (B 49) corrected—tr.]
64. A 33, B 49f.
65. A 34, B 50.

a. On time and modes of time see SS 1930 [Vom Wesen der menschlichen Freiheit. Einleitung in die Philosophie. GA, vol. 31], p. 152ff., in particular p. 158f.; WS 1935/36 [Die Frage nach dem Ding. Zu Kants Lehre von den transzendentalen Grundsätzen. GA, vol. 41], p. 231ff.; see below p. 72f., p. 75f.

precisely these determinations—in the movement of the stars and in natural events in general (growth and decay)—that time is found and indeed so immediately that time comes to be equated with the "heavens." However, Kant does not simply reject out of hand the external appearances of the determination of time, if [indeed] time is to be the formal a priori condition for all appearances. One thesis denies within-time-ness[12] to physical beings which are at hand, the other grants it. How can these contradictory assertions be reconciled? If Kant reduces time as pure intuition to the givens of the inner senses, i.e., to representations in the broadest sense, then in this reduction lies an extension of precisely the possible scope within which it can function as the preliminary way of intuiting. Among the representations are found those which, as representations, also allow beings to be encountered which are not the same as the representing creature itself. Hence, Kant's reflections take this path:

Because all representations, as states of representing, fall immediately in time, what is represented in representing belongs as such in time. By the digression into the immediate within-time-ness of representing, a mediate within-time-ness of what is represented, i.e., of those "representations" determined through external sense, is given. Hence, since the external appearances are only mediately within time, in one sense the determination of time belongs to them and in another sense it does not. The argument from the within-time-ness of the external intuitings as a psychic event to the within-time-ness of what is intuited in these intuitings, becomes essentially facilitated for Kant through the ambiguity of the expression "intuition," or rather "representation." On the one hand, the expressions mean states of mind, but at the same time they mean that which they, as such states, have as their objects.

Whether this grounding of the universality of time as pure intuition, and with it [the grounding of] its central ontological function, continues to be valid and can be decisive must here remain open for the present, as must the question of whether space as pure intuition was thereby displaced from a possible central ontological function.[66]

If in general the grounding of the universality of time as pure intuition is to be possible, [this can only happen if it can be shown that] although space and time as pure intuitions both belong "to the subject," time dwells in the subject in a more original way than space. Time immediately reduced to the givens of inner sense, however, is at the same time only ontologically more universal if the subjectivity of the subject exists in the openness for the being. The more subjective time is, the more original and extensive is the expansiveness [Entschränkung] of the subject.

The universal ontological function that Kant assigns to time at the beginning

---

66. See §35 below, p. 137ff.

of the ground-laying can hence only be sufficiently justified because it is precisely time itself, and indeed time in its ontological function (i.e., as essential bit of pure ontological knowledge), which forces us to determine the essence of subjectivity in a more original way.[67]

The "Transcendental Aesthetic" has as its task to set forth the ontological αἴσϑησις which makes it possible "to disclose a priori" the Being of beings. To the extent that intuition retains the leading role in all knowledge, "one of the pieces required for the solution of the general problem of transcendental philosophy"[68] (Ontology) has been attained.

To whatever small degree pure intuition as essential element of ontological knowledge begins to dissipate, even in the slightest, then to just as small a degree can the isolated interpretation of one of these elements, already in its elementary function, be made visible. It is not the elimination of the Transcendental Aesthetic as a provisional occurance of the problem, but rather the preservation and refining of its problematic which must be the most proper goal for the ground-laying which Kant carried out, provided that it is certain of its own task.

First of all, however, by looking at it in the same way and isolating it, we must set forth the second essential element of pure finite knowledge: pure thinking.

B) Pure Thinking in Finite Knowing

§11. *The Pure Concept of Understanding (Notion)*

The other element in the finitude of human knowledge is thinking which, as determinative representing, is directed toward what is intuited in intuition and thus is in service to intuition alone. The object of an intuition, which is always a particular, is nevertheless determined as "such and such" in a "universal representation," i.e., in the concept. The finitude of thinking intuition is therefore a knowing through concepts; pure knowing is pure intuition through pure concepts. It is a matter of exhibiting this if the full essential existence of pure knowledge in general is to be secured. In order to be able

---

67. See §34 below, p. 132.
68. B 73.

to find such pure concepts, however, what is required first of all is the clarification of what is being sought under this name.

In the representing of a linden, a beech or a fir as a tree, for example, the particular which is intuited as such and such a thing is determined on the basis of a reference to the sort of thing which "applies for many." Indeed, this applicability to many [instances] characterizes a representation as concept, but nevertheless it does not yet hit upon its original essence. For its part, then, this applicability to many [instances] as a derivative character is grounded in the fact that represented in the concept is the one [*das Eine*] in which several objects agree. Conceptual representing is the allowing of the agreement of many in this one. The oneness of this one must be anticipatively kept in view in conceptual representing, therefore, and it must allow for all assertions concerning the many which are determinative. This preliminary keeping in view of the one within which the many should be able to agree is the basic act of the forming of a concept. Kant calls it "Reflection." It is "the deliberation whereby various representations can be grasped in one consciousness."[69] Such deliberating achieves a unity which as such encompasses many, so that with reference to this oneness the many can be likened to one another (comparison). At the same time, what is not in accord with the one that has been held out to us is disregarded (abstraction in the Kantian sense). What is represented in conceptual representing is "a representation *insofar as it can be embodied in various [things]*."[70] In the concept, something is not simply represented which tactically belongs to many; instead it is this belonging, insofar as it belongs, i.e., in its oneness, [which is represented]. What is thus represented as this encompassing one is the concept, and thus Kant rightly says: "It is a mere tautology to speak of universal or common concepts."[71]

Because the representation is formed into a concept in the basic act of the preliminary keeping-in-view of the one which applies to many, i.e., in reflection according to Kant, the concepts also are called reflected, i.e., [they are] representations which spring forth from reflection. The conceptual character of a representation—what is represented in it has the form of the one which applies to many—springs forth each time from reflection. However, according to the content of the determinative one, this arises for the most part from the empirical intuiting which compares and which learns from that. The origin of the content [*Wasgehalt*][13] of such empirical concepts is hence no problem.

Under the heading "pure concept," however, a "reflected" representation was sought whose content [*Wasgehalt*] essentially cannot be read from appearances. Also, its content [*Inhalt*] must be obtainable a priori. Concepts which

---

69. *Logikvorlesung*, VIII, §6, p. 402.
70. Ibid., §1, note 1, p. 399.
71. Ibid., note 2.

are also given their content [*Inhalt*] a priori, Kant calls notions, *conceptus dati a priori.*[72]

Are there such concepts? Are they found already prepared in human understanding? How can the understanding be capable of giving a content [*Wasgehalt*] where it is only an empty function of binding-together, directly dependent on the given intuition? And can such a what [*ein solches Was*] which was represented as given come to be found completely in the understanding if, as it should happen, it is isolated precisely from all intuition? If the understanding itself is to be the origin not only of the form of every concept as such, but also of the content of determinate concepts, then this origin can only lie in the basic act[a] of concept-formation as such, in reflection.

Every determining of something as something (judging) includes the "unity of the act of ordering various representations under a common one."[73] This act of reflecting unifying, however, is only possible in this way if in itself it is already guided by the preliminary reference to a unity in light of which a unifying in general is possible. The reflecting itself, quite apart from whatever concept arises from its action, is already the preliminary representing of a unity which, as such, guides the unification. If, accordingly, the representing of unity lies in the reflecting itself, then this means: representing of unity belongs to the essential structure of the basic act of understanding.

The essence of understanding is original comprehending or grasping. The representations of the guiding unity lie already prepared in the structure of the act of understanding as representing unification. These represented unities are the content [*Inhalt*] of the pure concepts. The content [*Wasgehalt*] of these concepts is the unity which in each case makes a unification possible. The representing of these unities is in itself already conceptual a priori on the grounds of its specific content [*Inhalts*]. The pure concept no longer need be endowed with a conceptual form; it is itself this form in an original sense.

Hence the pure concepts do not first arise by means of an act of reflection, they are not reflected concepts. Rather, they belong in advance to the essential structure of reflection, i.e., they are representations which act in, with, and for reflection, i.e., reflecting concepts. "All concepts generally, no matter from where they may take their material [*Stoff*], are reflected, i.e., representation[s] raised to the logical relation of general applicability. Yet there are concepts, the entire sense of which is to be nothing other than one reflection or another, to which occurring representations can be subject. They can be called concepts of reflection (*conceptus reflectentes*); and because every kind of reflection occurs in judgments, so they become the mere action of the understanding

---

72. Ibid., §4, p. 401. See also A 320, B 377.
73. A 68, B 93.

a. Basic act—representing from *unity*—*gathering*

which, in the judgments applied to the relation, are apprehended absolutely in themselves as grounds for the possibility of judging."[74]

Hence there are pure concepts in the understanding as such, and the "analysis of the faculty of understanding itself" must bring to light these representations which are co-constitutive of the essential structure of reflection.

§12. Notions as Ontological Predicates (Categories)

The pure understanding in itself yields a manifold, the pure unities of possible unification. And if indeed the possible ways of unification (judgments) constitute a closed cohesiveness, i.e., the closed nature of understanding itself, then in pure understanding there lies concealed a systematic totality of the manifoldness of pure concepts. However, this totality is then the system of those predicates which function in pure knowledge, i.e.,[a] which state something about the Being of beings. The pure concepts have the character of ontological predicates, which have been called "categories" since ancient times. The Table of Judgments is thus the origin of the categories and their table.

This origin of the categories has often been disputed and always will be. The primary objection centers around the questionable nature of the source of the origin [Ursprungsquelle] itself, around the Table of Judgments as such and the sufficiency of its grounding. In fact, Kant does not develop the manifold nature of the functions in judgment from the essence of the understanding. Instead he presents a finished table which is organized according to the four "primary moments" of Quantity, Quality, Relation, and Modality.[75] Whether and the extent to which these four moments are grounded in the essence of the understanding is likewise not indicated.[b] Whether in general they can be grounded through pure, formal logic is questionable.

In general, then, the character of this Table of Judgments is uncertain. Kant himself vacillates, calling it at times a "transcendental table,"[76] and at other times a "logical table of judgments."[77] As such, does not the charge which Kant made concerning Aristotle's Table of Categories also apply to his own Table of Judgments?

---

74. Erdmann, *Reflexionen II*, p. 554. In *Kants handschriftlicher Nachlaß*, vol. V, no. 5051.
75. *Logikvorlesung*, §20, p. 408.
76. A 73, B 98.
77. *Prolegomena*, §21.

a. how so?
b. In that regard see Klaus Reich, *Die Vollständigkeit der Kantischen Urteilstafel*, 1932; see in that regard my lectures and exercises from 1929-32.

But it is not to be decided here whether and to what extent the frequent criticisms of the Kantian Table of Judgments are justified and whether they even so much as hit upon the deficiency of the ground. Rather, we must see that such a critique of the Table of Judgments, as supposed critique of the source of the origin of the categories, has already fundamentally missed the decisive problem. Not only are the categories not deduced [abgeleitet] tactically from the Table of Judgments, but in no way can they have conduced [hergeleitet] to it,[14] and for this reason: because at the present stage of the discussion of the isolated elements of pure knowledge, the essence and the idea of the category in general has not yet been determined and indeed cannot even be made into a problem.

But if in principle the question concerning the origin of the categories cannot yet arise at this point, then the Table of Judgments must have another function than that specified above in the preparation of the question concerning the possibility of ontological knowledge.

It seems easy to be satisfied with the task posed by the first stage of the ground-laying, for what is more obvious than the elements of pure knowledge, pure intuition, and the pure concept, presented side by side? Yet, even with this isolation, from the very beginning we must not lose sight of the fact that pure finite knowledge has become a problem. This was said earlier: the second element, pure thinking, is essentially subservient to intuition. As a consequence, dependency on pure intuition is not secondary or supplemental to pure thinking but belongs essentially to it. If the pure concept is apprehended initially as notion, then the second element of pure knowledge has by no means yet been attained in its elementary character. On the contrary, it has been shorn of the decisive, essential moment, namely, the inner reference to intuition. The pure concept as notion is therefore only a fragment of the second element of pure knowledge.

As long as pure understanding is viewed with regard to its essence, i.e., its pure relatedness to intuition, an origin of the notions as ontological predicates cannot be unveiled at all. Hence the Table of Judgments is not also the "origin of the categories," but rather is merely the "guiding text for the discovery of all the concepts of the understanding." In it we should find guidance concerning the closed totality of pure concepts, although it cannot grant the unveiling of the full essence of the pure concepts as categories. Whether the Table of Judgments as Kant introduces and presents it can indeed also assume just this limited function of sketching out a systematic unity of the pure concepts of the understanding remains open here.

From what has been presented it has just now become clear: the more radically one seeks to isolate the pure elements of a finite [act of] knowledge, the more compelling becomes the impossibility of such an isolation and the more obtrusive is the dependency of pure thinking on intuition. With that, however, the artificiality of the first point of departure for a characterization of pure knowledge is revealed. Pure concepts, then, can only be determined as ontological predicates if they are understood as based on the *essential unity* of finite, pure knowledge.

THE SECOND STAGE OF THE GROUND-LAYING: THE ESSENTIAL UNITY OF PURE KNOWLEDGE

The isolated pure elements of pure knowledge are: time as universal, pure intuition and the notions as what is thought in pure thinking. If, however, the consideration which isolates the elements is not even allowed to comprehend them fully as such, then it is all the more likely that we will not be able to achieve its unity through a supervenient linking of the isolated parts. The problem of the essential unity of pure knowledge is made more precise, however, if we do not allow the matter to rest with the negative characterization that this unity cannot be a bond stretching between the elements which is merely an afterthought.

The finitude of knowledge directly demonstrates a peculiar inner dependency of thinking upon intuition, or conversely: a need for the determination of the latter by the former. The pull of the elements toward one another indicates that their unity cannot be "later" than they are themselves, but rather that it must have applied to them "earlier" and must have laid the ground for them. This unity unites the elements as original in such a way that even at first in the uniting, the elements as such spring forth, and through it they are maintained in their unity. In spite of his point of departure from the isolated elements, to what extent does Kant nevertheless succeed in making this original unity visible?

Kant gives the first characterization of the original, essential unity of the pure elements, which is preparatory for all further elucidation, in the third section of the first chapter of the "Analytic of the Concepts," namely, in the part bearing the heading "On the Pure Concepts of the Understanding, or Categories."[78] Understanding these paragraphs is the key to understanding the *Critique of Pure Reason* as a laying of the ground for metaphysics.

Because the notions, as belonging to the finitude of knowledge, are related essentially to pure intuition and because this relatedness of pure intuition and pure thinking at the same time constitutes the essential unity of pure knowledge, the essential delimitation of the categories in general is at the same time

---

78. A 76-80, B 102-105; in B it is designated as §10.

the elucidation of the inner possibility of the essential unity of ontological knowledge. It is now a matter of presenting Kant's answer to the question concerning the essential unity of pure knowledge by means of the interpretation of the above-named section. First, of course, the question itself still requires further clarification.

§13. The Question Concerning the Essential Unity of Pure Knowledge

If the elements of finite, pure knowledge are essentially dependent upon one another, then this already keeps them from attaching to one another, their unity is like an after-the-fact togetherness, so to speak. Even the fact that the unity of the elements lies at the root [of this], and how this is so, has been concealed and made unknowable by the preceding isolation. If, however, an analysis sees the tendency for unveiling the original unity through to its end, this nevertheless does not guarantee a complete grasping of it. On the contrary, in view of the rigor with which the isolation was carried out, and the peculiarity of the second element which emerges still more clearly, it is to be expected that this isolation can no longer be completely undone, so that in the end the unity will not be expressly developed on the basis of its own most origin.

That the unity is not to be the result of a collision of the elements, that instead it is now itself to be the original unifying, is announced by naming it "synthesis."

Now in the full structure of finite knowledge, however, various syntheses have necessarily played off of one another.[79] To the Veritative Synthesis belongs the Predicative, into which in turn the Apophantical has been incorporated. Which of these syntheses is meant when the essential unity of pure knowledge is asked about? Apparently the Veritative, for it has to do with the unity of intuition and thinking. Those which remain, however, are necessarily included in it.

The essential unity of pure knowledge, however, ought to form the unity of the togetherness of all the structural syntheses as a whole. Hence the Veritative Synthesis maintains a priority in the question concerning the essential unity of pure knowledge only insofar as the problem of synthesis is concentrated in it. This does not exclude the possibility that it is oriented just as necessarily toward the remaining forms of synthesis. With regard to the question concerning the essential unity of ontological knowledge, moreover, it revolves around the pure Veritative Synthesis. What is asked about is the original union of pure, universal intuition (time) and pure thinking (the notions). Now pure intuition in itself, however—as the representing of a

---

79. See above, §7, p. 26; and §9, p. 31f.

unified whole—is already something like an intuiting unifying. Thus Kant speaks with justification of a "Synopsis" in intuition.[80] At the same time, the analysis of the notion as a "reflecting concept" has proven that pure thinking as representing the pure unities is in itself originally giving of unity, and in this sense it is "synthetic."

The problem of the pure veritative or ontological synthesis must hence be brought to the question: How does the original (veritative) "synthesis" of the pure Synopsis and the pure reflecting (predicative) synthesis appear? Already from the form of this question we might assess the synthesis being sought as one having a truly superior character if indeed it is to unite such things which in themselves already demonstrate synthetic structure. The synthesis being sought must from the first already have been on a par with the forms of "Synthesis" and "Synopsis" which are to be unified; it must itself form these originally in the course of unifying them.

§14. *The Ontological Synthesis*

The question concerning the essential unity of pure intuition and pure thinking is a consequence of the previous isolation of these elements. Hence the character of their unity may be sketched out initially in such a way that it shows how each of these elements structurally supports the other. They indicate seams [*Fugen*] which point in advance to a having-been-joined together [*Ineinandergefügtes*]. The Veritative Synthesis, then, is that which not only dovetails the elements joined together at these seams, but is rather what "fits" them together in the first place.[15]

Kant therefore introduces the general characterization of the essential unity of pure knowledge with the following reference: "Transcendental logic, on the other hand, has lying before it a manifold of a priori sensibility which the transcendental aesthetic offered to it in order to provide material for the concepts of pure understanding. Without this material, those concepts would be without any content and therefore would be entirely empty. Now space and time contain a manifold of pure a priori intuition, but at the same time they are the conditions for the receptivity of our mind—conditions under which alone it can receive representations of objects and which therefore must also always affect the concept of these objects. And yet, the spontaneity of our thought requires that this manifold first be gone through in a certain way, taken up, and bound together in order to produce knowledge. This act I name synthesis."[81]

---

80. A 94.
81. A 76f., B 102.

The dependency of pure intuition and pure thinking on one another is introduced here in a remarkably superficial form. Now, strictly speaking, "transcendental logic" does not have the pure manifold of time "lying before it," but instead this pattern belongs to the essential structure of pure thinking as analyzed by transcendental logic. Correspondingly, the transcendental aesthetic does not "offer" the pure manifold, but rather pure intuition is offered in its own right, namely, in the direction of pure thinking.

This pure offering is introduced even more precisely as an "affecting," which is not to be thought of in terms of affection through the senses. Insofar as this affection "always" belongs to pure knowledge, that says: our pure thinking always stands before the time which approaches it. How this is possible remains unclear for the present.

With this essential dependency of our pure thinking upon the pure manifold, the finitude of our thinking "demands" that this manifold fit [fügt] with thinking itself, i.e., fit with it as a conceptual determining. In order for pure intuition to be determinable through pure concepts, however, its manifold must have been gathered from dispersion, i.e., it must be gone through and assembled. This reciprocal preparing-themselves-for-each-other takes place in that act which Kant generally calls synthesis. In it, both pure elements come together from themselves from time to time; it joins together the seams allotted to each, and so it constitutes the essential unity of pure knowledge.

This synthesis is neither a matter of intuition nor of thinking. Mediating "between" both, so to speak, it is related to both. Thus in general it must share the basic character of the two elements, i.e., it must be a representing. "Synthesis in general, as we shall hereafter see, is the mere result of the *power of imagination*, a blind but indispensable function of the soul without which we would have no knowledge whatever, but of which we are seldom conscious even once."[82]

With this we have the first indication that apparently everything about synthetic structures in general which shows in the essential construction of knowledge is brought about through the power of imagination. Now, in particular and above all, however, it is a matter of the essential unity of pure knowledge, i.e., of "pure synthesis." It is called pure "if the manifold . . . is given a priori."[83] Hence, the pure synthesis fits in with that which, as synopsis, unifies in pure intuition.

At the same time, however, it requires us to take a look at a guiding unity. Hence to pure synthesis pertains the fact that, as representing unifying, it represents in advance the unity which belongs to it as such, i.e., in general. General-representing (*Allgemein-Vorstellen*) of this unity which is essentially peculiar to it, however, means: with respect to the unity that is represented

---

82. A 78, B 103. [Italics are Heidegger's—tr.]
83. A 77, B 103.

in it, pure synthesis is brought to the concept which itself gives it unity. Thus pure synthesis acts purely synoptically in pure intuition and at the same time purely reflectively in pure thinking. From this it is evident that there are three parts belonging to the full essence of pure knowledge: "What must first be given to us—with a view to the a priori knowledge of all objects—is the *manifold* of pure intuition; the *synthesis* of this manifold by means of the power of the imagination is the second, but even this does not yet yield knowledge. The concepts which give *unity* to this pure synthesis, and which consist solely in the representation of this necessary synthetic unity, furnish the third requisite for the knowledge of a proposed object [*eines vorkommenden Gegenstandes*], and they rest on the understanding."[84]

In this triad, the pure synthesis of the power of imagination holds the central position. Nevertheless, this is not mentioned in a superficial sense, as if in the enumeration of the conditions for pure knowledge the power of imagination was merely between the first and third. Rather, this center is a structural one. In it, the pure synopsis and the pure, reflecting synthesis meet and join together. This joining-into-one is expressed for Kant in the fact that he discovers the sameness of pure synthesis in the sticking-together [*Synhaften*] of intuition and the understanding.

"The same function which gives unity to the various representations *in a single judgment* also gives unity to the mere synthesis of various representations *in a single intuition* which, expressed generally, is called the pure concept of the understanding."[85] With this sameness of the synthetic function, Kant does not mean the empty identity of a tying-together which is formal and which works everywhere, but instead the original, rich wholeness of one which is composed of many members and which, like intuiting and thinking, is a particularly efficacious unifying and giving of unity. At the same time, this says: the modes of synthesis named earlier—the formal, apophantic [mode] of the judging function, and the predicative [mode] of conceptual reflection— belong together in the oneness of the essential structure of finite knowledge as the veritative synthesis of intuition and thinking. Here sameness means: an essential, structural belonging-together.

"Therefore the same understanding—namely, through exactly the same actions by means of which it achieves the logical form of a judgment in concepts through analytical unity—also brings a transcendental content into its representations by means of the synthetic unity of the manifold in intuition in general. . . ."[86] What now becomes visible as the essential unity of pure knowledge is far removed from the empty simplicity of an ultimate principle. On the contrary, it is revealed as a multiform action which remains obscure

---

84. A 78f., B 104.
85. A 79, B 104f.
86. A 79, B 105.

in its character as action as well as in the fact that its unification is composed of many members. This characterization of the essential unity of ontological knowledge cannot be the conclusion, but must instead be the correct *beginning* of the laying of the ground for ontological knowledge. This ground-laying has been transformed into the task of bringing to light pure synthesis as such. But because it is an action, its essence can only become apparent to the extent that it is itself traced out in its springing-forth. Now we can see for the first time, from what forces itself upon us as theme for the groundlaying, why a laying of the ground for ontological knowledge must become an unveiling of the origin of pure synthesis, i.e., why it must come to be unveiled as such a synthesis in its being-allowed-to-spring-forth.

If the laying of the ground for metaphysics now comes to the point where "the matter itself is deeply veiled"[87] and hence, if laments about this obscurity are not allowed to emerge, then so much greater is our need to accept a short delay for the sake of a methodological consideration of the present situation regarding the ground-laying and of the further course indicated by it.

§15. The Problem of the Categories and the Role of Transcendental Logic

The problem of the essential unity of ontological knowledge first provides the basis for the determination of the essence of the categories. If a category (as the name indicates) is not only, nor first and foremost, a mode of "assertion," σχῆμα τοῦ λόγου, but if instead it can satisfy its ownmost essence as σχῆμα τοῦ ὄντος, then it may not function as an "element" (notion) of pure knowledge.[a] Instead, the known Being of beings must lie in it directly. The knowing of Being, however, is the unity of pure intuition and pure thinking. Hence, for the essence of the categories it is precisely the pure intuitability of the notions that becomes decisive.

Now the "metaphysical exposition" of pure intuition was the task of the Transcendental Aesthetic. The elucidation of the other element of pure knowledge, pure thought, fell to the Transcendental "Logic," namely, to the Analytic of the Concepts. The problem of the essential unity of pure knowledge has led the inquiry to a point beyond the isolation of the elements. Hence pure synthesis falls neither to pure intuition nor to pure thought. For this reason, the elucidation of the origin of pure synthesis which is about to begin can be neither a transcendental-aesthetic nor a transcendental-logical one. Accordingly, the category is neither a problem of the Transcendental Aesthetic nor of the Transcendental Logic.

---

87. A 88, B 121.

a. unclear

But in which transcendental discipline, then, does the discussion of the central problem of the possibility of ontology fall? This question remains foreign to Kant. He assigns not only the elucidation of the pure concepts as elements of pure knowledge, but also the determination and grounding of the essential unity of pure knowledge to the "Analytic of the Concepts." In this way, logic maintains an incomparable priority over the aesthetic whereas, on the other hand, it is precisely intuition which is presented as primary[b] in knowledge as a whole.

This peculiarity requires clarification if in fact the problematic of the subsequent stages of the laying of the ground for metaphysics is to remain transparent. This clarification becomes all the more urgent because in interpreting the *Critique of Pure Reason* the tendency to accept it as a "logic of pure knowledge" constantly wins out. Indeed, this remains true even where the intuition, and hence the Transcendental Aesthetic, has been granted a relative right.

In the end, the priority of the Transcendental Logic in the whole of the laying of the ground for *Metaphysica Generalis* remains, in a certain sense, valid.[c] But precisely for this reason, the interpretation must free itself from the Kantian architectonic, and it must make the idea of transcendental logic problematic.

First of all, it is necessary to reach agreement concerning the extent to which Kant justifiably treats not only the discussion of the two elements of pure knowledge, but also the problem of the unity of both elements in the "Analytic of the Concepts."

If the essence of thinking remains in its servile relationship to intuition, then a properly understood analytic of pure thinking must draw precisely this relationship, as such, with it into the sphere of its problematic. That this happened with Kant shows on its surface that the finitude of thinking is contained in the theme. If one gives the supremacy of Transcendental Logic this sense, then what follows with certainty from it is something quite other than a diminution, to say nothing of a complete elimination, of the function of the Transcendental Aesthetic. However, with insight into the grounds for[d] the priority of Transcendental Logic, this [priority] itself is superseded—certainly not in favor of the Transcendental Aesthetic, but rather in favor of the posing of a question which again takes up, on a more original basis, the central problem of the essential unity of ontological knowledge and its grounding.

For this reason Kant also assigns to the Analytic of the Concepts the discussion of the conditions and principles of their "use." Indeed, under the heading

---

b. See p. 15 above. [The reference is to Heidegger's marginal note "e" on that page—tr.]

c. Because the entire starting point for the Question of Being from antiquity is λόγος (χατηγορίαι) [*logos* (*kategoria!*)]; Question of Being—as Onto-logy [*Onto-logie*], where "logy" means not only its character as a discipline, but rather Ontologico-logy [*Ontologo-logie*]!

d. and the manner of

of the use of the pure concepts, the relationship of intuition to pure thinking necessarily enters into the theme. Nevertheless, the element of thinking is always situated as the point of departure for the question of the essential unity of pure knowledge. The inclination in this direction thus constantly allows the categories, which at bottom [im Grunde] include the problem of essential unity, always to present themselves at the same time as notions under the heading of pure concepts of the understanding.

It has come to the point, however, that, along with this primary orientation toward the element of thinking, Kant must also draw the universal knowledge of thinking in general in the sense of traditional formal logic.[16] In this way, what leads to the problem of the pure concepts as categories on the transcendental [level], preserves the character of a logical, albeit a transcendental-logical, discussion.

Finally, however, the orientation toward *logos* and *ratio*, which corresponds to their meaning in Western Metaphysics, boasts from the start of a priority in the laying of the ground for metaphysics. In the determination of this ground-laying, this priority comes to be expressed as a *Critique of Pure Reason*.

For all that, Kant needed a certain conclusive framework for the architectonic control and presentation of this "very complicated web of human knowledge"[88] that was first disclosed through his analytic; [he needed] a framework which a newly created logic of pure knowledge could most easily take over from formal logic.

As self-evident as this multifaceted predominance of "Logic" might be in the *Critique of Pure Reason*, the following interpretation of the later and decisive stages of the laying of the ground for ontology must break through the architectonic of the extrinsic succession and pattern of problems. It must bring to our attention the impetus intrinsic to the problematic that initially allowed Kant to come to such a presentation.

THE THIRD STAGE OF THE GROUND-LAYING: THE INNER POSSIBILITY OF THE ESSENTIAL UNITY OF ONTOLOGICAL SYNTHESIS

The answer, apparently firmly established, to the question concerning the essential unity of ontological knowledge progressively dissolves with a closer determination of this unity within the problem of the possibility of such a

---

88. A 85, B 117.

unification. In pure synthesis, pure intuition and pure thinking should be able to meet one another a priori.

What and how must the pure synthesis itself be if it is to satisfy the requirements of such a unification? It is now a matter of exhibiting the pure synthesis, as it were, in such a way that it shows how it is able to unify time and notion. The sense and task of what 'Kant calls the "Transcendental Deduction of the Categories" is the exhibition of the original self-forming of the essential unity of ontological knowledge.

Therefore, if the basic intention of the "Deduction" lies in the analytical opening-up of the basic structure of pure synthesis, then its true content cannot be expressed if it is presented as "*quaestio juris.*" From the start, then, the *quaestio juris* may not be taken as a guide for the interpretation of this central Kantian doctrine. On the contrary, the motive and magnitude of the juridical formulation of the Transcendental Deduction must instead be clarified on the basis of the tendency of the problem proper to it.

For reasons that will be discussed later,[89] the present interpretation will consider exclusively the working out of the Transcendental Deduction in the first edition. Kant repeatedly stressed the "difficulty" of the Transcendental Deduction and sought to "remedy" its "obscurity." The diversity and complexity of the references, which are always increasingly disclosed in the content of the problem itself, from the start prevented Kant's being satisfied with a single point of departure for the Deduction, and prevented his being mollified by a single way of carrying it out. But the repeated carrying-out itself still shows Kant struggling with the work. It often happens that the goal toward which the Transcendental Deduction strives is suddenly seen and stated clearly for the first time when [already] underway. And what should first be presented in and through the analytical unveiling is mentioned beforehand in a "Preliminary Remark." Now the inner complexity of the problem also gives rise to the situation in which those references, the clarification of which causes particular difficulty, frequently are treated in a way which overemphasizes them, and in turn they are deceptive in that their treatment inflates their actual meaningfulness. This applies in particular to the discussion of pure thinking in the whole of the essential unity of pure knowledge.

The following interpretation will not follow each of the twisted paths of the Transcendental Deduction, but will instead lay bare the original impetus for the problematic. Herewith, the first requirement is to make sufficiently clear the proper goal of the Transcendental Deduction with a view to the guiding problem of the laying of the ground for metaphysics.

---

89. See below, §31, p. 115ff.

§16. The Elucidation of the Transcendence of Finite Reason as Basic Intention of the Transcendental Deduction

A finite, knowing creature can only relate itself to a being which it itself is not, and which it also has not created, if this being which is already at hand can be encountered from out of itself. However, in order to be able to encounter this being as the being it is, it must already be "recognized" generally and in advance as a being, i.e., with respect to the constitution of its Being. But this implies: ontological knowledge, which here is always pre-ontological, is the condition for the possibility that in general something like a being can itself stand in opposition to a finite creature.[17] Finite creatures need this basic faculty of a turning-toward . . . which lets-[something]-stand-in-opposition.[18] In this original turning-toward, the finite creature first allows a space for play [Spielraum] within which something can "correspond" to it. To hold oneself in advance in such a play-space, to form it originally, is none other than the transcendence which marks all finite comportment to beings. If, however, the possibility of ontological knowledge is grounded in pure synthesis and if ontological knowledge nevertheless constitutes precisely the letting-stand-against of . . . , then the pure synthesis must be revealed as that which complies with and supports the unified whole of the inner, essential structure of transcendence. Through the elucidation of this structure of pure synthesis, the innermost essence of the finitude of reason is then unveiled.

Finite knowledge is intuition which takes things in stride. As such, it requires determinative thinking. Therefore, in the problem of the unity of ontological knowledge, pure thinking demands a central significance, without prejudice, and indeed does so precisely because of the preeminence which intuition has in all knowledge.

To what essential service [Dienst] is pure thinking called in its serving appointment [Dienststellung]? What purpose does it serve within the making-possible of the essential structure of transcendence? Precisely this question concerning the essence of pure thinking, apparently isolated once again, must lead to the innermost kernel of the problem of essential unity.

It is not accidental that in the "Transition to the Transcendental Deduction of the Categories"[90] Kant alludes to the clearly perceived finitude of our representing, namely, to that of what is purely known; "for we are not here speaking of its causality by means of the will." The question is rather: what is the representing able to accomplish for itself with respect to the beings to which it relates itself? Kant says that the "representation in itself" "cannot bring forth its object *so far as its existence [Dasein] is concerned.*" Our knowing is not ontically creative; it is not able, from out of itself, to place the being before

---

90. A 92f., B 124f.

itself. In the middle of the discussion of the Transcendental Deduction, Kant emphasizes that "outside our knowledge we have nothing which we could ever set over against this knowledge as corresponding to it."[91]

As a consequence, if our knowing, as finite, must be an intuiting which takes things in stride, then it is not enough merely to establish this fact. On the contrary, the problem now arises for the first time: What then necessarily belongs to the possibility of this taking of beings in stride, which is in no way self-evident?

Obviously this, that beings are encountered from out of themselves, i.e., they can appear as that which stands-against [als Gegenstehendes]. If, however, we are not in control of the Being-at-hand of the being, then precisely the dependency upon the taking-in-stride of the same requires that the being have in advance and at all times the possibility of standing-against.

An intuiting which takes things in stride can take place only in a faculty of letting-stand-against of . . . , in the turning-toward . . . which first of all forms a pure correspondence. And what is it that we, from out of ourselves, allow to stand-against? It cannot be a being. But if not a being, then just a nothing [ein Nichts]. Only if the letting-stand-against of . . . is a holding oneself in the nothing can the representing allow a not-nothing [ein nich-Nichts], i.e., something like a being if such a thing shows itself empirically, to be encountered instead of and within the nothing. To be sure, this nothing is not the *nihil absolutum*. What it has to do with this letting-stand-against of . . . is worth discussing.

If finitude is placed at the point of departure for transcendence as clearly as it is by Kant, then it is not necessary, in order to escape an alleged "subjective idealism," to invoke a "turn to the Object"[19]—a turn which is praised again today all too noisily and with all too little understanding of the problem. In truth, however, the essence of finitude inevitably forces us to the question concerning the conditions for the possibility of a preliminary Being-oriented toward the Object, i.e., concerning the essence of the necessary ontological turning-toward the object in general. Thus in the Transcendental Deduction, i.e., in connection with the task of an illumination of the inner possibility of ontological knowledge, Kant poses the decisive question, and what is more, it is the first one.

"And here, then, it is necessary that we make clear to ourselves what we mean by the expression an object [Gegenstand] of representations."[92] It is a matter of investigating the character of that which stands opposed to us [entgegensteht] in the pure letting-stand-against [im reinen Gegenstehenlassen]. "Now we find that our thought of the relation of all knowledge to its object carries with it an element of necessity, where indeed this [the object] is viewed

91. A 104.
92. A 104.

as that which opposes so that our knowledge is not haphazard or arbitrary, but is instead determined a priori in a certain way. . . ."[93] In the letting-stand-against as such, something reveals itself as "that which opposes."

By emphasizing this resistance, Kant refers to an immediate find. He does not fail to characterize the unique structure of this resistance more closely. We should note well, however, that it is not a matter here of a resisting character in the being or perhaps even of the pressing in of sensations. Rather, it is a question of the previous resistance of Being. That which is objective in objects[20] "carries with it" a constraint ("necessity"). By means of this constraint, all that is encountered is forced together in advance into a concordance with reference to which we can also first refer to as something discordant. Hence, a setting-forth of unity can be found in this preliminary and constant drawing-together into unity. The representing of a representative, unifying unity, however, is the essence of those kinds of representations which Kant calls concepts. This is called "a consciousness" in the sense of the representing of unity.[94] The letting-stand-against . . . is hence the "primal concept" and, to the extent that the conceptual representing comes to be assigned to the understanding, the primal activity of the understanding. However, as a closed totality this contains in itself a multitude of ways of unification. Consequently, the pure understanding reveals itself as the faculty of letting-stand-against. . . . As a totality, the understanding gives in advance that which is contrary to the haphazard. Representing unity originally, namely, as unifying, it represents to itself a connectedness which in advance rules all possible gathering together. "Now, however, the representation of a universal condition according to which a certain manifold (thus, in uniform fashion) can be posited is called a *rule*."[95] The concept "may indeed be as imperfect or as obscure as it wants"; "its form is always something that is universal and that serves as the rule."[96][a]

Now the pure concepts (*conceptus reflectentes*), however, are those which have such ruling unities as their unique content. They serve not only as rules, but also, as pure representings, they give first of all and in advance something rulable. Thus, in conjunction with the elucidation of the letting-stand-against, Kant first attains the more original concept of understanding. "We may now characterize it as the *faculty of rules*. This characterizing is more fruitful and approximates its essence more closely."[97]

If the understanding is now to make possible the letting-stand-against and

---

93. A 104.
94. A 103f.
95. A 113.
96. A 106.
97. A 126.

a. On rule, see *Duisburgscher Nachlaß* 10.[30] [*Der Duisburg'sche Nachlaß und Kants Kritizismus um 1775*, ed. Th. Haering, Tübingen, 1910.]

if it is empowered to regulate in advance all that "intuition" brings forth, then is it not expounded as the supreme faculty? Has the servant not changed into the master? How does it stand, then, with its subservient position, which hitherto has constantly been given as its essence and as the authentic index of finitude? If his explanation of the understanding as the faculty of rules comes nearer the mark, has Kant in the middle of the central problematic of the Transcendental Deduction forgotten the finitude of the understanding?

If this unreasonable suggestion is impossible, however, to the extent that the finitude of reason gives rise to, determines, and supports the whole problem of the possibility of Metaphysics in general, how then may the dominant position of the understanding, which is now becoming apparent, be brought into accord with its subservient position? Are its mastery and governing, as the letting-stand-against of the rules of unity, fundamentally a serving? Does it govern a service by means of which it betrays its finitude at the deepest level, because in the letting-stand-against it reveals precisely the most original neediness of the finite creature?

In fact, the understanding is the supreme faculty—in finitude, i.e., [it is] finite to the highest degree. If this is so, however, then its dependency on the intuition must come to light most clearly, even in the letting-stand-against as the primal activity of the pure understanding. Of course, this cannot be an empirical intuition, but rather it must be pure.

Only insofar as the pure understanding, as understanding, is the servant of pure intuition can it remain master of empirical intuition.

But again, pure intuition itself, and it alone, is finite essence. First of all, their essential structural unity immerses pure intuition and pure thinking in their full finitude, which reveals itself as transcendence. However, if pure synthesis originally unifies the elements of pure knowledge, then the unveiling of the full synthetic structure of pure synthesis must suggest itself as that task which alone leads to the goal of the Transcendental Deduction: to the elucidation of transcendence.

§17. The Two Ways of the Transcendental Deduction

From the determination of the problematic of ontological knowledge, the sense of the Transcendental Deduction has been revealed. It is the analytical unveiling[21] of the structural whole of pure synthesis. At first, this interpretation of the Transcendental Deduction hardly corresponds to its lexical concept [Wortbegriff]. It even appears to contradict Kant's own explicit explanation of what deduction means. Nevertheless, before we can decide this, the Transcendental Deduction must first have been consummated by being carried out, and in this way it must be laid out concretely. In this connection, the interpretation will confine itself to "Section Three"[98] of the "Deduction of the Pure Concepts of the Understanding," in which Kant represents the Deduction "in its interconnectedness."[99]

This section's heading clearly expresses [the fact] that the problem of the inner possibility of ontological knowledge is nothing other than the unveiling of transcendence. According to this heading, the Deduction treats "the relationship of the understanding to objects in general, and the possibility of knowing them a priori." Now in order to understand the twofold way in which Kant allows the Deduction to be taken, we must remind ourselves anew of its task.

For a finite creature, beings are accessible only on the grounds of a preliminary letting-stand-against which turns-our-attention-toward. In advance, this takes the beings which can possibly be encountered into the unified horizon of a possible belonging-together. In the face of what is encountered, this a priori unifying unity must grasp in advance. What is encountered itself, however, has already been comprehensively grasped in advance through the horizon of time which is set forth in pure intuition. The unifying unity of pure understanding which grasps in advance, therefore, must itself already have been united previously with pure intuition as well.

This a priori unified whole made up of pure intuition and pure understanding "forms" the play-space for the letting-stand-against in which all beings can be encountered. With regard to this whole of transcendence, it is a matter of showing how (which here means, at the same time) pure understanding and pure intuition are dependent upon one another a priori.

This proof of the inner possibility of transcendence can apparently be conducted in two ways.

First, [it can be conducted] so the presentation starts with the pure understanding, and through the elucidation of its essence the innermost dependency upon time is shown. This first way begins, as it were, "from above" with the understanding and leads down to the intuition (A 116-120).

The second way proceeds "from below,"[100] beginning with the intuition and proceeding to pure understanding (A 120-128).

Each of the two ways accomplishes the unveiling of "both extreme endpoints, namely, sensibility and understanding," which must "necessarily be interconnected."[101] For all that, what is essential here is perhaps not a connection of two faculties thought of in a linear fashion, but rather the structural elucidation of their essential unity. What proves decisive is that in which they can be interconnected in general. Hence, in both ways this unifying middle

---

98. A 115-128.
99. A 115.
100. A 119.
101. A 124.

must be run through and thereby brought to light as such. In this going back and forth between both endpoints, the unveiling of pure synthesis takes place. This twofold course of the Deduction shall now be presented, although indeed only in its basic features.

a) The First Way

The necessary dependency of pure understanding on pure intuition must be unveiled, thereby making manifest the mediating unity of both, the pure synthesis, as mediator. This requires that pure understanding, as the point of departure for the first way, be so clarified that from its structure the dependency upon a pure synthesis, and hence upon a pure intuition, becomes visible.

The "Deduction" is hence wholly different from a deductive, logical developing of the previously mentioned relations of the understanding to pure synthesis and to pure intuition. Rather, from the outset the Deduction already has the whole of pure, finite knowledge in view. While holding fast to what is caught sight of in this way, the explicit taking-up of the structural references that join the whole together proceeds from one element to the other. Without the lasting premonition of the finitude of transcendence, every statement of the Transcendental Deduction remains incomprehensible.

The character of the Being-in-opposition that makes the standing-against possible reveals itself in an anticipatory holding of the unity. In this representing of unity, the representing itself is revealed as that which is bound to the unity, and indeed as the selfsame which maintains itself in the act of the pure representing of unity.[102] Only in the openness that it—the representing unity as such—is, in opposition to which the unifying unity as regulating has been set, can this representing come to meet something. Only in such a turning-oneself-toward can what is encountered be "something which matters to us."[103]

The representing of unity, as pure thinking, necessarily has the character of the "I think." The pure concept, as consciousness of unity in general, is necessarily pure self-consciousness. This pure consciousness of unity is not just occasionally and tactically carried out, but rather it must always be possible. It is essentially an "I am able."[22] "This pure, original, unchangeable consciousness I will now name *Transcendental Apperception*."[104] The representing of unity which lets something stand against it is grounded in this apperception "*as a power*."[105] Only as the constant, free "I can" does the "I think"

---

102. A 108.
103. A 116.
104. A 107.
105. A 117, note. Emphasis Kant's.

have the power to allow the Being-in-opposition of the unity to stand against itself, if in fact linking remains possible only with reference to an essentially free comporting. The pure understanding, in its original holding of unity before itself, acts as Transcendental Apperception.

Now what is represented in the unity which is held before itself in this way? Perhaps it is simultaneously the universe of beings [*das All des Seienden*], in the sense of the *totum simul*, which the *intuitus originarius* intuits? But this pure thinking is certainly finite, and as such it cannot from itself, through its representing, set the being in opposition to itself, not to mention simultaneously setting everything in its unity. The represented unity first awaits the encountered being; and as such awaiting, it makes possible the encountering of objects which show themselves with one another. As nonontic, this unity supports the essential tendency of a unifying of that which is not yet unified in itself. That is why, following the clarification of Transcendental Apperception, Kant says of the unity which is represented in it: it "presupposes a synthesis however, or includes one."[106]

Characteristically, Kant wavers here in the unequivocal determination of the structural relationship of the unity to the unifying synthesis. In any case, the latter belongs with characteristic necessity to the former. The unity is unifying by nature. The reason is: the representing of unity takes place as a unifying whose structural wholeness demanded the having-in-advance of unity. Kant is not afraid to say that Transcendental Apperception "presupposes" the synthesis.

Now it was already established in the second stage of the ground-laying that all synthesis is brought about from the power of imagination. Accordingly, Transcendental Apperception was related essentially to the pure power of imagination. As pure, this cannot re-present[23] something given in advance which is empirical, in opposition to which it would only be reproductive. Rather, as pure power of imagination [*Einbildungskraft*] it is necessarily formative [*bildend*] a priori, i.e., purely productive. Kant also calls the pure, productive power of imagination "transcendental." "Thus the principle of the necessary unity of the pure (productive) synthesis of the power of imagination, prior to apperception, is the ground for the possibility of all knowledge, especially of experience."[107]

What does the expression "prior to apperception" mean here? Does Kant want to say that the pure synthesis precedes Transcendental Apperception in the order of the grounding of the possibility of pure knowledge? This interpretation would coincide with the above assertion that apperception "presupposes" the pure synthesis.

Or does the "prior to" have yet another meaning? In fact, Kant uses the

106. A 118.
107. Ibid.

"prior to" in a way that first gives the whole statement the decisive structural sense, to the effect that in it the interpretation which was attempted first would indeed simultaneously be included with it. At one point, Kant speaks "of an object prior to [vor] a wholly other intuition."[108] It is superfluous, and at the same time it would weaken the passage, if the "prior to" is changed to "for" ["für"], especially if we recall the Latin expression "coram intuitu intellectuali" which Kant also uses.[109] If we understand the "prior to" in the sentence just cited as coram, then the character of the structural unity of Transcendental Apperception and the pure power of imagination first comes to light. Accordingly, the representing of unity has essentially before itself, in view, a unifying unity, i.e., the representing is in itself one which unifies.

Pure synthesis, however, should unify a priori. What it unifies must have been given for it a priori. But the intuition which in advance is pure, given, universal, and which takes things in stride is time. Hence the pure power of imagination must be related to it essentially. Only in this way is [the pure power of imagination] unveiled as the mediator between Transcendental Apperception and time.

For this reason, Kant prefaces all discussions of the Transcendental Deduction with a "general observation which must serve as the ground for what follows. . . ."[110] It says that all "modifications of the mind . . . are subject to time . . . as that in which they must all be ordered, connected, and brought into relation with one another."[111] It might initially seem striking that in neither the first nor the second way does Kant discuss in more detail and explicitly the a priori essential relationship of the pure power of imagination to time. Instead, the entire analysis is concentrated on the task of making visible the essential relatedness of pure understanding to the pure synthesis of the power of imagination. It is then through this relatedness that its ownmost nature—finitude—is most clearly expressed. It is only understanding to the extent that it "presupposes or includes" the pure power of imagination. "*The unity of apperception in relation to the synthesis of the power of imagination* is the *understanding*; and this same unity, with reference to the *transcendental synthesis* of the power of imagination, [is] the *pure understanding*."[112]

b) The Second Way

The necessary dependency of pure intuition on pure understanding, i.e., the unity which mediates between both of them, the pure synthesis, is to

---

108. A 287, B 343f.; see Nachträge zur Kritik (from Kant's posthumous works, ed. B. Erdmann) (1881), p. 45.
109. A 249.
110. A 99.
111. Ibid.
112. A 119.

become manifest as mediator. As a result, the second way begins with the following words: "we want now to start from below, that is, with the empirical, in order to bring out the necessary connection in which understanding, by means of the categories, stands to appearances."[113]

Even here, where it would be obvious to set forth explicitly the pure condition of the receptivity of finite knowledge, Kant does not dwell upon a discussion of pure intuition (time). Instead, he goes immediately to the proof that, although "sense" takes things in stride, in itself it "has nothing" like a connectedness between things that are encountered. Nevertheless, this connectedness must be capable of being experienced in finite knowing because the finite creature never has the being as *totum simul*. Rather, as Kant expressly states here, what is encountered is found "scattered and individually."[114] With that, however, if what comes along is to be capable of being encountered as something which stands within connectedness, the sense of something like "connection" must be understood in advance. To pre-present[24] connection in advance, however, means: first of all to form something like relation in general by representing it. However, this power—which first and foremost "forms" relations—is the pure power of imagination.

According to the "general observation,"[115] time as pure universal intuition is at once that wherein [things] can be joined in general and that wherein it is possible to form connections. The letting-[itself]-be-encountered of a being, which should be capable of showing itself in the connectedness in which it stands-against, must be grounded in the pure power of imagination that is essentially related to time. In the pure forming of determinate relations it asserts a normative unification, but this is opposed in advance to the fact that what is encountered is haphazardly taken in stride. This horizon of normative connection contains the pure "affinity" of appearances. "That the affinity of appearances . . . only becomes possible by means of this transcendental function of the power of imagination is indeed strange, based solely on what is clearly obvious from what we have seen so far."[116]

All connecting, however, and particularly the pure forming of unification in general, structurally incorporates a previous representing of unity. This, if the pure synthesis is to function a priori, must itself be a priori, so that this representing of unity constantly accompanies all forming of unities as invariably one and the same. This "fixed and lasting" self, however, is the I of transcendental apperception. Just as time belongs to all empirical intuition, so the previous forming of affinity in the transcendental power of imagination also belongs to this same intuition as an [instance of] letting the being be

---

113. A 119.
114. A 120.
115. A 99.
116. A 123.

encountered in its own original order. Pure apperception, however, must be added to this if the taking-in-stride is to be capable of being sustained by a pure turning-toward, i.e., a letting-stand-against of . . . .[117]

Now the first way has shown, however, that transcendental apperception, which must be added to pure intuition through the essential mediation of the pure power of imagination, is itself not at hand as something original and isolated, and hence it also is not just joined to the pure power of imagination because the latter occasionally needs it. On the contrary, for its part even this transcendental apperception, as representing of unity, must have before it a unity which forms itself in the unifying. And thus in the second way as well, everything forces us to the point at which the transcendental power of imagination as mediator is allowed to come forward. "We thus have a pure power of imagination as a fundamental faculty of the human soul which serves as a basis for all knowledge a priori. By means of this, we bring the manifold of intuition {into connection} on the one hand, and we bring {this} into connection with the condition of the necessary unity of pure apperception on the other."[118][25]

The triad of pure intuition, pure power of imagination, and pure apperception is no longer a juxtaposition of faculties. Through the revelation of the mediating forming of pure synthesis, the Transcendental Deduction has established the intrinsic possibility of the essential unity of pure knowledge. This forms the pure letting-something-stand-against . . . [das reine Gegenstehenlassen von . . .], and, as this forming, it thus first makes evident something like an horizon of objectivity [Gegenständlichkeit] in general. And because pure knowledge in this way first opens up the space for play necessary for a finite creature and in which "all relation of Being or Not-Being takes place,"[119] this [knowledge] must be termed ontological.

Now, since finitude was made conspicuous by the understanding, it plays a special role in the Deduction. But precisely in the course of the hither-and-thither movement of the two ways, the understanding gives up its preeminence, and through this giving-up it reveals itself in its essence. This [essence] consists of its having to be grounded in the pure synthesis of the transcendental power of imagination which is relative to time.

---

117. A 124.
118. A 124. Striking out the "and" as proposed by Erdmann and Riehl takes away from the colloquial and perhaps difficult presentation precisely the decisive sense according to which the transcendental power of imagination on the one hand unifies pure intuition in itself and on the other hand unites this with pure apperception.
119. A 110.

§18. The External Form of the Transcendental Deduction

For what reason does the Transcendental Deduction, as a "laying before the eyes" of transcendence, take on the form of a "*quaestio juris*"? Wherein is the right, and where lie the limits, to this "juridical" posing of the question, which to be sure obtrudes only in the first introduction to the Transcendental Deduction and not in the course of its being carried out?

Kant did not use "deduction" in the philosophical sense of *deductio* as opposed to *intuitus*,[120] but rather in a way that a "professor of law" would understand. In a lawsuit, "rights" are validated, and "unwarranted claims" are overruled. To this end, two factors are necessary: first, the establishment of the facts of the case and the points of dispute (*quid facti*), and, second, the exhibiting of what, as underlying authority,[26] continues to be legally valid (*quid juris*). Jurists call the exhibition of the legal possibility of [such] an authority "Deduction."

Why does Kant now put the problem of the possibility of metaphysics into the form of the task of such a juridical deduction? Does a "legal action" underlie the problem of the inner possibility of metaphysics?

We have already seen how for Kant the question concerning the possibility of *Metaphysica Generalis* (ontology) arises from the question concerning the possibility of traditional *Metaphysica Specialis*.[121] The latter wants to know the supersensible being rationally (from mere concepts). The claim to a priori ontic knowledge lies in the pure concepts (categories). Does it have a right to this power or not?

The debate with traditional metaphysics regarding "its ultimate purpose" relative to its own possibility has become a legal action. Pure reason must "open the trial," the "witnesses" must be interrogated. Kant speaks of a "tribunal."[122] The legal action falling within the problem of ontological knowledge requires the Deduction, i.e., the proof for the possibility of the a priori ability of pure concepts to refer to objects. Since the authority for the use of these concepts, which do not come from experience, is never to be shown by means of a reference to their tactical use, the pure concepts "always [demand] the Deduction."[123]

The authority of the categories must be determined through the elucidation of their essence. As pure representations of unities within a finite representing,

---

120. Descartes, *Regulae ad Directionem Ingenii*, in *Opera*, ed. Adam and Tannery, vol. X, p. 368ff. [Translation: "Rules for the Direction of the Mind," in *The Philosophical Works of Descartes*, ed. Elizabeth Haldane and G. R. T. Ross (Cambridge: Cambridge University Press, 1911; reprinted, 1975), vol. 1, p. 7ff.]

121. See above, §2, p. 6ff.

122. A 669, B 697; A 703, B 731.

123. A 85, B 117.

they are essentially dependent upon pure synthesis and hence upon pure intuition. In other words: The solution to the problem, which was formulated simply as *quaestio juris*, exists in the unveiling of the essence of the categories: they are not notions, but rather pure concepts which, by means of the pure power of imagination, refer essentially to time. To the extent that they are this essence, however, they constitute transcendence. They are formed with the letting-stand-against-of. . . . For this reason they are, in advance, determinations of the objects, i.e., of the being insofar as it is encountered by a finite creature.

Through the analytical elucidation of the essence of the categories as the essentially more necessary building blocks, or rather hinges [*Fugen*] of transcendence, their "objective reality" is demonstrated. In order to understand the problem of the objective reality of the categories as a problem of transcendence, however, it is imperative not to take the Kantian term "reality" ["*Realität*"] in the same sense as modern "epistemology" does, according to which "reality" ["*Realität*"] means the same as "actuality" ["*Wirklichkeit*"] — which Kant indicates with the terms "*Dasein*" or "existence" ["*Existenz*"]. Instead, as Kant himself aptly translates it, "*realitas*" means "fact-ness" ["*Sachheit*"], and it alludes to the content[27] of the being which comes to be delimited by means of the *essentia*. Under the heading of the objective reality of the categories, the following comes into question: To what extent can the content (reality [*Realität*]) which is represented in the pure concepts be a determination of that which stands-against finite knowledge, i.e., of the being as something which stands-against (as an Object)?[28] The categories are objectively real to the extent that they belong to ontological knowledge, which "forms" the transcendence of the finite creature, i.e., the letting-stand-in-opposition of . . . .

Now it is easy to see: If one interprets the expression "objective reality" based not on the essence of the pure synthesis of the transcendental power of imagination as what forms the essential unity of ontological knowledge, but if instead one clings primarily and exclusively to the expression "objective validity," a term which Kant, with a view to the external, introductory formulation of the Transcendental Deduction, used as a juridical way of putting the question, and if in opposition to the sense of the Kantian problem one takes validity as the logical value of judgment—then the decisive problem will be completely lost from view.

The problem of the "origin and the truth"[124] of the categories, however, is the question of the possible manifestness of Being from beings in the essential unity of ontological knowledge. If this question is to be grasped concretely and taken hold of as a problem, however, then the *quaestio juris* cannot as

---

124. A 128.

such be taken as a question of validity. Instead, the *quaestio juris* is only the formula for the task of an analytic of transcendence, i.e., of a pure phenomenology of the subjectivity of the subject, namely, as a finite subject.

However, if the fundamental problem presented by the traditional *Metaphysica Specialis* has been solved by means of the Transcendental Deduction, then has not the ground-laying already achieved its goal in general terms with the stage we just discussed? And at the same time, regarding the interpretation of the *Critique of Pure Reason*, does not what has been said attest to the right of previous usage to consider the Transcendental Deduction as the central discussion within the positive part of the Doctrine of the Elements? What need is there, then, for yet another stage to the laying of the ground for ontological knowledge? What is it that demands a still more original going-back to the ground of the essential unity of ontological knowledge?

THE FOURTH STAGE OF THE GROUND-LAYING: THE GROUND FOR THE INNER POSSIBILITY OF ONTOLOGICAL KNOWLEDGE

The inner possibility of ontological knowledge is exhibited from the specific totality of the constitution of transcendence. The medium holding it together is the pure power of imagination. Kant not only finds this result of the groundlaying to be "strange," but he also repeatedly stresses the obscurity into which all discussions of the Transcendental Deduction must move. At the same time, the laying of the ground for ontological knowledge certainly strives—over and above a mere characterization of transcendence—to elucidate it in such a way that it can come to be developed as the systematic totality of a presentation of transcendence (transcendental philosophy=ontology).

Now the Transcendental Deduction has indeed made precisely the totality of ontological knowledge in its unity into a problem. For all that, with the central meaning of finitude and the dominance of the logical (rational) way of posing the question in metaphysics, it is the understanding—or rather its relation to the unity-forming medium, to the pure power of imagination— which comes to the foreground.

However, if all knowledge is primarily intuition and if finite intuition has the character of taking things in stride, then for a fully valid illumination of transcendence the reference of both the transcendental power of imagination and the pure understanding to pure intuition must be explicitly discussed. Such a task, however, leads the transcendental power of imagination and the self-forming of transcendence and its horizons to demonstrate their unifying function in their innermost occurrence. Kant undertakes the freeing-up of the essential ground for ontological knowledge as finite, pure intuition in the section which adjoins the Transcendental Deduction and which bears the heading "On the Schematism of the Pure Concepts of the Understanding."[125]

The very fact of this allusion to the systematic place of the Schematism chapter within the ordering of the stages of the ground-laying betrays the fact that these eleven pages of the *Critique of Pure Reason* must constitute the central core of the whole voluminous work. Of course, this central significance of Kant's Doctrine of the Schematism can [only] stand out legitimately and for the first time on the basis of the interpretation of its content. This interpretation has to keep to the fundamental question regarding the transcendence of the finite creature.

But once again, Kant introduces the problem in a more superficial form as a guide to the question concerning the possible subsumption of the appearances under the categories. The justification of this way of posing the question, corresponding to the treatment of the "*quaestio juris*," should first follow [after] a working-out of the inner dynamic of the problem of the schematism.

§19. Transcendence and Making-Sensible

A finite creature must be able to take the being in stride, even if this being would be directly evident as something already at hand. Taking-in-stride, however, if it is to be possible, requires something on the order of a turning-toward, and indeed not a random one, but one which makes possible in a preliminary way the encountering of the being. In order for the being to be able to offer itself as such, however, the horizon of its possible encountering must itself have the character of an offering. The turning-toward must in itself be a preparatory bearing-in-mind of what is offerable in general.

In order for the horizon of the letting-stand-against as such to be able to function, however, this character of an offering needs a certain perceivability. Perceivable means: immediately capable of being taken in stride in intuition. Hence the horizon, as a distinct offering, must present itself in a preliminary way and constantly as a pure look.[29] From this it follows that the letting-stand-against of finite understanding must intuitively offer objectivity as such, i.e., that the pure understanding must be grounded in a pure intuition which guides and sustains it.

But now, what belongs to this making-perceivable of the horizon of the preliminary turning-toward? The finite creature which turns-toward must itself be able to make the horizon intuitable, i.e., it must be able to "form" the

---

125. A 137–147; B 176–187.

look of the offering from out of itself. Now if, however, as the Transcendental Deduction indicates, pure intuition (time) stands in an essential relation to pure synthesis, then the pure power of imagination carries out the forming of the look of the horizon. But then it does not just "form" ["*bildet*"] the intuitable perceivability of the horizon in that it "creates" [this horizon] as a free turning-toward. Although it is formative in this first sense, it is so in yet a second sense as well, namely, in the sense that in general it provides for something like an "image" ["*Bild*"].

The expression "image" is to be taken here in its most original sense, according to which we say that the landscape presents a beautiful "image" (look), or that the collection presented a sorry "image" (look). And already during the Second Way of the Deduction, which proceeds from the inner connectedness of time and the pure power of imagination, Kant also says of the power of imagination ("imagination")[30] that it "must bring . . . into an *image*."[126]

In the occurrence of this double forming (the creating of the look), the ground for the possibility of transcendence is first visible, and the necessary look-character of its preliminary essence, which stands against and offers, is first understandable. Now, transcendence, however, is finitude itself, so to speak. If in the letting-stand-against, the horizon which is formed therein is to be made intuitable (and again, finite intuition is called sensibility), then the offering of the look can only be a making-sensible of the horizon. The horizon of transcendence can be formed only in a making-sensible.

The letting-stand-against, seen from the standpoint of pure reason, is a representing of unities as such which regulate all unification (pure concepts). Hence, transcendence is formed in the making-sensible of pure concepts. Because it is a preliminary turning-toward, this making-sensible must likewise be pure.

The pure making-sensible occurs as a "Schematism." The pure power of imagination gives schema-forming in advance the look ("image") of the horizon of transcendence. That the reference to such a making-sensible is nevertheless insufficient overlooks the fact that factically it cannot be established at all if its essence is not known beforehand—this fact can already be extracted from the idea of a pure making-sensible.

For Kant, sensibility means finite intuition. Pure sensibility must be the sort of intuition that takes what is intuitable in stride in advance —prior to all empirical receiving. Now in the intuiting, however, finite intuition cannot exactly produce an intuitable being. Pure making-sensible must therefore be the taking of something in stride which

---

126. A 120. [I have rendered the quote from Kant just as Heidegger cited it—with the ellipses. The passage makes much more sense, however, if the words Heidegger omitted are restored. Thus Kant wrote "*Die Einbildungskraft soll nämlich das Mannigfaltige der Anschauung in ein Bild bringen*": "That is to say, the power of imagination must bring the manifold of intuition into an image"—tr.]

indeed is formed first of all in the taking-in-stride itself; that is, [it must be] a look, but one which all the same does not offer the being.

What then is the character of what is intuitable in pure sensibility? Can it have the character of an "image"? What does image mean? How is the look "formed" ["*bildende*"] in the pure power of imagination [*Einbildungskraft*], the pure schema, to be distinguished from images [*Bilde*]? And finally, in what sense can the schema be called an "image"? Without preliminary interpretation of this phenomenon of making-sensible, the schematism as the ground of transcendence remains veiled in complete darkness.

§20. Image and Schema[a]

In general, making-sensible means the manner in which a finite creature is able to make something intuitable, i.e., is able to create a look (image) from something. According to what and how something comes into view, look or image means something different. First of all, image can mean: the look of a determinate being to the extent that it is manifest as something at hand. It offers the look. As a derivation of this meaning, image can also mean: the look which takes a likeness of something at hand (likeness),[31] i.e., a look which is the after-image of something no longer at hand or a look which is the premonition of a being [yet] to be produced for the first time.[32]

Then, however, "image" can also have the full range of meaning of look in general, in which case whether a being or a non-being will be intuitable in this look is not stated.

Now in fact, Kant used the expression "image" in all three senses: as immediate look of a being, as the at-hand, likeness-taking look of a being, and as the look of something in general. Moreover, these meanings of the term "image" were not specifically taken up in opposition to each other; indeed, it is even questionable whether the specified meanings and ways of the Being of image [*das Bildseins*] are sufficient to clarify what Kant discusses under the heading of "Schematism."

The best-known way of creating a look (giving an image) is the empirical intuiting of what shows itself. That which shows itself here always has the character of the immediately seen particular ("this-here"). To be sure, this does not exclude the possibility that a multitude of such particulars might be intuited, namely, as a richer "this-here"; for example, this particular totality of this landscape. This [landscape] is called a look (image), species, just as it looks to us. Thus the image is always an intuitable this-here, and for this

---

a. See *Philosophischer Anzeiger I.* 1925/26. Linke, *Bild und Erkenntnis*, p. 302ff.

reason every likeness—for example, a photograph[b]—remains only a transcription of what shows itself immediately as "image."

Now the expression "image" likewise is used frequently in this second sense as likeness. This thing here, this photograph which is at hand, immediately offers a look as this thing. It is image in the first and broad sense. But while it shows itself, it wants to show precisely that from which it has taken its likeness. To obtain an image in this second sense now no longer means merely to intuit a being immediately, but instead means, for example, to buy or to produce a photograph.

It is possible to produce a copy (photograph)[33] again from such a likeness, [a photograph] of a death mask for example. The copy can only directly copy the likeness and thus reveal the "image" (the immediate look) of the deceased himself. The photograph of the death mask, as copy of a likeness, is itself an image—but this is only because it gives the "image" of the dead person, shows how the dead person appears, or rather how it appeared. According to the meaning of the expression "image" hitherto delimited, making-sensible means on the one hand the manner of immediate, empirical intuiting, but on the other hand it also means the manner of immediate contemplation of a likeness in which the look of a being presents itself.

Now the photograph, however, can also show how something like a death mask appears in general. In turn, the death mask can show in general how something like the face of a dead human being appears. But an individual corpse itself can also show this. And similarly, the mask itself can also show how a death mask in general appears, just as the photograph shows not only how what is photographed, but also how a photograph in general, appears.

But what do these "looks" (images in the broadest sense) of this corpse, this mask, this photograph, etc., now show? Which "appearance" (εἶδος, ἰδέα) do they now give? What do they now make sensible? In the one which applies to many, they show how something appears "in general." This unity applicable to several, however, is what representation represents in the manner of the concepts. These looks must now serve the making-sensible of concepts.

This making-sensible can now no longer mean: to get an immediate look, intuition from a concept; for the concept, as the represented universal, can not be represented in a *repraesentatio singularis*, which the intuition certainly is. For that reason, however, the concept is also essentially not capable of having a likeness taken.

Now what in general is meant by the making-sensible of a concept? What pertains to it? With this making-intuitable, how is the look of what is empirically, accessibly at hand or visualized—that is to say, the look of its possible likenesses—shared?

---

b. light-image

We say: this house which is perceived, e.g., shows how a house in general appears, and consequently it shows what we represent in the concept house. In what way does the look of this house show the 'how' of the appearing of a house in general? Indeed, the house itself offers this determinate look, and yet we are not preoccupied with this in order to experience how precisely this house appears. Rather, this house shows itself in exactly such a way that, in order to be a house, it must not necessarily appear as it does. It shows us "only" the "as . . ." in terms of which a house can appear.[34]

This 'as,' which goes with the ability something has to appear empirically,[35] is what we represent in connection with this determinate house. A house could so appear. By appearing within the range of possibilities of appearing, this house which is straightforwardly at hand has assumed one determinate [appearing]. But the result of this assuming interests us just as little as the result of those determinations that have failed due to the factical appearing of other houses. What we have perceived is the range of possible appearing as such, or, more precisely, we have perceived that which cultivates this range, that which regulates and marks out how something in general must appear in order to be able, as a house, to offer the appropriate look. This initial sketching-out [Vorzeichnung] of the rule is no list [Verzeichnis] in the sense of a mere enumeration of the "features" found in a house. Rather, it is a "distinguishing" ["Auszeichnen"] of the whole of what is meant by [a term] like "house."

But what is thus meant is in general only capable of being meant to the extent that it is represented as what regulates the possible belonging of this interconnectedness[36] within an empirical look. The unity of the concept in general can come to be represented as unifying, as something which applies to many, only in the representing of the way in which the rule regulates the sketching-out within a possible look. If the concept in general is that which is in service to the rule, then conceptual representing means the giving of the rule for the possible attainment of a look in advance in the manner of its regulation. Such representing, then, is structurally necessary with reference to a possible look, and hence is in itself a particular kind of making-sensible.

It [this particular type of making-sensible] gives no immediate, intuitable look of the concept. What is in it, and what necessarily comes forward with it in the immediate look, is not, properly speaking, meant as something thematic. Rather, it is meant as that which is possibly capable of being presented in the presentation whose manner of regulation is represented. Thus, in the empirical look it is precisely the rule which makes its appearance in the manner of its regulation.

However, this making-sensible not only yields no immediate look of the concept as unity, but rather this [unity] is not even meant thematically as the suspended content of a representation. Only as regulative unity is the conceptual unity what it can and must be as unifying. The unity is not grasped, but rather only if we look away from it in its determining of the rule is it then just as substantially the regulation which is determined in the view. This looking-away-from-it does not lose sight of it in general, but rather has in view precisely the unity as regulative.

The representing of the process of regulation as such a [representing] is properly conceptual representing. What has hitherto gone by that name, namely, the representing of unity which applies to many, was only an isolated element of the concept which remains veiled precisely with respect to its function as the rule governing the specific making-sensible which was pointed out.

However, if what is thematically represented in the making-sensible is neither the empirical look nor the isolated concept, but is rather the "listing" of the rule governing the providing of the image, then this also requires further characterization. The rule is represented in the 'how' of its regulating, i.e., according to how it regulates the presentation dictated within the presenting look. The representing of the 'how' is the free "imaging" ["*Bilden*"] of a making-sensible as the providing of an image in the sense just characterized, an imaging which is not bound to a determinate something at hand.

Such making-sensible occurs primarily in the power of imagination. "This representation of a general procedure of the power of imagination in providing an image for a concept I entitle the schema of this concept."[127] The formation of the schema in its fulfillment as the manner of making the concept sensible is called Schematism. The schema is indeed to be distinguished from images, but nevertheless it is related to something like an image, i.e., the image-character belongs necessarily to the schema. It (the character of the image) has its own essence. It is neither just a simpler look ("image" in the first sense) nor a likeness ("image" in the second sense). It will therefore be called the schema-image [*das Schma-Bild*].

§21. Schema and Schema-Image

A closer characterization of the Schema-Image will clarify its relationship to the schema and, at the same time, the type of relationship the concept has to the image. The formation of the schema [*Schemabildung*] is the making-sensible of concepts. How is the look of the immediately represented being related to what is represented of it in concepts? In what sense is this look an "image" ["*Bild*"] of the concept? This question must be discussed with respect to two kinds of concepts: those which are empirical and sensible (the concept

---

127. A 140, B 179f.

of a dog), and those which are pure and sensible, mathematical (the concept of a triangle or of a number).

Kant stresses that an "object of experience," i.e., the look that is accessible to us of a thing which is at hand, "or an image of the same," i.e., a likeness or copy of a being which is at hand, never "attains" the empirical concept of the same.[128] This not-attaining means, first of all, presenting it in a way which is "not adequate." However, at no time is this to be interpreted as meaning that there can be no adequate likeness of the concept. An empirical look of a being, with reference to its concept, can have absolutely no function as a likeness. This unsuitability pertains instead precisely to the schema-image, which in a true sense is the image of the concept. If anything, one could say that the empirical look contains exactly everything which the concept also contains, if not even more. But it does not contain it in the same way that the concept represents it: as one which applies to many. Instead, the content of the empirical look is given as one from among many, i.e., as isolated within what is thematically represented as such. The particular has dismissed the possibility of being just anything, but, nevertheless, for this reason it is a possible example[a] of the one which regulates the possibility of being just anything as such that applies to many. In this regulation, however, the universal has its own specific, clear determinacy, and it is in no way an indeterminate, dissolving "anything and everything" in contrast to what has been isolated.

The representing of the rule is the schema. As such, it necessarily remains relative to possible schema-images, of which no uniqueness can be demanded. "The concept of dog signifies a rule according to which my power of imagination can specify the form [Gestalt] of a four-footed animal in general, without being limited to any particular form which experience offers to me, or also to any possible image which I can present in concreto."[129]

That the empirical look does not attain its empirical concept expresses the positive structural relationship of the schema-image to the schema, according to which it is a possible presentation of the rule of presentation represented in the schema. At the same time, this means that, beyond the representation of this regulative unity of the rule, the concept is nothing. What logic refers to as a concept is grounded in the schema.[b] The concept "always refers immediately to the schema."[130]

Kant says of the empirical object that it is "even less" able to come up to

---

128. A 141, B 180.
129. Ibid.
130. Ibid.

a. See Kr[itik] d. U[rteilskraft], §59, p. 254 [Critique of Judgment, tr. J. H. Bernard (New York: Hafner Press, 1951), p. 196].
b. Here already we can see how it has been for "the" Logic!!

the standard set by its concept than is the "image" of the pure sensible concept. Is it perhaps for this reason that the schema-images of mathematical concepts are more adequate to their concepts? Obviously we are not to think here of a correspondence in the sense of a likeness either. The schema-image of a mathematical construction is equally valid whether it is empirically exact or roughly sketched out.[131]

Kant is obviously thinking of the fact that a mathematical schema-image, e.g., a specific triangle, must necessarily be either acute, right, or obtuse. With that, however, the possibility of being just anything is already exhausted [in the case of the triangle] whereas it is greater in the case of the presentation of a house. On the other hand, however, the sphere of the presentability of an acute or right triangle has a greater breadth. This schema-image, then, with its restriction, comes closer to the unity of the concept; with this greater breadth it comes closer to the universality of this unity. But as always, the image still has the appearance of an individual, while the schema has the unity of the universal rule governing many possible presentations "as its intention."

From this, what is essential to the schema-image first becomes clear: it does not get the character of its look only or first of all from the content of its directly discernible image. Rather, it gets the character of its look from the fact that it springs forth and how it springs forth from out of the possible presentation represented in its regulation; thus, as it were, bringing the rule into the sphere of possible intuitability. Only if the expression "image" is understood in this sense of the schema-image is it possible to call five points set one after another . . . . . "an image of the number five."[132] The number itself never looks like the five points, but it also never looks like the symbols '5' or 'V'. These are, indeed, looks, in still another way, of the number in question. In general, the shape '5' sketched out in space has nothing in common with the number, whereas the look of the five points . . . . . is certainly enumerable by means of the number five. Of course, this row of points does not indicate the number because it is visible at a glance and because we can apparently extract the number from it, but rather because it conforms to the representation of the rule for the possible presentability of this number.

But again, we do not first apprehend the number on the basis of this conformity. Rather, we already possess every number in the "representation of a method whereby a multiplicity, for instance a thousand, may be represented in an image in conformity with a certain concept."[133] In the representing of the rule of presentation, the possibility of the image is already formed.[37] This, and not the isolated look of a multiplicity of points, is already the true look

---

131. *Über eine Entdeckung*, p. 8, note.
132. A 140, B 179.
133. A 140, B 179.

which belongs structurally to the schema, the schema-image. For a real, delineated row of points, or rather one which has only been represented, the intuitable capacity to be viewed at a glance or not to be viewed at a glance remains unimportant for the "seeing" of the schema-image. It is for this reason as well that mathematical concepts are never grounded on the simply discernible images, but instead on the schemata. "In fact, it is not images {immediate looks} of the objects which lie at the foundation of our pure, sensible concepts, but rather the schemata."[134]

The analysis of the image-character of the schema-image of empirical and pure, sensible concepts has already proven: the making-sensible of concepts is a completely specific procuring of characteristic images. In the Schematism, the making-sensible which forms the schema can be understood neither by analogy to the customary "image-like presentation" ["*bildlichen Darstellung*"] nor even by being traced back to this. The latter is possible to such a small degree that, on the contrary, even the making-sensible in the sense first described—the immediate, empirical looking at things and the production of likenesses of it which are at hand—is only possible on the grounds of the possible making-sensible of concepts in the manner of the Schematism.

According to its essence, all conceptual representing is schematism. All finite knowing, however, as thinking intuiting, is necessarily conceptual.[c] Thus in the immediate perception of something at hand, this house for example, the schematizing premonition [*Vorblick*] of something like house in general is of necessity already to be found. It is from out of this pro-posing [*Vorstellung*][38] alone that what is encountered can reveal itself as house, can offer the look of a "house which is at hand." So the schematism occurs of necessity on the grounds of our knowing as finite knowing. For that reason Kant must say, "This schematism . . . is an art concealed in the depths of the human soul. . . ."[135] However, if the Schematism belongs to the essence of finite knowledge and if finitude is centered in transcendence, then the occurrence of transcendence at its innermost [level] must be a schematism. For this reason, Kant necessarily comes across a "transcendental schematism" if indeed he is to bring to light the ground for the inner possibility of transcendence.

---

134. A 140f., B 180. [In the second edition the words added by Heidegger were enclosed in parentheses and gave the impression of being part of Kant's text, an oversight corrected in the fourth edition—tr.]

135. A 141, B 180.

c. Here we must distinguish between: thinking *in* concepts, or bringing *out* concepts and proving *from* concepts—see *Critique of Judgment*.

§22. The Transcendental Schematism[a]

By means of the general characterization of schematism as a particular kind of making-sensible, it has been shown that schematism belongs necessarily to transcendence. On the other hand, the characterization of the full structure of ontological knowledge, which is necessarily intuition, has led to the insight: making-sensible, and indeed a pure making-sensible, belongs of necessity to transcendence. We have asserted that this pure making-sensible occurs as a schematism. It is now a question of grounding this assertion by means of a proof that the necessary, pure making-sensible of the pure understanding and its concepts (notions) happens in a transcendental schematism. What this [schematism] itself is, will be clarified with the unveiling of the manner in which it occurs.

The schema-forming making-sensible has as its purpose to procure an image for the concept. What is meant in [this concept], therefore, has an ordered relation to a discernibility. In such intuitability, what is conceptually intended becomes perceivable for the first time. The schema brings itself, i.e., brings the concept, into an image. The pure concepts of the understanding, which were thought in the pure "I think," require an essentially pure discernibility if in fact that which stands-against in the pure letting-stand-against is to be capable of being perceivable as a Being-in-opposition.[39] The pure concepts must be grounded in pure schemata, which procure an image for them.

Now Kant expressly says, however: "On the other hand, the schema of a pure concept of the understanding is something which can never be reduced to any image whatsoever. . . ."[136] However, if it belongs to the essence of a schema that is to be brought into an image, then the expression "image" in the preceding sentence can only mean a specific kind of image to the exclusion of others. From the start, it can only be a question of the schema-images. The refusal, then, of a possible symbolization [Verbildlichung] of the schemata of notions first of all means merely this: the presentable look, whose rule of presentation is represented in the schema of the notion, can never be taken out of the sphere of the empirically intuitive. If image is taken to mean empirical look in the broadest sense, then the schema of the notion obviously does not allow itself to be brought "into any image whatever." Yet even the looks which specify the mathematical construction of concepts are also, as images of "magnitudes" ["Größen"], reduced to a determinate region of the

---

136. A 142, B 181.

a. See *Duisburgscher Nachlaß* 10.[18ff.] Connection with the *transcendental* "subject" of *Judgment*; judgment and schema; construction; intuition! Haering certainly does *not* see through the *problem*, p. 66f.!

objective. Moreover, the notions as primal concepts cannot be brought into images like this either, to the extent that they represent those rules in which objectivity in general as preliminary horizon for the possible encountering of all objects is formed [bildet]. Hence, in the phrase cited above, "image" ["Bild"] means the kinds of schema-images which belong to the schemata of empirical and mathematical concepts. The schema of the pure concepts of the under-standing cannot be brought into any images of this kind whatsoever.

Now the elucidation of the inner possibility of ontological knowledge in the Transcendental Deduction has shown: through the mediation of the pure synthesis of the transcendental power of imagination, the pure concepts are essentially relative to pure intuition (time), and vice versa. Up to now, how-ever, only the essential necessity of the relation between notion and time has been discussed. On the other hand, the innermost structure of this relation as the innermost construction of transcendence has not yet been elucidated.

As pure intuition, however, time is such as to procure a look prior to all experience. The pure look which gives itself in such pure intuition (for Kant, the pure succession of the sequence of nows) must therefore be called a pure image. And in the chapter on Schematism, Kant himself even says: "The pure image . . . of all objects of sense in general,[b] however, [is] time."[137] Moreover, the same thing is expressed in a later passage, no less important, in which Kant determines the essence of the notion: the notion is "the pure concept, insofar as it has its origin simply in the understanding (not in the pure image of sensibility)."[138]

Hence the schema of the pure concept of the understanding can also be brought very nicely into an image, provided that "image" is now taken as "pure image."

As "pure image," time is the schema-image and not just the form of intuition which stands over and against the pure concepts of the understanding. Hence the schema of notions has a character of its own. As schema in general it represents unities, representing them as rules which impart themselves to a possible look. Now according to the Transcendental Deduction, the unities represented in the notions refer essentially and necessarily to time. The sche-matism of the pure concepts of the understanding, therefore, must necessarily regulate these internally in time. But as the Transcendental Aesthetic shows, time is the representation of a "unique object."[139] "Different times are but parts of one and the same time. The representation which can only be given through a unique object, however, is intuition."[140] Hence time is not only the necessary

---

137. A 142, B 182.
138. A 320, B 377.
139. A 31f., B 47.
140. Ibid.

b. i.e., in their objectivity

pure image of the schemata of the pure concepts of the understanding, but also their sole, pure possibility of having a certain look. This unique possibility of having a certain look shows itself in itself to be nothing other than always just time and the temporal.

Now if the closed multiplicity of the pure concepts of the understanding is to have its image in this unique possibility of having a certain look, then this image [*Bild*] must be one which is pure and which is formable [*bildbar*] in a variety of ways. Through internal self-regulation in time as pure look, the schemata of the notions pass their image off from this and thus articulate the unique pure possibility of having a certain look into a variety of pure images. In this way, the schemata of the pure concepts of the understanding "determine" time. "The schemata are thus nothing but a priori *determinations of time* according to rules,"[141] or put more succinctly, "transcendental determinations of time."[142] As such, they are "a transcendental product of the power of imagination."[143] This schematism forms transcendence a priori and hence is called "Transcendental Schematism."

The letting-stand-against of that which is objective and which offers itself, of the being-in-opposition-to, occurs in transcendence due to the fact that ontological knowledge, as schematizing intuition, makes the transcendental affinity of the unity of the rule in the image of time discernible a priori and therewith capable of being taken in stride. Through its pure schema-image, the transcendental schema necessarily has an a priori character which corresponds. Hence the interpretation carried out of the individual, pure schemata as transcendental determinations of time must point out this correspondence-forming character.

Now Kant extracts the complete unity of the pure concepts of the understanding from the Table of Judgments, and correspondingly, he gives the definitions of the schemata of the individual, pure concepts of the understanding to the Table of Notions. According to the four moments of the division of the categories (Quantity, Quality, Relation, Modality), the pure look of time must exhibit four possibilities of formability as "time-series, time-content, time-order, and time-inclusiveness."[144] These characters of time are not so much developed systematically through and out of an analysis of time itself, but instead are fixed in it "according to the order of the categories."[145] The interpretation of the individual schemata begins first of all with a relation-measuring, comprehensive analysis of the pure schemata of Quantity, Reality, and Substance, then becomes more concise, and ends with mere definitions.[146]

---

141. A 145, B 184.
142. A 138, B 177.
143. A 142, B 181.
144. A 145, B 184f.
145. Ibid.
146. A 142ff., B 182ff.

In a certain sense, Kant has a right to such a lapidary presentation. For if the Transcendental Schematism determines ontological knowledge on the basis of its essence, then the systematic working-out of ontological knowledge in the presentation of the system of synthetic principles must necessarily come across the character of the schematism a priori and must set forth the corresponding transcendental determinations of time. Now this also occurs, although only within certain limits.[147]

It is easy to recognize: the more clearly the essential structure of the Transcendental Schematism and, in general, all that belongs to the whole of transcendence is brought to light, then all the more clearly do the paths appear by which to find our way in the darkness of these most original structures "in the depths of our soul." The universal essence of the schematism in general, and of the transcendental in particular, has indeed been determined with sufficient clarity. That a further advancing is possible, however, is divulged by Kant himself in the following remark: "That we may not be further delayed by a dry and tedious dissection of what is demanded by transcendental schemata of the pure concepts of the understanding in general, we prefer to present them according to the order of the categories and in connection with them."[148]

Is it only the dryness and tediousness of this affair which restrains Kant from attempting a further dissection? The answer to this question cannot as yet be given.[149] [When given, the answer] will also clarify why the present interpretation refrains from attempting a concrete unfolding of the Kantian definitions of the pure schemata. However, in order to show that Kant's doctrine of the Transcendental Schematism is no baroque theory but instead is created out of the phenomena themselves, I would like to give an interpretation—admittedly only a short and rough one—of the transcendental schema of a category, namely, of substance.

"The schema of Substance is the persistence of the real in time. . . . "[150] For the full elucidation of the schematism of this schema, we must refer to the "First Analogy," i.e., to the "Principle of Persistence."[40]

Substance, as a notion, signifies first of all just: that which forms the ground (subsistence).[151] Its schema must be the representation of that which forms the ground, provided that it presents itself in the pure image of time. Now time, as pure sequence of nows, is always now. In every now it is now. Time thus shows its own permanence. As such, time is "immutable and lasting," it

---

147. A 158ff., B 197ff.
148. A 142, B 181.
149. See below, §35, p. 133.
150. A 143, B 183.
151. A 182ff., B 224ff.

"does not itself pass."[152][41]c Stated more precisely: time is not one thing among others which lasts. Rather, precisely on the grounds of the essential character previously mentioned—to be now, in every now—time gives the pure look of something like lasting in general. As this pure image (immediate pure "look"), it presents that which forms the ground in pure intuition.

This function of presentation, however, will first become genuinely clear when the full content of the notion "Substance" is examined—which Kant neglects to do here. Substance is a category of "Relation" (between Subsistence and Inherence). It signifies that which forms the ground for a "thing which adheres" [ein "Anhängendes"]. Thus time is only the pure image of the notion Substance if it presents precisely this relation in the pure image.

Time, however, is as sequence of nows precisely because in every flowing now it is a now, even another now. As the look of what lasts, it offers at the same time the image of pure change in what lasts.

So, even this rough interpretation of the transcendental schema of Substance, which at its longest cannot advance into the more original structures, must show: what is meant by the notion Substance can itself procure a pure image a priori in time. For this reason, the objectivity in the letting-stand-against becomes discernible and distinct a priori, provided that Substance belongs to it as constitutive element. Through this schematism the notion as schematized stands in view in advance, so that in this preliminary view of the pure image of persistence, a being which as such is unalterable in the change can show itself for experience. "To time, itself immutable and lasting, there corresponds in appearance that which is immutable in existence"[153] (i.e., Being-at-hand).[42]

The Transcendental Schematism is consequently the ground for the inner possibility of ontological knowledge. It forms [bildet] that which stands against in the pure letting-stand-against in such a way that what is represented in pure thinking is necessarily given intuitably in the pure image [Bilde] of time. Thus it is time, as given a priori, which in advance bestows upon the horizon of transcendence the character of the perceivable offer. But not only that. As the unique, pure, universal image, it gives a preliminary enclosedness to the horizon of transcendence. This single and pure ontological horizon is the condition for the possibility that the being given within it can have this or that particular, revealed, indeed ontic horizon. But time does not give just the preliminary, unified coherence to transcendence. Rather, as the pure self-giving[43] it simply offers to it, in general, something like a check.[44] It makes

---

152. A 144, B 183.
153. Ibid.

c. See A 41, B 58: "time itself is not changed, but rather, something which is in time."

perceivable to a finite creature the "Being-in-opposition-to" of objectivity,[45] which belongs to the finitude of the transcending turning-toward.

§23. Schematism and Subsumption

In the preceding pages, the Kantian doctrine of the schematism of the pure concepts of the understanding was intentionally interpreted in light of the unique orientation toward the innermost occurrence of transcendence. Now with his laying of the ground for metaphysics, however, Kant does not simply follow the problematic, the impulse for which arises anew with every step. Rather, even with the first introduction to the decisive elements of the doctrine, he clings first of all to the most feasible, known formulations which should lead in a preliminary way to the problem. Thus the Transcendental Deduction begins as a legal action [*Rechtshandel*] within traditional metaphysics. It is decided by the proof that the notions must be categories, i.e., that according to their essence they must belong to Transcendence itself if they are to be able a priori to determine empirical, accessible beings. At the same time, however, the condition for the "use" of these concepts is fixed.

To use concepts means in general: to apply them to objects, or rather—seen from the standpoint of the objects—to bring these objects "under" concepts.[a] In the language of traditional Logic, this use of concepts is called subsumption.[b] To use the pure concepts as transcendental determinations of time a priori, i.e., to attain pure knowledge, means: the process of the Schematism. Seen from this point of view, the problem of the Schematism in fact initially allows itself to be discussed quite adequately in the textbooks on subsumption. But it must be observed that here—in ontological knowledge—it is from the first a matter of ontological concepts, and consequently also a matter of a peculiar, i.e., an ontological, "subsumption."

Already with the first characterization of the essential unity of ontological knowledge, then, Kant has not neglected to allude to the fundamental difference between "bringing under concepts" (which concerns the objects) and "bringing to concepts" (which concerns the pure synthesis of the transcendental power of imagination).[154] The "bringing to concepts" of the pure synthesis occurs in the Transcendental Schematism. It "forms" the unity represented in the notion into the essential element of pure, discernable objectivity.[c] In the

---

154. See A 78ff., B 104ff.

a. (judgment)
b. *place* [something] *under* [something]
c. "reflection" to what degree?

Transcendental Schematism the categories are formed first of all as categories. If these are the true "primal concepts," however, then the Transcendental Schematism is the original and authentic concept-formation as such.

Therefore, if Kant introduces the chapter on Schematism with a reference to subsumption, it is because he wants thereby to point to transcendental subsumption as the central problem in order to show that in the essential structure of pure knowledge, the question concerning the inner possibility of original conceptuality as such has burst open.

The empirical concepts were drawn from experience and are therefore "homogeneous" with the content of the being they determine. Their application to objects, i.e., their use, is no problem. "Now pure concepts of the understanding, however, in comparison with empirical intuitions (indeed, with sensible intuitions in general), are completely nonhomogeneous and can never be encountered in any intuition. Now how is the subsumption of the latter under the former, and consequently how is the application of the category to appearances, possible? For no one will say that this [category], e.g., causality, can also come to be intuited through sense and is contained in appearance."[155] In the question concerning the possible use of the categories, their particular essence itself first becomes a problem. These concepts present us with the question of their "formation" in general. Hence, the talk of the subsumption of appearances "under categories" is not the formula for a solution to the problem, but rather it contains precisely the question of the sense in which we can speak here in general of subsumption "under concepts."

If we take the Kantian formulation of the problem of schematism as the problem of subsumption simply in the sense of an introduction to the problem, then it gives us an indication of the central purpose, and with it an indication of the core content of the chapter on Schematism.

To represent conceptually means to represent something "in general" ["*im allgemeinen*"]. With concept formation as such, the "universality" ["*Allgemeinheit*"][d] of the representing must become a problem. But now, if the categories as ontological concepts are not homogeneous with the empirical objects and the concepts of those objects, then neither can their "universality" be that of a level which is higher only by degree of the universality of a higher, or rather of a highest ontic "class" or "genus." What character of "generality" ["*Generalität*"] does the universality of the ontological (i.e., the metaphysical) concepts have? But that is merely the question: What does the "*generalis*" mean in the characterization of Ontology as *Metaphysica Generalis*? The problem of the Schematism of the pure concepts of the understanding is the question concerning the innermost essence of ontological knowledge.

---

155. A 137f., B 176f.

d. "sameness" as grounds for universality [*Allgemeinheit*]; sameness and "*reflection*"

Hence, the following stands out: If Kant poses the problem of the conceptuality of the primal concept in the Schematism chapter and if he resolves it with the help of the essential determination of these concepts as Transcendental Schemata, then the Doctrine of the Schematism of the pure concepts of the understanding is the decisive stage of the laying of the ground for *Metaphysica Generalis*.

The orientation with respect to the idea of subsumption, as a first discussion of the problem of the transcendental schematism, has a certain justification. But then Kant is also already permitted to gather from it a preliminary sketch of the possible solution to the problem and to characterize the idea of the transcendental schematism in a provisional way in terms of subsumption. If the pure concept of the understanding is fully nonhomogeneous with appearances, but if it is still to determine them, then there must be a mediator which bridges the nonhomogeneity. "This mediating representation must be pure (void of everything empirical), and indeed on the one hand it must be *intellectual* while on the other hand it must be *sensible*. The *Transcendental Schema* is such a [mediating representation]."[156] "Thus, an application of the category to appearances becomes possible by means of the transcendental determination of time which, as the schema of the concepts of the understanding, mediates the subsumption of the latter under the former."[157]

Thus the innermost meaning of the Transcendental Schematism is shown to be the question of Subsumption, even in the closest and most superficial form of the problem of Schematism. There is not the least cause to keep complaining ever anew of a disunity and confusion to the Schematism chapter. If anything in the *Critique of Pure Reason* was thoroughly articulated in the clearest way and was measured in each word, then it would be this part which is crucial for the whole work. Because of its significance, we have shown its division explicitly:[46]

1. The introduction to the problem of the Schematism with guidance from the traditional idea of Subsumption (A 137, B 176; A 140, B 179: "The schema in itself is . . . ").
2. The preparatory analysis of the structure of the Schematism in general and of the Schematism of the empirical and mathematical concepts (up to A 142, B 181: "On the other hand, the schema of a pure concept of the understanding is . . . ").
3. The analysis of the Transcendental Schema in general (up to A 142, B 182: "The pure image of all magnitudes . . . ").
4. The interpretation of the individual, transcendental schemata with guidance from the Table of Categories (up to A 145, B 184: "Now one sees from all of these . . . ").

156. A 138, B 177.
157. A 139, B 178.

5. The characterization of the four classes of categories with a view to the corresponding four possibilities for a pure formability [*Bildbarkeit*] of time (up to A 145, B 185:[47] "Now from this is illuminated . . . ").

6. The determination of the Transcendental Schematism as the "true and sole condition" of transcendence (up to A 146, B 185: "But it is also evident . . . ").

7. The critical application of the essential determination of the categories which is grounded through the Schematism (to the end of the section).

The Schematism chapter is not "confused," but rather is constructed in an incomparably lucid way. The Schematism chapter is not "confusing," but rather leads with an unheard-of certainty into the core of the whole problematic of the *Critique of Pure Reason*. Admittedly, all of that only becomes evident if the finitude of transcendence is grasped as ground for the inner possibility (and that means here a necessity) of metaphysics, so that the interpretation can get a toehold on these grounds.

But admittedly, Kant wrote in his last years (1797): "In general, the Schematism is one of the most difficult points. Even Herr Beck cannot find his way therein. —I hold this chapter to be one of the most important."[158]

THE FIFTH STAGE OF THE GROUND-LAYING:
THE FULL ESSENTIAL DETERMINATION OF
ONTOLOGICAL KNOWLEDGE

In the previous stage, the ground for the inner possibility of ontological synthesis, and thereby the goal of the ground-laying, was attained with the Transcendental Schematism. If we now add a fifth stage, it can no longer lead the ground-laying further along. Rather, it should take possession explicitly of the ground which has been won as such, i.e., with a view to its possible cultivation.

For this to happen, the stages we have just run through must be adopted in their unity, not in the sense of an adding-together which comes after the fact, but rather in the manner of an independent, full determination of the essence of ontological knowledge. Kant lays down this decisive determination of essence in the "highest principle of all synthetic judgments."[159] However, if ontological knowledge is none other than the original formation of transcen-

158. *Kants handschriftlicher Nachlaß*, vol. V, no. 6359.
159. A 154–158, B 193–197.

dence, then the highest principle must contain the most central determination of the essence of transcendence. That this is so is now to be shown. The prospect for the further tasks and consequences of the Kantian laying of the ground for *Metaphysica Generalis* will arise from the ground and soil we have attained in this way.

§24. The Highest Synthetic Principle as the Full Determination of the Essence of Transcendence

Kant also introduces this central piece of doctrine in [the context of] a critical attitude toward traditional metaphysics. This [latter] wants to know the being "from mere concepts," i.e., from thinking alone. The peculiar essence of mere thinking is delimited by general logic. Mere thinking is the joining of subject and predicate (judging).[a] Such joining explains only what is represented in the joined representations as such. It must be merely explanatory, "analytic," because it has "played merely with representations."[160][48] Mere thinking, if it wants to be such, must "remain" with what is represented as such. Of course, even in this binding-together it also has its own rules, fundamental principles, of which the highest is reputed to be the "Principle of Contradiction"[161] In general, mere thinking is not knowing; rather, it is just an element, although a necessary one, of finite knowledge. However, we can expand upon mere thinking, provided that it is taken in advance as an element of finite knowledge; we can make visible its necessary relation to something which first determines full knowledge in a primary way.

If the predicate is to be an element in an [instance of] knowledge, then it is not so much a matter of its relationship to the subject (apophantic-predicative synthesis), but rather of its (better: of the whole subject-predicate relation's) "relationship" to "something wholly other."[162] This other is the being itself, with which the knowing—thus also the judging relationship which belongs to it—is to be "in accord." Hence the knowing must "go beyond" that [point] at which every mere thinking as such, which previously was bound together in itself, necessarily "remains." Kant calls this the "relationship" to the "wholly other" synthesis (the Veritative Synthesis). As such, insofar as it

---

160. A 155, B 195.
161. A 150ff., B 189ff.
162. A 154, B 193f.

a. Distinguish between Subject-Object relationship in general, and formal and analytic judgments; the two are not the same; see the highest principle of Analytic Judgment and negative determination of *all* judgments in general—WS 1935/36. [*Die Frage nach dem Ding. Zu Kants Lehre von den transzendentalen Grundsätzen.* GA, vol. 41], p. 173ff. [*What Is a Thing?* tr. W. B. Barton and V. Deutsch (South Bend: Gateway, 1967), p. 169ff.]

knows something wholly other, knowledge is synthetic. But now, however, since the predicative-apophantic joining in mere thinking can also be called synthesis, it is best to distinguish the synthesis specific to knowledge, which was done earlier, as the one which brings-forth (namely, the wholly other).

This going-beyond to the "wholly other," however, requires a Being-in-there [Darinnensein], in a "medium"[163] within which this "wholly other"—that the knowing creature itself is not and over which it is not the master—can be encountered. But with the following words, Kant now paraphrases what it is that makes possible and makes up this going-beyond which turns-toward and which lets something be encountered: "It is but one[49] quintessence [Inbegriff] in which all our representations are contained, namely, the inner sense and its a priori form, time. The synthesis of the representations rests on the power of imagination, but their synthetic unity (which is required for judgment) [rests] on the unity of apperception.[b][164]

As a consequence the triad of elements, which was introduced in the second stage of the ground-laying along with the initial characterization of the essential unity of ontological knowledge, explicitly recurs here. The third and fourth stages, however, show how these three elements form a structural unity whose formative center is the transcendental power of imagination. What is formed there, however, is transcendence. If Kant now recalls this triad for the purpose of the decisive elucidation of transcendence, then it may no longer be taken according to the still-obscure succession with which they were introduced in the second stage. Rather, it [the triad] must be fully present in the transparency of its structure, which is finally revealed in the Transcendental Schematism. And if this fifth stage now merely summarizes, then the essential unity of transcendence, first indicated in the second stage only as a problem, must be taken as illuminated and must be appropriated as explicitly elucidated on the grounds of its essential possibility.

Thus, Kant now brings the whole problem of the essence of finitude in knowledge together in the short formula of the *"possibility of experience."*[165] Experience means: finite, intuiting knowledge of beings which takes them in stride. The being must be given to knowledge as something which stands-against. Now in the expression "possibility of experience," on the other hand, the term "possibility" has a characteristic ambiguity.

"Possible" experience could mean "possible" as distinct from real. But in the "possibility of experience," the "possible" experience[c] is no greater a problem

---

163. A 155, B 194.
164. Ibid.
165. A 156ff., B 195ff.

b. See A 216; B 263. the Analogies as exponents; the essence of exponents! See SS 1930 [Vom Wesen der menschlichen Freiheit. Einleitung in die Philosophie. GA, vol. 31], p. 152ff.
c. something—as object of possible experience

than the actual; instead they both [are a problem] with respect to what makes them possible in advance. "Possibility of experience" means, therefore, that which makes a finite experience possible, i.e., that which is not necessarily but rather possibly actual. This "possibility" which first makes possible the "possibly" is the *possibilitas* of traditional metaphysics,[50] and is synonymous with *essentia* or *realitas*. Definitions of the real [*Real-Definitionen*] are taken "from the essence of the matter, from the initial ground of possibility."[51] They serve "for knowledge of the matter according to its inner possibility."[166]

"Possibility of experience" therefore means primarily: the unified wholeness of what finite knowledge makes possible in its essence. "The *possibility of experience*, then, is that which a priori gives objective reality to all our cognitions [*Erkenntnisse*]."[167] Possibility of experience is therefore synonymous with transcendence. To circumscribe this in its full, essential wholeness means: to determine "the conditions for the possibility of experience."

"Experience," understood as experiencing in distinction from what is experienced, is intuiting which takes things in stride[d] and which must let the being give itself. "That an object is given" means that it "is presented immediately in intuition."[168] But what does this mean? Kant answers: "to relate the representation {of the object} to experience (be it actual or still possible)."[169] This relating, however, wants to suggest: in order for an object to be able to give itself, there must in advance already be a turning-toward such an occurrence, which is capable of being "summoned." This preliminary turning-one's-attention-toward . . . [*Sichzuwenden zu* . . .] occurs, as the Transcendental Deduction shows and as the Transcendental Schematism explains, in the ontological synthesis. This turning-one's-attention-toward . . . is the condition for the possibility of experiencing.

And yet, the possibility of finite knowledge requires a second condition. Only true knowledge is knowledge. Truth, however, means "accordance with the Object [*Objekt*]."[170] In advance, then, there must be something like a with-what [*ein Womit*] of the possible accordance[52] which can be encountered, i.e., something which regulates by giving a standard. It must open up in advance the horizon of the standing-against, and as such it must be distinct. This horizon is the condition for the possibility of the object [*Gegenstand*] with respect to its being-able-to-stand-against [*Gegenstehenkönnens*].[e]

---

166. *Logikvorlesung*, §106, note 2, vol. VIII, p. 447. See also B 302, note, and A 596, B 624, note.
167. A 156, B 195.
168. Ibid.
169. Ibid.
170. A 157, B 196f.

d. *incomplete*—but important here
e. See A 237, the basic principles of pure understanding as source of all truth.

Hence the possibility of finite knowledge, i.e., the experiencing of what is experienced as such, stands under two conditions. These two conditions together must delimit the full essence of transcendence. This delimitation can be carried out with one proposition which states the ground for the possibility of synthetic, i.e., finite, knowing judgments, and which as such applies in advance to "all."

What conclusive formulation does Kant give to this "highest fundamental principle of all synthetic judgments"? It reads: "the conditions for the *possibility of experience* in general are at the same time conditions for the *possibility of the objects of experience*."[171]

The decisive content of this proposition lies not so much in what Kant italicized, but rather in the "are at the same time" ["*sind zugleich*"]. What, then, does this "to be at the same time" ["*zugleich sein*"] mean? It gives expression to the essential unity of the full structure of transcendence, which lies in the fact that the letting-stand-against which turns itself toward as such forms the horizon of objectivity in general. The going-out-to . . . , which was previously and at all times necessary in finite knowing, is hence a constant standing-out-from . . . (*Ecstasis*). But this essential standing-out-from . . . , precisely in the standing, forms and therein holds before itself—a horizon. In itself, transcendence is ecstatic-horizonal. The highest principle gives expression to this articulation of transcendence unified in itself.

Accordingly, it may also be understood concisely as follows: what makes an experiencing possible at the same time makes possible the experienceable, or rather experiencing [an experienceable] as such. This means: transcendence makes the being in itself accessible to a finite creature. The "Being-at-the-same-time" in the formula for the highest synthetic principle[53] does not just mean that both conditions always come forth at the same time, or that if we think of the one then we will also have had to think of the other, or even that both conditions are identical. The grounding proposition [*Grundsatz*] is no principle [*Prinzip*] that is arrived at in the drawing of a conclusion that we must put forth as valid if experience is to hold true. Rather, it is the expression of the most original phenomenological knowledge of the innermost, unified structure of transcendence, laboriously extracted in the stages of the essential projection of ontological synthesis that have already been presented.[172]

---

171. A 158, B 197.
172. The above interpretation of the highest synthetic principle shows the extent to which it determines the essence of synthetic judgments a priori and, at the same time, the extent to which it can be claimed as the properly understood, metaphysical Principle of Sufficient Reason [*Satz vom Grunde*]. In this regard, see Heidegger, *Vom Wesen des Grundes, Festschrift* for Edmund Husserl (supplementary volume to the *Jahrbuch für Philosophie und phänomenologische Forschung*) (1929), p. 71ff., and in particular p. 79f. (also appearing as a reprint, 6th edition, [1973], p. 16f.). [This essay has also been reprinted in the anthology *Wegmarken* (1967), which has been reissued as vol. 9 of the *Gesamtausgabe* with Heidegger's own marginalia, pp. 123–175—tr.]

§25. Transcendence as the Laying of the Ground for Metaphysica Generalis

The unveiling of the ground for the inner possibility of the essence of ontological synthesis was determined to be the task of the laying of the ground for *Metaphysica Generalis*. Ontological knowledge has proven itself to be that which forms transcendence. Hence, the insight into the full structure of transcendence now makes it possible for the first time to have a clear view of the complete range of characteristics peculiar to ontological knowledge—its knowing as well as what it knows.

The knowing, as finite, must be a thinking intuiting of what gives itself which takes [what gives itself] in stride, and hence it must be pure. It is a pure schematism. The pure unity of the three elements of pure knowledge is expressed in the concept of the transcendental schema as "transcendental determination of time."

If ontological knowing is schema-forming, then therewith it creates (forms) from out of itself the pure look (image). Is it not the case, then, that even ontological knowledge which occurs in the transcendental power of imagination is "creative"? And if ontological knowing forms transcendence, which in turn constitutes the essence of finitude, then is not the finitude of transcendence burst asunder because of this "creative" character? Does not the finite creature become infinite through this "creative" behavior?

But is ontological knowledge, then, as "creative" as *intuitus originarius*, for which the being in intuiting is in and as what stands forth and can never become object?[54] Do beings come to be "known," then, in this "creative" ontological knowledge—i.e., are they created as such? Absolutely not. Ontological knowledge not only does not create beings, but also it does not relate itself at all, thematically or directly, to the being.

But to what [is it related] then? What is the known of this knowing? A Nothing. Kant calls it the "X" and speaks of an "object." To what extent is this X a Nothing, and to what extent is it still a "Something"? The answer to this question regarding the known in ontological knowledge can be given through a short interpretation of both of the main passages in which Kant speaks of this X. Characteristically, the first passage is found in the introduction to the Transcendental Deduction.[173] The second is found in the section entitled "On the Grounds for the Distinction of all Objects in General into Phenomena and Noumena"[174] that, according to the structure of the *Critique Of Pure Reason*, concludes the positive laying of the ground for *Metaphysica Generalis*.

The first passage reads: "Now we are also able to determine more correctly our concept[55] of an *object* in general. All representations, as representations,

---

173. A 108f.
174. A 235ff., B 294ff.

have their object and can themselves in turn be objects of other representations. Appearances are the only objects which can be given to us immediately, and what in them immediately relates to the object is called intuition. Now these appearances, however, are not things in themselves; rather, they are themselves only representations which in turn have their object—an object which can no longer be intuited by us and which may therefore be named the nonempirical, i.e., transcendental object = X."

What stands immediately in opposition to what is in the appearance is that which is given by intuition. Now the appearances, however, are themselves "only representations," not things in themselves. What is represented in them only shows itself in and for a turning-oneself-toward . . . which takes-in-stride. This, however, must itself "have its object in turn." Indeed, in general, it must give something in advance which has the character of a standing-against in general in order to form the horizon within which original beings can be encountered. This terminus of the preliminary turning-toward, therefore, can no longer be intuited by us in the sense of empirical intuition. However that does not exclude—indeed, it includes—the necessity of its immediate distinguishability in a pure intuition. This terminus of the preliminary turning-toward, therefore, can "be termed the nonempirical object = X."

"All our representations are in fact referred to some Object through the understanding, and since appearances are nothing but representations, the understanding refers them to a *Something* as the object of the sensible intuition: but this Something *as object of an intuition in general* is to that extent only the transcendental Object. But this means a Something = X, of which we know nothing and, according to the present organization of our understanding, of which we can know nothing at all, but rather which, as just a *correlatum* of the unity of apperception, can serve only for the unity of the manifold in sensible intuition. By means of this, the understanding unifies them in the concept of an object."[175]

The X is a "Something" of which in general we can know nothing at all. But it is not therefore not knowable, because as a being this X lies hidden "behind" a layer of appearances. Rather, it is not knowable because it simply cannot become a possible object of knowing, i.e., the possession of a knowledge of beings. It can never become such because it is a Nothing.

Nothing means: not a being, but nevertheless "Something." It "serves only as *correlatum*," i.e., according to its essence it is pure horizon. Kant calls this X the "transcendental object," i.e., the Being-in-opposition [*das Dawider*]

---

175. A 250. This is the text as corrected by Kant himself. See *Nachträge*, CXXXIV. [The "correction" consists of Kant's adding the words "*als Gegenstand einer Anschauung überhaupt*" ("as object of an intuition in general") to qualify the word "something" following the colon at the end of the first sentence. I have used asterisks to distinguish the added words. Kemp Smith did not include this correction in his translation, but I have rendered Heidegger's text verbatim—tr.]

which is discernable in and through transcendence as its horizon. Now if the X which is known in ontological knowledge is, according to its essence, horizon, then this knowing must also be such that it holds open this horizon in its character as horizon. But then, this Something may not even stand as what is directly and exclusively meant in the theme of an apprehending. The horizon must be unthematic, but must nevertheless be regularly in view. Only in this way can it push forward into the theme [of the apprehending] what is encountered in it as such.

The X is "object in general." This does not mean: a universal, indeterminate being which stands-against. On the contrary, this expression refers to that which makes up in advance the rough sizing up of all possible objects as standing-against, the horizon of a standing-against. This horizon is indeed not object but rather a Nothing, if by object we mean a being which is apprehended thematically. And ontological knowledge is no knowledge if knowledge means: apprehending of beings.

Ontological knowledge is rightly termed knowledge, however, if it attains truth. But it does not just "have" truth; rather, it is the original truth, which Kant therefore terms "transcendental truth," the essence of which is elucidated by means of the Transcendental Schematism. "In the whole of all possible experience, however, lies all our knowledge, and transcendental truth consists in the general relation to the same, which precedes all empirical truth and makes it possible."[176]

Ontological knowledge "forms" transcendence, and this forming is nothing other than the holding-open of the horizon within which the Being of the being becomes discernable in a preliminary way. If truth indeed means: unconcealment of . . . , then transcendence is original truth. Truth itself, however, must bifurcate into the unveiledness of Being and the openness [Offenbarkeit] of beings.[177] If ontological knowledge unveils the horizon, then its truth lies precisely in [the act of] letting the being be encountered within the horizon. Kant says: ontological knowledge only has "empirical use," i.e., it serves for the making-possible of finite knowledge in the sense of the experience of the being which shows itself.

Hence, it must at least remain open as to whether this "creative" knowledge, which is always only ontological and never ontic, bursts the finitude of transcendence asunder, or whether it does not just plant the finite "subject" in its authentic finitude.

According to this essential determination of ontological knowledge, ontology is none other than the explicit unveiling of the systematic whole of pure knowledge, to the extent that it forms transcendence.

---

176. A 146, B 185.
177. See *Vom Wesen des Grundes*, p. 75ff; 6th ed. (1973), p. 12ff.

Nevertheless, Kant wants to replace "the proud name of an ontology"[178] with that of a "Transcendental Philosophy," i.e., with an essential unveiling of transcendence. And he is justified in doing this as long as the title "Ontology" is taken in the sense of traditional metaphysics. This traditional ontology "presumes to give synthetic a priori knowledge of things in general." It raises itself to an a priori ontic knowledge which can only come to an infinite creature. But if this ontology, with its "presumption," takes off its "pride," i.e., if it grasps itself in its finitude—or rather grasps itself as the necessary structure of the essence of finitude—then the expression "ontology" will have been given its true essence for the first time, and thereby its use will have been justified. It is in this sense, then, which was first won and guaranteed through the laying of the ground for metaphysics, that Kant himself also uses the expression "ontology," and indeed [he does so] in the decisive passage in the *Critique of Pure Reason* which sets forth the outline of metaphysics as a whole."[179]

With the transformation of *Metaphysica Generalis*, however, the ground upon which traditional metaphysics is built is shaken, and for this reason the proper edifice of *Metaphysica Specialis* begins to totter. This problematic leads off in further directions, however, and will not be treated here. Moreover, it requires a preparation which can only be accomplished through a more original appropriation of what Kant had achieved as a laying of the ground for *Metaphysica Generalis* in the unity of the Transcendental Aesthetic and Logic.

---

178. A 247, B 303.
179. A 845, B 873. See also the use of the term "ontology" in *Über die Fortschritte der Metaphysik*.

Part Three

The Laying of the Ground for Metaphysics in Its Originality

But is it then possible in general to grasp the ground-laying which has now been achieved in a still more original way? Is this continual insisting upon originality not idle curiosity? Is it not punished with the wretchedness which is the fatal distinction of all those who want to know better? But above all, does it not force upon the Kantian philosophizing a standard which remains foreign to it, so that everything ends in a critique "from without," which would always be unjust?

From the start, the question concerning the originality of the Kantian ground-laying does not want to negotiate this steep path. If the discussion of originality in general is not to become critique in the sense of polemic, but instead is still to remain interpretation, then the leading idea of originality must be taken from the Kantian ground-laying itself. It is a matter of interrogating the premonition guiding Kant's entering into the dimension of origin and with it his striving for the ground for the source of the "basic sources of knowledge."[1] In order for this to happen, what the ground itself is, as already established in the ground-laying, must be clearly delimited.

A. THE EXPLICIT CHARACTERIZATION OF THE GROUND LAID IN THE GROUND-LAYING

§26. The Formative Center of Ontological Knowledge as Transcendental Power of Imagination

The laying of the ground for *Metaphysica Generalis* is the answer to the question concerning the essential unity of ontological knowledge and the ground of its possibility. Ontological knowledge "forms" transcendence, i.e., the holding-open of the horizon which is discernable in advance through the pure schemata. These "spring forth" as the "transcendental product"[180] of the transcendental power of imagination. As original, pure synthesis, it forms the essential unity of pure intuition (time) and pure thinking (apperception).

The transcendental power of imagination, however, did not first become the central theme in the Doctrine of the Transcendental Schematism. Rather, it already [had that status] in the preceding stage of the ground-laying, the Transcendental Deduction. Because it is to undertake the original unification, it must already have been mentioned in the second stage, with the first characterization of the essential unity of ontological knowledge. The transcendental power of imagination is hence the ground upon which the inner possibility of ontological knowledge, and with it that of *Metaphysica Generalis*, is built.

Kant introduces the pure power of imagination as an "indispensable function of the soul."[181] To clear the already-laid ground for metaphysics in an explicit way, therefore, means: to determine more precisely a faculty of the human soul. That the laying of the ground for metaphysics finally arrives at such a task is "self-evident," if indeed metaphysics, in Kant's own words, belongs to "human nature." As a consequence, the "Anthropology" which Kant dealt with over the years in his lectures must provide us with information concerning the already-laid ground for metaphysics."[182]

"The power of imagination (*facultas imaginandi*) [is] a faculty of intuition, even without the presence of the object."[183] Hence, the power of imagination belongs to the faculty of intuition. According to the definition cited above, by intuition we understand first and foremost the empirical intuition of beings. As "sensible faculty," the power of imagination belongs among the faculties of knowledge, which have been divided into sensibility and understanding, and of these the first is presented as the "lower" faculty of knowledge. The power of imagination is a way of sensible intuiting "even without the presence of the object." The intuited being itself does not need to be presenting [*anwesend*], and furthermore, the imagination does not intuit what it has taken in stride as intuition, as something really and only at hand, as is the case with perception for which the Object "must be represented as present."[184] The power of

---

180. A 142, B 181.
181. A 78, B 103.
182. In his Marburg dissertation, *Die Einbildungskraft bei Kant* (1928), H. Mörchen undertook the task of [preparing] a monographic presentation and interpretation of Kant's teachings concerning the power of imagination in his *Anthropology*, in the *Critique of Pure Reason*, in the *Critique of Judgment*, and in the other writings and lectures. The work will appear in volume XI of the *Jahrbuch für Philosophie und phänomenologische Forschung*. The present exposition is limited to what is most necessary for an exclusive orientation to the guiding problem of the laying of the ground for metaphysics.
183. Kant, *Anthropologie in pragmatischer Hinsicht, Werke*, vol. VIII, §28, p. 54.
184. Reicke, *Lose Blätter aus Kants Nachlaß* (1889), p. 102.

imagination "can" intuit, "can" take the look of something in stride, without showing the intuited which is referred to, itself, as being, and without getting the look from itself alone.

Thus we find in the power of imagination, to begin with, a peculiar nonconnectedness to the being. It is without strings in the taking-in-stride of looks, i.e., it is the faculty which in a certain way gives itself such [looks]. The power of imagination can hence be called a faculty of forming [Vermögen des Bildens] in a peculiar double sense. As a faculty of intuiting, it is formative [bildend] in the sense of providing the image [Bild] (or look). As a faculty which is not dependent upon the presence of the intuitable, it fulfills itself, i.e., it creates and forms the image. This "formative power" is simultaneously a "forming" which takes things in stride (is receptive) and one which creates (is spontaneous). In this "simultaneously" lies the proper essence of its structure. But if receptivity means the same as sensibility and if spontaneity means the same as understanding, then in a peculiar way the power of imagination falls between both.[185] This gives it a remarkably iridescent character which also comes to light in the Kantian determinations of these faculties. With the division of the faculties of knowledge into the two fundamental classes, he includes [imagination] in sensibility in spite of its spontaneity. Hence in this case, forming in the sense of providing images (intuiting) is decisive, a fact also revealed in the definition.

On the basis of its being without strings, however, it is for Kant a faculty of comparing, shaping, combining, distinguishing, and, in general, of binding-together (synthesis). "Imagining," then, refers to all representing in the broadest sense which is not in accordance with perception: conceiving of something, concocting something, devising something, wondering, having an inspiration, and the like.[2] The "power of forming,"[3] accordingly, is brought together with the faculty of wit[4] and the power of distinguishing, with the faculty of comparison in general. "The senses provide the matter for all our representations. From that the faculty first sets out to form representations independently of the presence of objects: power of forming, imaginatio; second, the faculty of comparison: wits and the power of distinguishing, iudicium discretum; third, the faculty of combining representations, not immediately with their objects but rather by means of a surrogate, i.e., [the faculty of] describing [them]."[186]

But with all this association of the power of imagination with the faculty of spontaneity, it still retains its intuitive character. It is subjectio sub aspectum, i.e., a faculty of intuitive presentation, of giving. Now the intuitive representing of an object which is not present can be twofold.

---

185. Already in Aristotle's De Anima, book G3, φαντασία stands "between" αἴσθησις and νόησις.

186. Erdmann, Reflexionen I, p. 118. Kants handschriftlicher Nachlaß, vol. II, 1, No. 339. See also Pölitz, I. Kants Vorlesungen über die Metaphysik, 2d ed., newly edited according to the edition of 1821 by K. H. Schmidt (1924), p. 141.

If it is restricted merely to bringing back via the visualizing of what was perceived earlier, then this look in itself is dependent upon the earlier one offered by the previous perception. This presentation falls back upon an earlier one and hence derives its content from there (*exhibitio derivativa*).

Yet, if in the imagination the outward appearance of an object was freely composed, then this presentation of its look is an "original" one (*exhibitio originaria*). Thus, the power of imagination is called "productive."[187] This original presenting, however, is not as "creative" as the *intuitus originarius*, which creates the being itself in the intuiting. The productive power of imagination forms only the look of an object which is possible and which, under certain conditions, is perhaps also producible, i.e., one which can be brought to presence. The imagining itself, however, never accomplishes this production. The productive forming of the power of imagination is never even "creative" in the sense that it can likewise form just the content of the image simply from out of the nothing, i.e., from out of that which has never before and nowhere been experienced. Hence it is "not powerful enough to bring forth a sensible representation which previously was *never* given to our sensible faculty, but rather we can always point out the stuff of that same [representation]."[188]

That is the essential part of what the *Anthropology* tells us about the power of imagination in general and the productive power of imagination in particular. It contains nothing more than what the ground-laying in the *Critique of Pure Reason* has already set forth. On the contrary: the discussions of the Transcendental Deduction and the Schematism brought to light in a much more original way the fact that the power of imagination is an intermediate faculty between sensibility and understanding.

But the definition of the power of imagination, that it can represent an object intuitively without its presence, was at the very least not found in the considerations of the ground-laying in the *Critique of Pure Reason*. Yet in this regard, to have seen that this definition occurs explicitly in the Transcendental Deduction, occurring for the first time in the second edition to be sure,[189] then has not the working-out of the Transcendental Schematism exhibited precisely that character mentioned in the definition of the power of imagination?

The imagination forms the look of the horizon of objectivity as such in advance, before the experience of the being. This look-forming [*Anblickbilden*] in the pure image [*Bilde*] of time, however, is not just prior to this or that experience of the being, but rather always is in advance, prior to any possible [experience]. Hence from the beginning, in this offering of the look, the power

---

187. *Anthropologie*, vol. VIII, §28.
188. Ibid.
189. B 151.

of imagination is never simply dependent upon the presence [*Anwesenheit*] of a being. It is dependent in this way to such a small degree that precisely its pre-forming [*Vor-bilden*] of the pure schema Substance, i.e., persistence over time, for example, first brings into view in general something like constant presence [*ständige Anwesenheit*]. In turn, it is first and foremost only in the horizon of such constant presence that this or any "present presence of an object"[5] as such can show itself. Hence in the Transcendental Schematism, the essence of the power of imagination—to be able to intuit without the present presence [*ohne Gegenwart*]—is grasped in a way that is fundamentally more original. Finally, the Schematism also shows quite straightforwardly and in a far more original sense the "creative" essence of the power of imagination. Indeed, it is not ontically "creative" at all, but [is creative] as a free forming of images. The *Anthropology* shows that the productive power of imagination as well is still dependent upon the representations of the senses. In the Transcendental Schematism, however, the power of imagination is originally pictorial[6] in the pure image of time. It simply does not need an empirical intuition. Hence, the *Critique of Pure Reason* shows both the intuitive character and the spontaneity in a more original sense.

The attempt to experience by means of Anthropology what is more original about the power of imagination as the previously laid ground for ontology, therefore, remains unsuccessful in any case. Not only that, but also such an attempt in general is a mistake because on the one hand it fails to recognize the empirical character of the Kantian Anthropology, and on the other hand it does not allow for the peculiar nature of the consideration of the ground-laying and of the unveiling of origin in the *Critique of Pure Reason*.

The Kantian Anthropology is empirical in a double sense. First, the characterization of the faculties of the soul moves within the framework of the knowledge which general experience offers concerning human beings. And second, in advance and solely on the strength of it, the faculties of the soul themselves, e.g., the power of imagination, will come to be considered with reference to [the fact] that they are related, and how they are related, to the experienceable being. The productive power of imagination, with which Anthropology is concerned, never has to do with anything but the forming of the looks of empirically possible, or rather impossible, objects.

On the other hand, the productive power of imagination in the *Critique of Pure Reason* never refers to the forming of objects, but refers instead to the pure look of objectivity in general. The pure productive power of imagination, free of experience, makes experience possible for the first time. Not all productive power of imagination is pure, but what is pure in the sense just characterized is necessarily productive. To the extent that it forms transcendence, it is rightly called the transcendental power of imagination.

Anthropology does not pose the question of transcendence at all. All the same, the abortive attempt to want to interpret the power of imagination in a more original way in light of Anthropology proved that a reference to transcendental structures always already lies in the empirical interpretation of the faculties of the soul, which, properly speaking, can never simply be purely empirical themselves. But these can neither be grounded in Anthropology nor in general can they come to be created from it by means of mere assumptions.

But then, what kind of knowing is it which carries out the unveiling of transcendence, i.e., the freeing of pure synthesis and with that the interpretation of the power of imagination? If Kant calls this kind of knowledge "transcendental," then it is only possible to gather from this that it has transcendence for a theme. But what is the methodological character of this knowing? How does the going-back to the origin occur? As long as the required clarity in this matter is lacking, then indeed it is also the case that no step in the ground-laying which might be more original may be carried out.

At this stage of our considerations, it no longer seems possible to avoid an explicit discussion of the "Transcendental Method." Indeed, assuming that this method may be clarified, the task still remains to deduce the direction of the going-back required by the dimension of origin itself and to do so from the already-laid ground itself. Of course, whether this falling-in behind the direction itself, which is marked out by the matters themselves, requires its possible, more original interpretation, depends upon whether Kant's ground-laying up to this point—or rather the interpretation of it—is original and ample enough to assume the guidance of such a falling-in-behind. However, only an actual attempt that is carried out can decide that. The way of Kant's Anthropology, which at first appears to be self-evident, has revealed itself to be the wrong way. All the more clearly, then, the necessity arises that we unflinchingly keep the further interpretation focused on the phenomenon which reveals itself as the ground for the inner possibility of ontological synthesis, on the transcendental power of imagination.

§27. The Transcendental Power of Imagination as the Third Basic Faculty

To understand the faculties of "our mind" as "transcendental faculties" means in the first place: to unveil them according to how they make the essence of transcendence possible. Faculty thus does not mean a "basic power" ["*Grundkraft*"] which is at hand in the soul. "Faculty" now means what such a thing "is able to do,"[7] in the sense of the making-possible of the essential structure of ontological transcendence. Faculty now means "possibility" in the sense laid out above.[190] Thus understood, the transcendental power of im-

---

190. See above, §24, p. 82f.

agination is not just, and not first and foremost, a faculty found between pure intuition and pure thinking. Rather, together with these, it is a "basic ability to do something"[8] as a making-possible of the original unity of both and with it the essential unity of transcendence as a whole. "Thus we have a pure power of imagination as a basic ability of the human soul to do something, which is the basis for all knowledge a priori."[191]

At the same time, "basic ability to do something" says that the pure power of imagination is not reducible to the pure elements together with which it forms the essential unity of transcendence. That is why, with the decisive characterization of the essential unity of ontological knowledge, Kant expressly enumerates three elements: pure intuition (time), pure synthesis by means of the power of imagination, and the pure concepts of pure apperception.[192] In the same connection, Kant emphasizes that "we shall hereafter see" the way in which the power of imagination acts as "an indispensable function of the soul, without which we should have no knowledge whatsoever."[9]

In the Transcendental Deduction, the previously named triad of elements is discussed in its possible unity, and it is grounded through the Schematism. Moreover, the introduction of the idea of the pure Schematism again yields the same enumeration of the three pure elements of ontological knowledge. And finally, the discussion of the highest principle of all synthetic judgments, i.e., the final determination of the full essence of transcendence, is introduced with the enumeration of the previously named three elements "as the three sources" for the "possibility of pure synthetic judgments a priori."[10]

In opposition to this unequivocal characterization of the transcendental power of imagination as a third basic faculty alongside pure sensibility and pure understanding, a characterization which grew from the inner problematic of the *Critique of Pure Reason* itself, the clarification which Kant explicitly gave at the beginning and at the end of his work now speaks:

There are but "two basic sources of the mind, sensibility and understanding," there are only these "two stems to our power of knowledge"; "aside from these two sources of knowledge, we have no others."[193] This thesis corresponds as well to the bifurcation of the whole transcendental investigation into a Transcendental Aesthetic and a Transcendental Logic. The transcendental power of imagination is homeless. It is not even treated in the Transcendental Aesthetic where, as a "faculty of intuition," it properly belongs. On the other hand, it is a theme of the Transcendental Logic where, strictly speaking, it may not be as long as logic remains confined to thought as such. But because from the beginning this Aesthetic and this Logic are oriented with respect to transcendence which is not just the sum of pure intuition and pure thinking

---

191. A 124.

192. A 78f., B 104.

193. See above, §6, p. 24ff. [Here Heidegger has taken slight liberties with these passages, which he quoted correctly on pp. 25-26, notes 48, 49, and 52—tr.]

but is rather a particular, original unity within which they function only as elements, its two-way result must lead out beyond itself.

Could this result have eluded Kant, or is it at least consistent with his way of thinking that he suppressed the previously named triad of basic faculties in favor of the theory of the duality of the stems, as it were? This is so little the case that Kant instead speaks explicitly of the "three original sources of the soul" in the midst of the progression of his ground-laying, both at the close of the Introduction to the Transcendental Deduction and also at the beginning of its actual enactment, just as if he had never established the duality of the stems.

"There are, however, three original sources (capacities or faculties of the soul) which contain the conditions for the possibility of all experience and which themselves can be derived from no other faculty of the mind, namely, *sense, power of imagination*, and *apperception* . . . . All of these faculties, besides the empirical use, have another, transcendental use which concerns merely the form and which is possible a priori."[194]

"There are three subjective sources of knowledge, upon which rest the possibility of an experience in general and knowledge of its objects: *sense, power of imagination*, and *apperception*. Each of these can be viewed as empirical, namely, in the application to given appearances. But a priori, all of them are also elements, or the groundwork [*Grundlagen*], which themselves make this empirical use possible."[195] In both of these passages, the fact explicitly arises that besides the empirical use of these faculties there is also the transcendental, with which the relationship to Anthropology is demonstrated anew.

Thus this triad of basic faculties stands in harsh opposition to the duality of basic sources and stems of knowledge. Yet what is it about the two stems? Is it accidental that Kant uses this image to characterize sensibility and understanding, or is it instead used just to indicate that they grow from a "common root"?

Now the interpretation of the ground-laying, however, shows: the transcendental power of imagination is not just an external bond which fastens together two ends. It is originally unifying, i.e., as a particular faculty it forms the unity of both of the others, which themselves have an essential structural relation to it.

What if this original, formative center was that "unknown common root" of both stems? Is it an accident that with the first introduction of the power of imagination Kant says that "we ourselves, however, are seldom conscious [of it] even once"?[196]

---

194. A 94.
195. A 115.
196. A 78, B 103. The explicit characterization of the power of imagination as a basic faculty must have driven home the meaning of this faculty to Kant's contemporaries. Thus Fichte and Schelling, and in his own way Jacobi as well, have attributed an essential role to the power of imagination. Whether in this way the essence of the power of imagination as seen by Kant was

B. THE TRANSCENDENTAL POWER OF IMAGINATION AS
ROOT OF BOTH STEMS

If the established ground does not have the character of a floor or base which is at hand, but if instead it has the character of a root, then it must be ground in such a way that it lets the stems grow out from itself, lending them support and stability. With that, however, we have already attained the direction we sought, by means of which the originality of the Kantian ground-laying can be discussed within its own particular problematic. This ground-laying becomes more original if it does not simply take the already-laid ground in stride, but if instead it unveils how this root is the root for both stems. But this means nothing less than that pure intuition and pure thinking lead back to the transcendental power of imagination.

And yet, apart from the question of its possible success, is not the questionableness of such an undertaking itself obvious? Through such a leading-back of the finite creature's faculties of knowledge to the power of imagination, does not all knowledge come to be reduced to mere imagination? Would the essence of the human being, then, not dissolve into an appearance [*Schein*]?

However, if the origin of pure intuition and pure thinking as transcendental faculties is shown to be based on the transcendental power of imagination as a faculty, this is not to say that we want to give evidence to the effect that pure intuition and pure thinking may be a product of the imagination and, as such, only something imaginary. The unveiling of the origin which has already been characterized means, rather: the structure of these faculties has been rooted in the structure of the transcendental power of imagination, so that indeed this latter can "imagine" something for the first time only in structural unity with those two.

But whether what is formed in the transcendental power of imagination is a mere appearance in the sense of "mere imagination" must at least remain open. First of all, what is not really at hand is reputed to be "merely imaginary." But according to its essence, what is formed in the transcendental power of imagination is in no way something at hand, if indeed the transcendental power of imagination can never be ontically creative. For that reason, what is formed therein can likewise never essentially be "mere imagination" in the above sense. Rather, in general it is the horizon of objects formed in the transcendental power of imagination—the understanding of Being—which first makes possible something like a distinction between ontic truth and ontic appearance ("mere imagination").

---

recognized, adhered to, and even interpreted in a more original way, cannot be discussed here. The following interpretation of the transcendental power of imagination grows out of another way of questioning and moves, so to speak, in the opposite direction from that of German Idealism. See below, §35, p. 137f.

But does not ontological knowledge, the essential ground for which is to be the transcendental power of imagination, also have, as essentially finite, a corresponding untruth which is at one with its truth? In fact, the idea of transcendental untruth conceals one of the foremost problems of finitude as such, which not only has not been solved, but also which has not even been posed because the basis for posing the problem must first be worked out. This, however, can only come to pass if in general the essence of finite transcendence, and with it that of the transcendental power of imagination, is successfully unveiled. Yet at no time are pure intuition and pure thinking to be explained as something imaginary because their essential possibility undergoes a leading-back to the essential structure of the transcendental power of imagination. The transcendental power of imagination does not imagine like pure intuition, but instead makes it possible for pure intuition to be what it "really" can be.

But just as the transcendental power of imagination itself is far from being merely something imaginary [*Eingebildetes*] because as a root it "forms" [*"bildet"*], likewise it is not something that could be thought of as a "basic power" in the soul. Nothing lies further from this going-back into the essential origin of transcendence than the monistic-empirical explanation of the remaining faculties of the soul based on the power of imagination. Accordingly, this intention is already self-prohibitive because in the end the essential unveiling of transcendence decides in the first place the sense in which one is permitted to speak of "soul" and "mind," the extent to which these concepts originally meet the ontologico-metaphysical essence of human beings.

On the contrary, the going-back to the transcendental power of imagination as the root of sensibility and understanding only means: in view of the essential structure of the transcendental power of imagination, which was attained within the problematic of the ground-laying, the constitution of transcendence is to be projected anew onto the grounds of its possibility. The going-back which lays the ground moves in the dimension of "possibilities," of the possible [instances of] making-possible. Above all, therein lies the fact that, in the end, what has hitherto been known as the transcendental power of imagination is broken up into more original "possibilities" so that by itself the designation "power of imagination" becomes inadequate.

The further unveiling of the originality of the ground-laying will be even less likely to lead to an absolute explanatory basis than did the stages of the setting-free of the ground covered by Kant that have already been presented. The strangeness of the previously laid ground which must have forced itself upon Kant cannot disappear. Rather, it will increase with the growing originality, if indeed man's metaphysical nature as a finite creature is at once the most unknown and the most actual to him.

If the transcendental power of imagination may be shown as the root of transcendence, then the problematic of the Transcendental Deduction and the

Schematism first achieves its transparency. The question concerning pure synthesis which was posed there aims for an original union in which what is unified must have grown in advance from the elements which were to be united. This forming of an original unity, however, is only possible to the extent that, according to its essence, what is unified allows what is to be unified to spring forth. Hence, the character of the already-laid ground as root first makes the originality of the pure synthesis, i.e., its letting-spring-forth, understandable.

In the following interpretation, it is true that the orientation continues to adhere to the way of the ground-laying which we have already run through, but the individual stages will no longer be described. The specific way in which the pure power of imagination, pure intuition, and pure thinking hang together should also come to be unveiled originally only to the extent that the Kantian ground-laying itself contains indications of it.

§28. The Transcendental Power of Imagination and Pure Intuition[a]

Kant calls the pure intuitions Space and Time "original representations." The "original" is not to be understood here ontically or psychologically, and it does not concern the Being-at-hand or perhaps the innateness[11] of these intuitions in the soul. Rather, the "original" characterizes the way according to which these representations are represented. The expression "original" corresponds to the "*originarius*" in the title *intuitus originarius* and means: to let [something] spring forth.[b] Now of course, as belonging to human finitude, the pure intuitions in their representing cannot allow any beings to spring forth.

And yet, they are formative in the peculiar sense that they pro-pose [*vorstellen*] the look of space and time in advance as totalities which are in themselves manifold. They take the look in stride, but in itself this taking-in-stride is the formative self-giving of that which gives itself. According to their essence, the pure intuitions themselves are "original," i.e., presentations of what is intuitable which allow [something] to spring forth: *exhibitio originaria*. In this presenting, however, lies the essence of the pure power of imagination. Pure intuition, therefore, can only be "original" because according to its essence it is the pure power of imagination itself which formatively gives looks (images) from out of itself.[12]

The rooting of pure intuition in the pure power of imagination becomes fully clear if we ask about the character of what is intuited in pure intuition.

---

a. certainly no relevant presentation with respect to its content of what springs forth [*Entspringens*] from space, but instead only indicated the essence of origin [*Ursprungs*]

b. See p. 33. [Reference is to Heidegger's marginal note "q" on that page—tr.]

Indeed, interpreters for the most part all too often and all too quickly deny that something is intuited in pure intuition in general, that indeed it may only be the "form of intuition." What is discerned in pure intuition is a whole which is unified in itself, although it is not empty, and whose parts are always just limitations of itself. But this unified whole must allow itself to be discerned in advance regarding this togetherness of its manifoldness which is for the most part indistinct. Pure intuition—originally unifying, i.e., giving unity—must *catch* sight of the unity.[13] Kant therefore rightly speaks here not of a synthesis, but rather of the "Synopsis."[197]

The totality of what is intuited in pure intuition does not have the unity which characterizes the universality of a concept. The unity of the totality of intuition, therefore, also cannot spring forth from the "synthesis of the understanding." It is a unity which is caught sight of in advance in the image-giving imagining [*im Bild-gebenden Einbilden*]. The "syn"[14] of the totality of space and time belongs to a faculty of formative intuition. The pure synopsis, if it constitutes the essence of pure intuition, is only possible in the transcendental power of imagination, and that is all the more so as this [transcendental power of imagination] is in general the origin of all that is "synthetic."[198] "Synthesis" must be taken here in a way which is quite wide enough to encompass the synopsis of intuition and the "synthesis" of the understanding.

In a reflection both graphic and immediate, Kant once said, "Space and Time are the forms [*Formen*] of the pre-forming [*Vorbildung*] in intuition."[199] In advance they form the pure look which serves as horizon for the empirically intuitable. But if pure intuition, in the manner of its intuiting, reveals the specific essence of the transcendental power of imagination, then is not what is pre-formed in it, as that which was formed in the imagination (*imaginatio*), itself imaginative? This characterization of what is intuited as such in pure intuition is no formal consequence of the previous analysis, but instead it lies enclosed in the essential content of what is accessible in pure intuition. This imaginative character of Space and Time, then, has nothing unheard of or strange about it if we adhere to the fact that it is a matter of pure intuition and pure imagination. As we have shown, what is formed in the imagination is not necessarily an ontic appearance.

Now Kant must have seen little of the essential structure of pure intuition; indeed, he would not have been able to grasp it at all, had not the imaginative character of what is intuited in it become visible to him. Kant says unambiguously: "The mere form of intuition, without substance, is in itself no object, but

---

197. A 94f. Kant expressly says here that he has treated the Transcendental Synopsis in the Transcendental Aesthetic.

198. A 78, B 103.

199. Erdmann, *Reflexionen II*, 408. *Kants handschriftlicher Nachlaß*, vol. V, No. 5934: With reference to Erdmann's reading, Andickes reads—erroneously in my opinion—"connection" ("*Verbindung*") instead of "pre-forming" ("*Vorbildung*"). See below, §32, p. 123.

is rather the merely formal condition of the same (as appearance), as pure space and pure time. As forms to be intuited, these are indeed Something, but they are not themselves objects which can be intuited (*ens imaginarium*)."[200] What is intuited in pure intuition as such is an *ens imaginarium*. Hence on the grounds of its essence, pure intuiting is pure imagination.[15]

The *ens imaginarium* belongs to the possible forms of the "Nothing," i.e., to what is not a being in the sense of what is at hand. Pure space and pure time are "Something," but certainly not "objects." If one says without hesitation that in pure intuition "nothing" is intuited and hence that it lacks objects, then in the first place this interpretation is only negative, and ambiguous as well, as long as we have not made it clear that Kant uses the expression "object" here in the decidedly restricted sense according to which the being which shows itself in the appearance is meant. Accordingly, an object is not just any "Something."

Pure intuitions, as "forms to be intuited," are indeed "intuitions without things,"[201] but they nevertheless have what is intuited in them. Space is nothing actual, i.e., it is not a being accessible in perception, but is rather "the representation of a mere possibility of Being-together."[202]

Now of course the inclination to deny an object in the sense of something intuited to pure intuition in general thereby becomes strengthened in particular by the fact that one can refer to a genuinely phenomenal character of pure intuition—to be sure, without being able sufficiently to determine this character. In the knowing relation to things which are at hand and which are "spatio-temporally" ordered, we are directed only at this. But for all that, space and time do not allow themselves to be flatly denied. The positive question must therefore read: How, then, are space and time there as well? If Kant says they may be intuitions, then we might reply: but in fact these were not intuited. Certainly they are not intuited in the sense of a thematic apprehension, but rather they are intuited in the manner of an original, formative giving. Precisely because the pure intuited is what and how it is, as essential for the forming—in accordance with the characterized double sense of the pure look which is to be created—the pure intuiting cannot intuit its "intuited" in the manner of a thematic, apprehending, taking-in-stride of something which is at hand.

Thus the original interpretation of pure intuition as pure power of imagination first provides the possibility to elucidate positively what the intuited is in pure intuition. As preliminary forming of a pure, unthematic, and (in the Kantian sense) unobjective look, pure intuition makes it possible that the

---

200. A 291, B 347. R. Schmidt remarks that in A, "(*ens imaginarium*)" appears three lines higher, after "time." [Indeed, that is the way Kemp Smith translates it as well, although I have chosen to follow Heidegger's citation exactly here—tr.]

201. *Reflexionen II*, p. 402. *Kants handschriftlicher Nachlaß*, vol. V, no. 5315.

202. A 374.

empirical intuiting of spatio-temporal things which moves within its horizon does not first need to intuit space and time in the sense of an apprehension which first^c ascertains these multiplicities.

Now, it is also through this interpretation of pure intuition that the transcendental character of transcendental intuition is first clarified, if indeed the innermost essence of transcendence is grounded in the pure power of imagination. Thus, standing as it does at the beginning of the *Critique of Pure Reason*, the Transcendental Aesthetic is fundamentally unintelligible. It has only a preparatory character and can be read properly for the first time [only] from the perspective of the Transcendental Schematism.

Thus as untenable as the effort by the Marburg School of Kant Interpretation is to apprehend space and time as "categories" in the logical sense and to absorb the Transcendental Aesthetic into the Logic, one of the motives suggested by that effort, however, is genuine: the insight, admittedly not clarified, that the Transcendental Aesthetic, taken by itself, cannot itself constitute the whole of what lies closed up within it as a possibility. However, based on the peculiar "syn"-character of pure intuition, the belonging-together of pure intuition with the synthesis of the understanding does not follow. Rather, the interpretation of this "syn"-character leads to the origin of pure intuition in the transcendental power of imagination. Absorbing the Transcendental Aesthetic into the Logic, moreover, becomes still more questionable when it is shown that the specific object of the Transcendental Logic, pure thinking, is also rooted in the transcendental power of imagination.[203]

§29. The Transcendental Power of Imagination and Theoretical Reason

The attempt to point out an origin for pure thinking in the transcendental power of imagination, and therewith for theoretical reason in general, already appears for now to be hopeless for the simple reason that such a project might be taken to be absurd in itself. Yet Kant expressly says that the power of imagination would be "always sensible."[204] But as essentially sensible (i.e., as a lower and inferior faculty), how is it to be capable of forming the origin for that which is higher and "superior"? In finite knowing, the fact that the understanding presupposes sensibility and with it the power of imagination as a "substratum" is understandable. However, the claim that the understand-

---

203. Only by means of a clear separation between a synopsis of pure intuition and the synthesis of the understanding is the difference between "form of intuition" and "formal intuition" to be elucidated, [a distinction] that Kant introduces in §26, p. B 160, footnote.

204. A 124.

c. previously

ing itself, according to its essence, should spring forth from out of sensibility, cannot hide its obvious absurdity.

And yet, prior to any formalistic argumentation, we must note that it is not a question here of the empirical, explanatory derivation of a higher faculty of the soul from an inferior one. Provided that in the consideration of the ground-laying the faculties of the soul are not substituted for the subject of the discussion in any way, then the order of precedence as to "lower" and "higher," which grows out of such an arrangement of the faculties of the soul, likewise cannot guide us—not even for purposes of an objection. First of all, however, what does "sensible" mean?

By design, the essence of sensibility was already delimited with the characterization of the point of departure for the ground-laying, just as Kant determined it for the first time.[205] Accordingly, sensibility and finite intuition mean the same thing. The finitude lies in the taking-in-stride of what gives itself. What gives itself and how it gives itself remain open. It is not that every sensible intuition (i.e., every intuition which takes things in stride) must already be sentient, empirical. The "more inferior" of the affections of the corporeally conditioned senses does not belong to the essence of sensibility. Thus, not only can the transcendental power of imagination as pure finite intuition be "sensible," it must be, even as the basic determination of finite transcendence.

Nevertheless, this sensibility of the transcendental power of imagination cannot be claimed as the basis for its assignment to the class of inferior faculties of the soul—especially not if, as transcendental, it is to be the condition for the possibility of all faculties. But at this point, the most difficult (because it is the most "natural") objection to a possible origin of pure thinking in the transcendental power of imagination has fallen.

Reason can now no longer be claimed as "higher." But another difficulty immediately presents itself. The fact that pure intuition springs forth from the transcendental power of imagination as a faculty of intuition is still conceivable. But the claim that thinking, which must indeed be sharply distinguished from all intuition, should have its origin in the transcendental power of imagination appears to be impossible, even if importance can no longer be attached to the order of precedence of sensibility and understanding.

And yet, thinking and intuiting, although different, are not separated from one another like two completely dissimilar things. Rather, as species of representing [Vorstellens] both belong to the same genus of pre-presenting [Vorstellens] in general. Both are modes of the representing of . . . [des Vorstellens von . . .]. The insight into the primary representational character of thinking is no less decisive for the interpretation which follows than is the correct understanding of the sensible character of the power of imagination.

---

205. See above, §5, p. 18ff.

By means of an original unveiling of the essence of understanding, its innermost essence must be brought into view: the dependency upon intuition. This Being-dependent characterizes the Being-understanding of the understanding.[16] And this "Being" is what and how it is in the pure synthesis of the pure power of imagination. To this one might reply: certainly the understanding is related to pure intuition "through" the pure power of imagination. But by no means is that to say that the pure understanding is itself the transcendental power of imagination and not something which stands on its own.

That the understanding is something which stands on its own is attested to by logic, which does not need to deal with the power of imagination. And in fact, Kant always introduces the understanding in a form which the apparently "absolute," at-hand logic has determined for it. The analysis must indeed depart from this independence of thinking if the origin of thinking in the power of imagination is to be shown.

That traditional logic does not treat the pure power of imagination is indisputable. Whether logic does not need to treat it in general if it understands itself, however—this, at least, must remain open. That Kant takes the point of departure for his questioning time and again from logic is similarly undeniable. But just as questionable is whether in this way logic, in a determinative sense, makes thinking its only theme, as well as whether it guarantees that this logic can delimit the full essence of thinking or can even approach it.

Does not Kant's interpretation of pure thinking in the Transcendental Deduction and in the Doctrine of the Schematism show that not only the functions of judgment, but also the pure concepts as notions, merely present artificially isolated elements of the pure synthesis which, for its part, is an essentially necessary "presupposition" for the "synthetic unity of apperception"? And does not Kant even absorb formal logic, with respect to which he indeed constantly orients himself as if with respect to an "Absolute," into what he calls Transcendental Logic,[a] which has the transcendental power of imagination as its central theme? Does the rejection of traditional logic not go so far that Kant—characteristically, for the first time in the second edition— must say: "And so the synthetic unity of apperception is the highest point to which we must ascribe all employment of the understanding, even the whole of logic, and in conformity with it, transcendental philosophy. Indeed, this faculty is the understanding itself"?[206]

Thus, the preconceptions concerning the ability of thinking to stand on its own—how they were suggested through the tactical existence of what was

---

206. B 133, note.

a. See the later formulation of the *Concept* of Judgment!

apparently the highest and irreducible discipline of formal logic—are not permitted to become the standard for a decision concerning the possibility of an origin of pure thinking in the transcendental power of imagination. Rather, it is worth our while to seek the essence of pure thinking in what the ground-laying itself has already brought to light in this regard. Only by beginning with the original essence of understanding, and in no way with a "logic" that slights this essence, can a decision be made concerning its possible origin.

The characterization of thinking as judging is indeed appropriate, but is still only a distant determination of its essence. The designation of thinking as "faculty of rules" already "comes closer to" this [essence],[207] and indeed it does so because from there a way leads out to the basic determination of the understanding as "pure apperception."

"Faculty of rules," however, means: to hold before us in advance the represented unities which give direction to every possible unification that is represented. These unities (notions, or rather categories) which are represented as regulative, however, must not only have learned to play their part based on their proper affinity, but this affinity must itself also be grasped comprehensively in advance in a lasting unity through a still more anticipatory pro-posing [*vorgreifenderes Vor-stellen*] of them.

The proposing[17] of this lasting unity, as the sameness of the totality of the rules of affinity, is the basic impulse of the letting-stand-against-of. . . . In such a proposing [*vorstellenden*] self-orienting toward . . . , the "self" in this orienting-toward . . . is, as it were, taken outside. In such an orienting-toward . . . , or rather in the "self" which was "thrown out" with it, the "I" of this "self" is necessarily apparent. In this way, the "I propose" "accompanies" all representing.[18] But it is not a question of a nearby, consummated act of knowing which is directed by thinking itself. The "I" "goes with" in the pure self-orienting. To the extent that it is itself only what it is in this "I think," the essence of pure thinking as well as that of the I lies in "pure self-consciousness." This "consciousness" of the self, however, can only be elucidated based on the Being of the self and not the reverse, whereby the latter might be elucidated based on the former, or rather whereby the latter might even be rendered superfluous through the former.

The "I think," however, is always an "I think substance," "I think causality" —or rather, "in" these pure unities (categories), always already "it means":[208] "I think substance," "I think causality," etc. The I is the "vehicle" of the categories to the extent that in its preliminary self-orienting toward . . . , it brings them along [to a point] from which, as represented, regulative unities, they can unify.

---

207. A 126.
208. A 343, B 401.

As a result, the pure understanding is a pre-forming of the horizon of unity which represents "from out of itself." It is a representing, forming spontaneity, the occurrence of which lies in the "Transcendental Schematism." Kant expressly calls this "the procedure of understanding with these schemata,"[209] and he speaks of the "schematism of our understanding."[210] And yet, the pure schemata are now "a transcendental product of the power of imagination."[211] How does this allow for reconciliation? The understanding does not bring forth the schemata, but "works with them." This working-with of the understanding, however, is *not* a way of putting-into-practice, which it *also* carries out on occasion. Rather, this pure schematism, which is grounded in the transcendental power of imagination, constitutes precisely the original Being of the understanding, the "I think substance," etc. As representing which forms spontaneously, the apparent achievement of the pure understanding in the thinking of the unities is a pure basic act of the transcendental power of imagination. This is all the more so since this representing, self-orienting toward . . . is no thematic asserting of the unity, but is instead the unthematic bringing-itself-before[-us] of what has been proposed [*das Vorgestellten*], as we have already indicated several times. This occurs, however, in a forming representing, i.e., one which brings-forth.

Now if Kant calls this pure, self-orienting, self-relating-to . . . , "our thought" ["*unseren Gedanken*"], then "thinking" ["*Denken*"] this thought [*Gedankens*] is no longer called judging, but is thinking in the sense of the free, forming, and projecting (although not arbitrary) "conceiving" ["*Sichdenkens*"] of something. This original "thinking" is pure imagining.

The imaginative character of pure thinking becomes even clearer if we attempt, based on the essential determination of the understanding which has now been achieved, to come nearer to pure self-consciousness, to its essence, in order to grasp it as reason. Here again, the difference between understanding which judges and reason which draws conclusions, a difference borrowed from formal logic, certainly may not be permitted to be decisive. Instead, what will be decisive is what arises in the transcendental interpretation of the understanding.

Kant calls the pure understanding a "closed unity." But from where does the projected whole of affinity take its wholeness? Insofar as it is a question of the wholeness of a representing as such an [affinity], that which gives the wholeness must itself be a representing. This occurs in the forming of the Idea [*Idee*]. Because the pure understanding is the "I think," on the grounds of its essence it must have the character of a "faculty of Ideas," i.e., of reason, for without

---

209. A 140, B 179.
210. A 141, B 180.
211. A 142, B 181.

reason we have "no coherent employment of the understanding."[212] Ideas "contain a certain completeness,"[213] they represent the "form of a whole,"[214] and hence in a more original sense are rule-giving.

Now one might object that precisely with the unfolding of the Transcendental Ideal, which "must serve . . . as rule and archetype"[215] Kant expressly says that it acts "completely differently . . . with creations of the power of imagination" "of the kind which painters and physiognomists profess to have in their heads."[216] Here the connection between the Ideas of pure reason and those of the power of imagination has indeed been expressly denied. However, this passage says simply that the Transcendental Ideal "must always rest on determinate concepts," and can be no arbitrary and "blurred sketch" of the empirical, productive power of imagination. This does not rule out that those "determinate concepts" are possible only in the transcendental power of imagination.

Now one could agree with the interpretation of theoretical reason with regard to its kinship with the transcendental power of imagination insofar as it highlights the representing, free forming in pure thinking. However, if the interpretation wants to conclude from this as to an origin of pure thinking in the transcendental power of imagination, then we must point out that spontaneity constitutes but one moment of the transcendental power of imagination and that, accordingly, while thinking indeed has a relationship with the power of imagination, this is never indicative of a full coinciding of their essences. For the power of imagination is also and precisely a faculty of intuition, i.e., of receptivity. And it is receptive, moreover, not just apart from its spontaneity. Rather, it is the original unity of receptivity and spontaneity, and not a unity which was composite from the first.

Now it has been shown that on the grounds of its purity pure intuition possesses the character of spontaneity. As pure, spontaneous receptivity, it has its essence in the transcendental power of imagination.

Now if pure thinking is to be of the same essence, then as spontaneity it must at the same time exhibit the character of a pure receptivity. But does Kant not generally suppose that understanding and reason are simply identical with spontaneity?

Nevertheless, if Kant equates the understanding with spontaneity, this no more excludes a receptivity of understanding than the equating of sensibility—finite intuition—with receptivity excluded a corresponding spontaneity. In the end, the view of empirical intuition merely justifies the emphatic and

---

212. A 651, B 679.
213. A 567f., B 595f.
214. A 832, B 860. See in this regard *Vom Wesen des Grundes*, 6th ed. (1973), p. 31f.
215. A 570, B 598.
216. Ibid.

exclusive characterization as receptivity, and, correspondingly, the view of the "logical" function of the understanding within empirical knowledge justifies the exclusive emphasis of its spontaneity and "function."

On the other hand, in the domain of pure knowledge, i.e., within the problem of the possibility of transcendence, the pure taking-in-stride of that which gives itself, i.e., the taking-in-stride which gives to itself (spontaneously), cannot remain concealed. But must not precisely a pure receptivity now emerge, just as compelling and with all its spontaneity, in the transcendental interpretation of pure thinking? Apparently. It has long since emerged in the preceding interpretation of the Transcendental Deduction and the Schematism.

In order to see the essential intuitive character of pure thinking, only the genuine essence of finite intuiting as a taking-in-stride of what gives itself must be grasped and adhered to. But now it has come out as the fundamental character of the "unity" of transcendental apperception that, constantly unifying in advance, it is opposed to everything random. Hence, in the representing self-turning-toward . . . , only this Being-in-opposition and no other is taken up. The free, formative projecting of the affinity is in itself a representing submitting to it which takes things in stride. The rules, which are represented in the understanding as the faculty of rules, are not grasped as something at hand "in consciousness." Rather, the rules of binding together (synthesis) are represented precisely as binding in their character as binding-together.[19] If something, such as a ruling rule, is only there in the letting-be-ruled which takes things in stride, then the "Idea" as representation of the rule can only be represented in the manner of something which takes things in stride.

In this sense, pure thinking in itself, not after the fact, is capable of taking things in stride: i.e., it is pure intuition. This structural, coherent, receptive spontaneity must, accordingly, spring forth from the transcendental power of imagination in order to be able to be what it is. As pure apperception, the understanding has the "ground for its possibility" in a "faculty" which "looks out in an infinity of self-made representations and concepts."[217] The transcendental power of imagination projects, forming in advance the totality of possibilities in terms of which it "looks out," in order thereby to hold before itself the horizon within which the knowing self, but not just the knowing self, acts. Only for this reason can Kant say: "Human reason is by its nature architectonic, i.e., it regards all knowledge as belonging to a possible system. . . ."[218]

The intuitive character which belongs to pure thinking as such, however, can appear much less strange if we consider that the pure intuitions, time and space, are just as "unintuitable" as the properly understood categories, i.e., as pure schemata—as long as "intuitable" just means: to be perceivable through a sense organ.

---

217. *Über die Fortschritte der Metaphysik*, VIII, p. 249.
218. A 474, B 502.

The necessity, however, revealed in the standing-against of the horizon of objectivity,[20] is only possible as encountered "compulsion" insofar as it happens in advance upon a Being-free for it. Freedom already lies in the essence of pure understanding, i.e., of pure theoretical reason, insofar as this means placing oneself under a self-given necessity. Hence understanding and reason are not free because they have the character of spontaneity, but because this spontaneity is a receptive spontaneity, i.e., because it is the transcendental power of imagination.

Along with the leading-back of pure intuition and pure thinking to the transcendental power of imagination, however, it should also become obvious that in this way the transcendental power of imagination reveals itself more and more as structural possibility, i.e., in its making-possible of transcendence as the essence of the finite self. Thus it loses not only the character of an empirical faculty of the soul which has been picked up, but also the restriction, hitherto in effect, of its essence to the root-Being [Wurzelsein] for the theoretical faculty as such. And so, then, the last step in the unveiling of the "originality" of the previously laid ground must be risked.

§30. The Transcendental Power of Imagination and Practical Reason

Kant already says in the Critique of Pure Reason: "Everything which is possible through freedom is practical."[219] Insofar as freedom belongs to the possibility of theoretical reason, however, it is in itself as theoretically practical. But if finite reason as spontaneity is receptive and thereby springs forth from the transcendental power of imagination, then of necessity practical reason is also grounded therein. Indeed, the origin of practical reason may not be "disclosed"[21] through argumentation, even though it perhaps seems legitimate to do so. Rather, what is required is an express unveiling by means of an elucidation of the essence of the "practical self."

According to what has been said about the "I" of pure apperception, the essence of the self lies in "self-consciousness." But as what and how the self is in this "consciousness," this is determined by the Being of the self, to which its manifestness belongs. This manifestness is what it is only insofar as it codetermines the Being of the self. If the practical self is now to be examined with regard to the ground of its possibility, then it is worth first delimiting that self-consciousness which makes this self as self possible. With the consideration of this practical, i.e., moral, self-consciousness, then, we must investigate the extent to which its essential structure refers back to the transcendental power of imagination as its origin.

---

219. A 800, B 828.

The moral I, the authentic self and essence of man, Kant also calls the person. In what does the essence of the personality of the person consist? Personality itself is the "idea of the moral law" along "with the respect which is inseparable from it."[220] Respect is "susceptibility" to the moral law, i.e., the making-possible of a being-susceptible to this law as a moral one. But if respect constitutes the essence of the person as the moral self, then according to what has already been said it must present a way of Being-self-conscious.[22] To what extent is it such?

Can it [respect] function as a way of Being-self-conscious if, according to Kant's own designation, it is a "feeling"? Feelings, pleasurable and unpleasurable states, indeed belong to sensibility. To be sure, this is not just determined through bodily states, so that the possibility of a pure feeling—one which is not determined by the affections, but rather one which is "self-produced"—remains open.[221] Therefore, we must first ask about the universal essence of feeling in general. The elucidation of this essence will allow us to decide for the first time the extent to which "feeling" in general—and with it, respect as a pure feeling—can present something like a way of Being-self-conscious.

Even in the "base" feelings of pleasure, a peculiar basic structure appears. Pleasure [Lust] is not just pleasure for something and in something, but rather it is always at the same time enjoyment [Belustigung], i.e., a way in which human beings experience themselves as enjoying [belustigt], in which they are happy [lustig]. Thus, in every sensible (in the narrower sense) and nonsensible feeling is found this clear structure: feeling is an instance of having a feeling for . . . , and as such it is at the same time a self-feeling of that which feels. The manner in which self-feeling from time to time makes the self manifest, i.e., the manner in which it lets it be, will always be codetermined essentially through the character of that for which the feeling [being], in the self-feeling, has a feeling. Now to what extent does respect correspond to this essential structure of feeling, and why is it a pure feeling?

Kant gives the analysis of respect in the *Critique of Practical Reason*.[222] The following interpretation will single out only what is essential.

Respect as such is respect for the moral law. It does not serve [as a basis] for the judgment of actions, and it does not first appear after the ethical

220. *Die Religion innerhalb der Grenzen der bloßen Vernunft, Werke*, vol. VI, p. 166. [*Religion within the Limits of Reason Alone*, trans. Theodore Greene and Hoyt Hudson (Chicago, 1934), p. 22f.—tr.]

221. *Grundlegung zur Metaphysik der Sitten*, 2d ed., *Werke*, vol. IV, p. 257, note. [*Kant: Foundations of the Metaphysics of Morals*, trans. Lewis White Beck, ed. Robert Paul Wolff (Indianapolis, 1978), pp. 20–21, note 2—tr.]

222. *Kritik der praktischen Vernunft*, Part I, Book 1, Division 3. *Werke*, vol. V, p. 79ff. [Meiner edition, ed. Vorländer (Hamburg: 1974), p. 86ff. *Critique of Practical Reason*, trans. Lewis White Beck (Indianapolis, 1978) p. 76ff.]

fact[23] to be something like the manner in which we take a position with respect to the consummated act. On the contrary, respect for the law first constitutes the possibility for action. The respect for . . . is the way in which the law first becomes accessible to us. At the same time we find therein: this feeling of respect for the law does not also serve, as Kant puts it, for the "grounding" of the law. The law is not what it is because we have respect for it, but rather the reverse: this respecting having-a-feeling for the law, and with it this determinate manner of making the law manifest, is the way in which the law, as such a respecting having-a-feeling for in general, can be encountered by us.

Feeling is having-a-feeling for . . . , so it is true that the feeling I at the same time feels itself herein. In respect before the law, therefore, the respecting I itself must at the same time become manifest in a determinate way. Furthermore, this way of becoming manifest is not something subsequent and occasional, but rather the respect before the law—this determinate way of making the law manifest as the determinative ground for action—is in itself a making-manifest of myself as acting self. Reason, as free, gives to itself that for which the respect is respect, the moral law. Respect before the law is respect before oneself as that self which does not come to be determined through self-conceit and self-love. Respect, in its specific making-manifest, thus refers to the person. "*Respect* is always directed toward persons, never toward things."[223]

In respect before the law, I subordinate myself to the law. The specific having-a-feeling for . . . which is found in respect is a submitting. In respect before the law, I submit to myself. In this submitting-to-myself, I am as I itself. As what, or more precisely, as who am I manifest to myself in the feeling of respect?

In submitting to the law, I submit to myself as pure reason. In this submitting-to-myself, I elevate myself to myself as the free creature which determines itself. This peculiar, submitting, self-elevating of itself to itself manifests the I in its "dignity." Negatively stated: In respect before the law, which as a free creature I give to myself, I cannot despise myself. Hence, respect is the manner of the Being-its-self of the I [*des Selbstseins des Ich*], on the grounds of which it "does not throw away the hero in its soul." Respect is the manner of the self's[24] Being-responsible, face to face with itself; it is authentic Being-its-self.

The submitting, self-projecting[25] onto the entire basic possibility of what authentically exists, which the law gives, is the essence of the acting Being-itself, i.e., of practical reason.

The preceding interpretation of the feeling of respect shows not only the extent to which it constitutes practical reason, but at the same time it makes it clear that the concept of feeling in the sense of an empirically intended

---

223. Ibid., p. 84. [Meiner ed., p. 89; *Critique of Practical Reason*, p. 79.]

faculty of the soul has disappeared, and into its place has stepped a transcendental, basic structure of the transcendence of the moral self. The expression "feeling" must come to be understood in this ontologico-metaphysical sense if we are to exhaust what Kant means by the characterization of respect as "moral feeling" and as "feeling of my existence." No further steps are now required in order to see that this essential structure of respect in itself allows the original constitution of the transcendental power of imagination to emerge.

The self-submitting, immediate, surrender-to . . . is pure receptivity; the free, self-affecting of the law, however, is pure spontaneity. In themselves, both are originally one. And again, only this origin of practical reason in the transcendental power of imagination allows us to understand the extent to which, in respect, the law as much as the acting self is not to be apprehended objectively. Rather, both are manifest precisely in a more original, unobjective, and unthematic way as duty and action, and they form the unreflected, acting Being of the self [Selbst-sein].

§31. The Originality of the Previously Laid Ground and Kant's Shrinking-Back from the Transcendental Power of Imagination

The "highest principle of all synthetic judgments" delimits the full essence of the transcendence of pure knowledge. The transcendental power of imagination manifests itself as the essential ground for this essence. The preceding, more original interpretation of the essence of this essential ground, however, first shows the scope of the highest principle. This principle speaks of the essential constitution of the human essence in general, to the extent that it is determined as finite, pure reason.

This original, essential constitution of humankind, "rooted" in the transcendental power of imagination, is the "unknown" into which Kant must have looked if he spoke of the "root unknown to us," for the unknown is not that of which we simply know nothing. Rather, it is what pushes against us as something disquieting in what is known. And yet, Kant did not carry through with the more original interpretation of the transcendental power of imagination; indeed, he did not even make the attempt in spite of the clear, initial sketching-out of such an analytic which he himself recognized for the first time. On the contrary:

Kant shrank back from this unknown root.[a]

---

a. That applies, certainly, for those who admit that Kant went *toward* the transcendental power of imagination; for *only then* can there also be a *back* [ein Zurück. Refers to the root of "zurückgewichen," translated as "shrank back"—tr.]. See Kritik d. U[rteilskraft], §59, pp. 258–59 [Critique of Judgment, tr. J. H. Bernard, p. 199] here as well the interpretation is fully upheld, and here again the *shrinking back* [Zurückweichen!] but in what sense.

In the second edition of the *Critique of Pure Reason*, the transcendental power of imagination as it came to light in the impassioned course of its first projection[224] was thrust aside and given a new interpretation—one favoring the understanding. If the entire ground-laying is not thereby to collapse into itself, then certainly the accomplishment of its transcendental grounding according to the first edition must still be maintained.

We cannot discuss here the sense in which the pure power of imagination recurs in the *Critique of Judgment* and above all whether it still recurs in express relationship to the laying of the ground for metaphysics as such which was pointed out earlier.

First of all, in the second edition Kant struck out both of the principle passages in which he had earlier expressly included the power of imagination as a third basic faculty, along with sensibility and understanding. The first passage[225] is replaced by a critical discussion of the analyses of the understanding by Locke and Hume, just as if Kant saw his own procedure in the first edition—although mistakenly—as still being close to Empiricism.

The second passage,[226] however, was omitted in the course of the revision of the Transcendental Deduction as a whole.

Indeed, Kant subsequently modified in a very telling way even the passage in which he first introduces the power of imagination in the *Critique of Pure Reason* as an "indispensable function of the soul,"[227] although only in his personal copy.[228] Instead of "function of the soul," he now wants to have written "function of the understanding." With that, the pure synthesis has been allocated to the pure understanding.[b] The pure power of imagination has become dispensable as a particular faculty, and thus the possibility that precisely it could be the essential ground for ontological knowledge has apparently been topped off, which indeed the chapter on Schematism (a chapter that remained unaltered in the second edition) shows clearly enough.

Now the transcendental power of imagination, however, is not revealed for the first time as the formative center of pure knowledge in the chapter on Schematism (fourth stage); on the contrary, this has already happened in the Transcendental Deduction (third stage). Hence, if the transcendental power of imagination is to be removed in the second edition with regard to its central

---

224. See above, §§24 and 25.
225. A 94.
226. A 115.
227. A 78, B 103.
228. See *Nachträge*, XLI.

b. understanding, however, conceived of "transcendentally"

function as a basic faculty,^{c} then before anything else the Transcendental Deduction must undergo a full revision. The transcendental power of imagination is the disquieting unknown that becomes the incentive for the new version of the Transcendental Deduction. From this incentive, however, the goal of the new reworking of the Transcendental Deduction first becomes visible as well.[229] This goal at first proves to be the correct guide for a more penetrating interpretation of this revision. Of course, this cannot be exhibited here. It must suffice to indicate the altered place of the transcendental power of imagination.

The changing of "function of the soul" into "function of the understanding" cited above characterizes Kant's new position with respect to the transcendental power of imagination. It is no longer a "function" in the sense of a particular faculty, but instead is now just a "function" as a proficiency^d of the faculty of the understanding. While in the first edition all synthesis, i.e., synthesis as such, sprang forth from the power of imagination as a faculty which is not reducible to sensibility or understanding, in the second edition the understanding alone now assumes the role of origin for all synthesis.^{e}

Already at the very beginning of the Transcendental Deduction in the second edition it is said: synthesis^f "is an act of the spontaneity of the power of representation" which we "must entitle understanding, in contrast to sensibility."[230] We should already notice here the indifferent expression "power of representation."

"Synthesis" in general is the name of an "act of the understanding."[231] "The

---

229. See below, p. 117ff.
230. B 130.
231. Ibid.

c. With the elimination of the power of imagination, the distinction between sensibility and understanding becomes clearer and sharper. The λογός comes more into its own, but as more transcendental, i.e., it is always related at the same time to intuition. The objectivity of the object becomes related more determinately to the "I connect" ["ich verbinde"] and the certainty more decisive for the grounding feature of Metaphysics (Being and thinking).

Now the possibility has also been accepted (with the sharp separation from sensibility (intuition) and thinking), of the necessary unity—to make understandable in general their togetherness and belonging to one another in some way.

They lie there like two blocks, and yet that is just not the sense and the intention of an investigation that would even call itself "Episteme-"ology ["Erkenntnis"-theorie].

Even then, the unity of both capacities (the possibility of the unity) must be grasped, or must at least become a problem.

The separation is the first fundamental [grundlegende] task, but only a first one.

[The German term Erkenntnistheorie referred to in this note literally means "theory of knowledge" and is often translated as "epistemology"; but Heidegger split it and used quotes to emphasize the "knowledge" part ("Erkenntnis"-theorie), requiring the awkward-sounding term "Episteme-" ology, which preserves an emphasis on "episteme," the Greek word for "knowledge"—tr.]

d. dependent

e. But the understanding is not the thinking of formal logic, but rather §19!

f. the "connection" conjunctio; see the "I connect," I judge!

faculty of binding-together a priori" is the "Understanding."[232] That is why the discussion is now concerned with the "pure synthesis of the understanding."[233] But it does not long remain a matter of a secret assignment of the function of synthesis to the understanding. Rather, Kant expressly states: "the transcendental synthesis of the power of imagination [is] . . . an effect of the understanding on sensibility."[234] The "transcendental act of the *power of imagination*" is conceived of as "the synthetic influence of the understanding on the inner sense,"[235] i.e., on time.

But at the same time, does this passage not also show that the transcendental power of imagination is still preserved? Certainly its complete elimination in the second edition would have been much too surprising, particularly if the "function" of the power of imagination remains indispensable for the problematic. Moreover, the power of imagination is named in the parts of the *Critique of Pure Reason* which were not revised and which stand before and after the Transcendental Deduction.

However—in the second edition, the transcendental power of imagination is still there in name only. "It is one and the same spontaneity which, there under the name power of imagination and here under that of the understanding, brings binding-together into the manifold of intuition."[236] Power of imagination is now just the name for empirical synthesis, i.e., for the synthesis related to intuition. As the passages cited above show clearly enough, this synthesis—according to the matter, i.e., as synthesis—belongs to the understanding. "Synthesis" is just "called" "power of imagination" insofar as it refers to intuition, but fundamentally it is understanding.[g][237]

The transcendental power of imagination no longer functions as independent grounding faculty, mediating in an original way between sensibility and understanding in their possible unity. Rather, this intermediate faculty now falls, so to speak, between the two separate grounding sources of the mind. Its function is relegated to the understanding. And even if Kant first introduces an apparently distinctive proper name for the transcendental power of imagination in the second edition with the title *Synthesis Speciosa*,[h][238] then it is precisely this expression which proves that the transcendental power of

---

232. B 135.
233. B 140; 153.
234. B 152. [Kant emphasizes the word *Einbildungskraft* (power of imagination) by printing it in spaced type; Heidegger does not preserve the emphasis here—tr.]
235. B 154. [Heidegger italicized *Einbildungskraft* in his fourth edition; the word is not emphasized in Kant's text—tr.]
236. B 162, note.
237. B 151.
238. Ibid.

g. as the *understanding itself*!
h. see Tradition

imagination has forfeited its former independence. It only has this name because in it the understanding refers to sensibility, and without this reference it is *Synthesis Intellectualis*.[i]

But why did Kant shrink back from the transcendental power of imagination? Did he, perhaps, not see the possibility for a more original ground-laying? Quite the opposite. The Preface to the first edition delimits the task of such a [ground-laying] with complete clarity. Kant distinguishes "two sides" to the Transcendental Deduction, one which is "objective" and one which is "subjective."[239]

According to the above-mentioned interpretation of the Transcendental Deduction, this says: the Transcendental Deduction poses the question of the inner possibility of transcendence, and through its answer it unveils the horizon of objectivity [*Gegenständlichkeit*].[26] The analysis of the Objectivity [*Objektivität*] of possible Objects [*Objekte*] is the "Objective" ["*objektive*"] side of the Deduction.

Objectivity [*Gegenständlichkeit*], however, is formed in the letting-stand-against [*Gegenstehenlassen*] which turns-toward, which takes place in the pure subject as such. The question regarding the faculties that are essentially concerned with this turning-toward and with its possibility, is the question of the subjectivity of the transcending subject as such. It is the "subjective" side of the Deduction.

Now, because what matters first and foremost to Kant is to make transcendence visible once in order to elucidate on the basis of it the essence of transcendental (ontological) knowledge, that is why the Objective Deduction is "also essential to my purposes. The other seeks to investigate pure understanding itself, according to its possibility and the powers of knowledge upon which it itself rests, and, consequently, seeks to consider it in a more subjective relationship. Although this discussion is of great importance with regard to my chief purpose, it does not belong to it essentially. For the chief question always remains: What and how much can understanding and reason know, free from all experience? and not: How is the *faculty of thinking* itself possible?"[240]

The Transcendental Deduction is in itself necessarily objective-subjective at the same time, for it is the unveiling of transcendence, essential for a finite subjectivity, which first forms the turning toward an Objectivity in general. The subjective side of the Transcendental Deduction can thus never be absent; however, its explicit working-out might be deferred. If Kant has resolved to do this, then he could do so only on the basis of a clear insight into the

---

239. A xvi ff.
240. Ibid.

i. remains [Presumably, it remains *Synthesis intellectualis* — tr.]

essence of such a working-out of the subjective side of the laying of the ground for metaphysics.

In the above-cited characterization of the Subjective Deduction, moreover, it was clearly stated that it [the Subjective Deduction] must go back to "powers of knowledge" "upon which the understanding itself rests." Furthermore, Kant sees with complete clarity that this going back to the origin cannot be any sort of empirico-explanatory, psychological consideration which only "hypo-thetically" sets forth a ground. And yet, this task of a transcendental unveiling of the essence of the subjectivity of the subject (the "Subjective Deduction") was not first posed in the Preface as an afterthought. Rather, in the preparation of the Deduction Kant already speaks of this "still completely untrodden path" which necessarily carries with it an "obscurity." He does not want to give any "far-ranging" theory of subjectivity, although the "Deduction of the Categories" "necessitates" that we "penetrate deeply into the first grounds for the possi-bility of our knowledge in general."[241]

Hence, Kant knew of the possibility for and necessity of a more original ground-laying, but it was not part of his immediate purpose. Nonetheless, this cannot be grounds for deleting the transcendental power of imagination, where indeed it directly forms the unity of transcendence and its objectivity [Gegenständlichkeit]. The transcendental power of imagination must itself pro-vide the occasion which turned Kant away from it as a basic transcendental faculty in its own right.

Because Kant does not carry out the Subjective Deduction, the subjectivity of the subject for him continues to be guided by *the* constitution and *the* characterization offered to him through traditional Anthropology and Psychol-ogy.[27] For these [disciplines], the power of imagination was just a base faculty within sensibility. In fact, the outcome of the Transcendental Deduction and the Schematism, i.e., the insight into the transcendental essence of the pure power of imagination, was not by itself strong enough to permit the subjec-tivity of the subject as a whole to be seen in a new light.

How is the baser faculty of sensibility also to be able to constitute the essence of reason? Does not everything fall into confusion if the lowest takes the place of the highest? What is to happen with the venerable tradition, according to which Ratio and Logos have claimed the central function in the history of metaphysics? Can the primacy of Logic fall? Can the architectonic of the laying of the ground for metaphysics in general, the division into Transcendental Aesthetic and Logic, still be upheld if what it has for its theme is basically to be the transcendental power of imagination?

Will not the *Critique of Pure Reason* have deprived itself of its own theme if pure reason reverts to the transcendental power of imagination? Does not this ground-laying lead us to an abyss?

---

241. A 98.

In the radicalism of his questions, Kant brought the "possibility" of meta-physics to this abyss. He saw the unknown. He had to shrink back. It was not just that the transcendental power of imagination frightened him, but rather that in between [the two editions] pure reason as reason drew him increasingly under its spell.

Through the laying of the ground for metaphysics in general, Kant for the first time won clear insight into the character of the "universality" of ontologico-metaphysical knowledge. Now for the first time he had "rod and staff" in hand, in order to wander critically through the region of Moral Philosophy and to repair the indeterminate, empirical universality of popular philosophical doctrines concerning morals by means of the essential origi-nality of the ontological analyses which alone can situate a "Metaphysics of Morals" and the ground-laying thereof. In the struggle against the superficial and obscured empiricism of the predominant moral philosophy, the decisive demarkation of the pure a priori in opposition to everything empirical has attained a growing significance. To the extent that the essence of the subjec-tivity of the subject lies in its personality, which, however, is synonymous with moral reason, the rational character of pure knowledge and of action must be solidified. All pure synthesis and synthesis in general must, as spontaneity, fall to the faculty which in a proper sense is free, the acting reason.

The pure rational character of personality which is thus unveiled more and more, of course, could likewise not impugn human finitude for Kant, if indeed a being generally determined through ethicality [Sittlichkeit] and duty can neither be nor become "infinite." On the contrary, Kant awoke to the problem of now searching for finitude precisely in the pure, rational creature itself, and not first in the fact that it is determined through "sensibility." Only in this way was ethicality able to be grasped as pure, i.e., as neither conditioned by nor even made for the factical, empirical human being.

This personal-ontological problem of a finite pure reason in general admit-tedly was not able to tolerate in proximity to itself that which recalls the specific constitution of a determinate kind of realization of a finite rational creature in general. Such, however, was the power of imagination, which was reputed to be not only a specifically human faculty, but also a sensible one.

The problematic of a pure reason amplified in this way must push aside the power of imagination, and with that it really first conceals its transcenden-tal essence.

It is unmistakable that the problem of this distinction between a finite, rational creature in general and the separate realization of such a creature, which is the human being, thrusts itself to the fore in the Transcendental Deduction of the second edition. Indeed, the first "improvement" which Kant appends to the first page of the second edition of his work already makes this clear. To the characterization of finite knowledge, namely, to that of finite intuition, he adds: "at least to us humans."[242] This should show that every finite intuition is indeed one which takes things in stride, but that the taking-in-stride must not necessarily be mediated through the sense organs, as with us humans.

The obscurity and "strangeness" of the transcendental power of imagination, of the ground cleared in the first ground-laying, and the sheer power of pure reason, were worked together in order to veil once more the line of vision into the more original essence of the transcendental power of imagination, a perspective which was broken open, so to speak, only for an instant.

This is the quintessential content of the observation, already long established in Kant interpretation on the basis of the fundamental problem of the *Critique of Pure Reason* and which for the most part has been expressed as follows: Kant changed from the "psychological" interpretation of the first edition to the more "logical" interpretation of the second.

To be sure, we should note that the ground-laying in the first edition was never "psychological," any more than that of the second edition was a "logical" one. On the contrary, both are transcendental, i.e., they are necessarily "objective" as well as "subjective." But in the transcendental, subjective ground-laying of the second edition, it decided in favor of the pure understanding as opposed to the pure power of imagination in order to preserve the mastery of reason. In the second edition, the subjective, "psychological" deduction recedes so little that, on the contrary, it intensifies precisely in the direction of the pure understanding as the faculty of synthesis. It now becomes superfluous to trace the understanding back to more original "powers of knowledge."[j]

The interpretation of the stages of the laying of the ground for metaphysics, which was carried out above from an exclusive orientation with respect to the first edition of the *Critique of Pure Reason*, had constantly shifted the finitude of human transcendence into the center of the problematic. Now, if Kant presented the problem of finitude more comprehensively in the second edition through the enlargement of the concept of a finite, rational creature that no longer coincides with the concept of the human being, then is this not grounds enough—even with the intention of [providing] a central interpretation of this work—to abide by the second edition? According to what has been said, this [second edition] is not therefore "better" because it proceeds "more logically." On the contrary, in a properly understood sense it is even "more psychological," namely, [in the sense of] a more exclusive orientation with respect to pure reason as such.

In this way, however, did not the preceding interpretation [*Interpretation*],

---

242. B 33.

j. because understanding and judgment (see §19) are grasped transcendentally beforehand, i.e., as referring to *intuition* and even the laying-out [*Auslegung*] of the transcendental power of imagination which in a more original way has outgrown it, discuss judgment?

But why, then, did the finitude of pure knowledge beset the problem from the beginning? Because metaphysics, the laying of the ground for which it [the problem] refers, belongs to "human nature." Consequently, the specific finitude of human nature is decisive for the laying of the ground for metaphysics. The apparently superficial question as to whether, in the interpretation of the *Critique of Pure Reason*, the second edition deserves priority in principle over the first or the reverse, is merely the pale reflection of the decisive question for the Kantian laying of the ground for metaphysics and the interpretation thereof: Is the transcendental power of imagination, as previously laid ground, solid enough to determine originally, i.e., cohesively and as a whole, precisely the finite essence of the subjectivity of the human subject? Or will the problem of a human pure reason, through the elimination of the transcendental power of imagination, already have been formed more comprehensively as a problem and thus have been brought closer to a possible solution? As long as this question is not decided, the more original interpretation of the transcendental power of imagination being sought also remains necessarily incomplete.

C. THE TRANSCENDENTAL POWER OF IMAGINATION AND THE PROBLEM OF HUMAN PURE REASON

It should first become clear by means of a distinctive proof that in the *Critique of Pure Reason*, as a laying of the ground for metaphysics, it is from the beginning and solely a matter of human pure reason. The formula for the problem of the possibility of *Metaphysica Generalis* runs: "How are synthetic a priori judgments possible?" Kant says the following concerning the solution to this problem:

"The above problem cannot be solved except as follows: that we consider it beforehand in relation to the human faculties by means of which man is capable of the expansion of his knowledge a priori and which in *him* constitute what one can specifically call *his* pure reason. For if we are to recognize under the pure reason of a creature in general the faculty of knowing things independently of experience and therefore of sensible representations, then with this nothing at all has been determined concerning the general manner in which such knowledge was possible in this creature (e.g., in God or another higher spirit), and the problem is therefore indeterminate. As for human beings, in contrast, all knowledge of the same consists of concept and intuition."[243]

This passage is found in the treatise *"Über die Fortschritte der Metaphysik"* ["On the Progress of Metaphysics"]. With the working-out of this treatise, Kant has certainly laid the problematic of metaphysics as such before us immediately and in its entirety. In a laying of the ground for metaphysics, then, the "specific" finitude of human subjectivity is the problem. It cannot exist merely as a possible "instance" of a finite, rational creature in general coinciding with what was extracted in the course of the consideration.

To human finitude belongs sensibility, meaning the intuition which takes things in stride. As pure intuition, i.e., pure sensibility, it is a necessary element in the structure of transcendence which distinguishes finitude. Human pure reason is necessarily a pure sensible reason. This pure reason must be sensible in itself, it does not first become sensible in this way because it is tied to a body. Rather, the reverse is true: the human being, as finite, rational creature, can thus only "have" its body in a transcendental (i.e., a metaphysical) sense because transcendence as such is sensible a priori.

Now, if the transcendental power of imagination is to be the original ground for the possibility of human subjectivity, namely, in its unity and wholeness, then it must make possible something like a pure, sensible reason. Pure sensibility, however, namely, in the universal meaning according to which it must come to be grasped in the laying of the ground for metaphysics, is time.

Should time as pure sensibility stand in an original unity with the "I think" of pure apperception? Should the pure I, which according to the generally prevailing interpretation Kant placed outside of all temporality and all time, be taken as "temporal"? And all this on the grounds of the transcendental power of imagination? How in general is this related to time?

§32. The Transcendental Power of Imagination and Its Relation to Time

The transcendental power of imagination has been revealed as the origin of pure, sensible intuition.[244] Thus, it has been proven in principle that time, as a pure intuition, springs forth from the transcendental power of imagination. Nevertheless, a specific, analytical elucidation of the manner in which time is now grounded precisely in the transcendental power of imagination is required.

Time "flows continually"[245] as the pure succession of the sequence of nows.

---

243. *Über die Fortschritte der Metaphysik*, VIII, p. 312.
244. See above, §28, p. 99ff.
245. B 291.

Pure intuition intuits this succession unobjectively. Intuiting means the taking-in-stride of what gives itself. Pure intuition, in the taking-in-stride, gives itself that which is capable of being taken in stride.

Taking-in-stride of . . . is understood first of all as the receiving of something at hand or present. But this narrow conception of taking-in-stride, still oriented with respect to empirical intuition, must be kept separate from pure intuition and its character as taking-in-stride. It is easily seen that the pure intuition of the pure succession of nows cannot be the taking-in-stride of a presence [Anwesenden]. If it were, then at most it would be able to "intuit" just the current now, and never the sequence of nows as such and the horizon formed in it. Indeed, strictly speaking, in the mere taking-in-stride of a "present moment" [eines "Gegenwärtigen"] it is not possible to intuit a single now insofar as it has an essentially continuous extension in its having-just-arrived and its coming-at-any-minute.[28] The taking-in-stride of pure intuition must in itself give the look of the now, so that indeed it looks ahead to its coming-at-any-minute and looks back on its having-just-arrived.

Now for the first time it is unveiled in a more concrete way that pure intuition, which is treated in the Transcendental Aesthetic, from the beginning cannot be the taking-in-stride of a "present moment." In pure intuition, the self-giving which takes things in stride is in principle not related to something which is only a presence and is related least of all to a being which is at hand.

Consequently, if pure intuiting has this free-moving character, does it not already follow from this that "at bottom" it is the pure power of imagination? This follows at best only insofar as pure intuition itself forms that which can be taken in stride in it. However, that this original forming, in itself and in particular, is to be a looking-at, a looking-ahead and a looking-back, indeed has nothing to do with the transcendental power of imagination!

If only Kant himself had not expressly set forth this threefold, trinitarian character of forming in the imagining of the power of imagination![29]

In his lectures on Metaphysics, namely, in the Rational Psychology, Kant analyses the "forming power" [bildende Kraft] in the following manner: this faculty "produces representations either of present time, or representations of past time, or even representations of future time. Hence the formative faculty [Bildungsvermögen] consists of:

1. The faculty of taking a likeness [Abbildung], the representations of which are of the present time: facultas formandi.

2. The faculty of reproduction [Nachbildung], the representations of which are of a past time: facultas imaginandi.

3. The faculty of prefiguration [Vorbildung], the representations of which are of a future time: facultas praevidendi."[246]

---

246. Pölitz, Kants Vorlesungen über die Metaphysik, p. 88; see p. 83.

The term "taking a likeness" ("*Abbildung*") requires a brief explanation. It does not mean the production of a likeness in the sense of a copy. Rather, it means the look which was itself gathered immediately from the presencing (present) object.[30] The forming-from [*Ab-bilden*] does not mean a forming-according-to [*Nach-bilden*], but rather form-giving [*Bild-gebend*] in the sense of the immediate distinguishing of the look of the object itself.

Although Kant does not speak in this passage of the transcendental power of imagination, still one point becomes clear: the forming [*Bilden*] of the "imagination" ["*Einbildung*"] is *in itself* relative to time. Pure imagining, however, which is called pure because it forms its fabric [*Gebilde*] from out of itself, as in itself relative to time, must first of all form time. Time as pure intuition means neither just what is intuited in pure intuiting nor just the intuiting which lacks the "object." Time as pure intuition is the forming intuiting of what it intuits *in one*. This gives the full concept of time for the first time.

Pure intuition, however, can only form the pure succession of the sequence of nows as such if in itself it is a likeness-forming, prefiguring, and reproducing power of imagination. Hence, it is in no way permissible to think of time, especially in the Kantian sense, as an arbitrary field which the power of imagination just gets into for purposes of its own activity, so to speak. Accordingly, time must indeed be taken as pure sequence of nows in the horizon within which we "reckon with time." This sequence of nows, however, is in no way time in its originality. On the contrary, the transcendental power of imagination allows time as sequence of nows to spring forth, and as this letting-spring-forth it is therefore original time.

But is it possible to sift out such a wide-ranging interpretation of the transcendental power of imagination as original time from Kant's few intimations? With the unforeseeable consequences which in the end would result from this interpretation, it must be grounded more concretely and securely.

§33. The Inner Temporal Character
of the Transcendental Power of Imagination

In the first edition, the power of imagination was termed the faculty of "synthesis in general." If the inner, temporal character of the power of imagination is now to be emphasized, then we must investigate where it is that Kant expressly treats synthesis. This occurs in the section which prepares the way for the carrying-out of the Transcendental Deduction according to the two ways previously presented, a section entitled: "On the a priori Grounds for the Possibility of Experience."[247] The location of the thematic analysis of

---

247. A 95ff.

synthesis as such is thus not arbitrary. And if in particular Kant still describes the discussion of synthesis as a "preliminary remark,"[247a] we should not therefore think of it as a casual and at bottom superfluous observation. Instead, what was treated therein must be kept in view from the start for the Transcendental Deduction and the Transcendental Schematism. The Transcendental Deduction, however, as the third stage of the ground-laying, has as its task to show the inner possibility for the essential unity of ontological synthesis.

The three elements of pure knowledge are: pure intuition, pure power of imagination, and pure understanding. Their possible unity, i.e., the essence of their original unification (synthesis), is the problem. Hence, an elucidation of the synthesis with a view toward these three elements of pure knowledge is required.

Accordingly, Kant divides his "Preliminary Remark" into three sections:
" 1. On the Synthesis of Apprehension in Intuition.
2. On the Synthesis of Reproduction in Imagination.
3. On the Synthesis of Recognition in Concepts."
Now are these modes of synthesis three in number because there are three elements belonging to the essential unity of pure knowledge? Or does this triplicity of modes of synthesis have a more original ground, one which at the same time elucidates why, especially as ways of pure synthesis, they are unified in order to "form" the essential unity of the three elements of pure knowledge on the grounds of their more original unity?

Are there three modes of synthesis because time appears in them and because they express the threefold unity of time as present, having-been, and future? And if the original unification of the essential unity of ontological knowledge occurs through time, but if the ground for the possibility of pure knowledge is the transcendental power of imagination, then is this not revealed as original time?

And yet, by naming the second of the three modes of synthesis "Synthesis of Reproduction in Imagination," Kant already says that the power of imagination is just one element among others and that it is in no way the root of intuition and concept. That turns out to be the case.

But just as indisputably, the Transcendental Deduction, which through this analysis of the threefold synthesis is to have provided the fundament, shows that the power of imagination represents not just one faculty among others, but rather their mediating center. That the transcendental power of imagination is the root of sensibility and understanding was admittedly first shown in the more original interpretation. No use can be made of this result here. Instead, the working-out of the inner temporal character of the three modes of synthesis should produce the ultimate, decisive proof for the fact that the

247a. A 98.

interpretation of the transcendental power of imagination as the root of both stems is not only possible, but also necessary. For a general understanding of the Kantian analysis of the three modes of synthesis, several points must first be clarified, and they must guide us in what follows.

First, Kant's manner of expression requires closer determination. What is meant by Synthesis "of" Apprehension, Synthesis "of" Reproduction, Synthesis "of" Recognition? It does not mean that apprehension etc. are subject to a synthesis nor that apprehension, or rather reproduction and recognition, consummate a synthesis. Rather, it means that synthesis as such has the character of either apprehension or reproduction or recognition. Hence the expressions mean: Synthesis in the mode of Apprehension, Reproduction, and Recognition, or synthesis as apprehending, as reproducing, as recognizing. Thus Kant treats synthesis, i.e., the faculty of synthesis, with regard to these three modes as peculiar to it in specific ways.

Second, it is worth noting: the modes of synthesis first come to be clarified in the individual sections through a description of the manner in which they function in empirical intuition, in empirical imagining, and in empirical thinking. This preparatory characterization, however, is intended to show that in pure intuition, in pure imagination, and in pure thinking, there is already in each case a corresponding pure apprehending, pure reproducing, and pure recognizing synthesis which is also constitutive. With that, it is shown at the same time that these modes of pure synthesis constitute the condition for the possibility of empirical synthesis in the knowing relation to the being.

Third, it is worth noting that the proper goal of the interpretation of the three modes of synthesis—even if it is not always formulated clearly enough and in advance—lies in demonstrating their intrinsic and essential belonging-together in the essence of pure synthesis as such.

And finally, we may not forget, as Kant himself expressly required, that "throughout what follows" it must be quite "fundamental": all "our representations . . . are subject to time." But if all intuiting, imagining, and thinking representings are governed by the threefold synthesis, then is it not the time-character of this synthesis which makes everything uniformly submissive in advance?

a) Pure Synthesis as Pure Apprehension[248]

In empirical intuition as the immediate taking-in-stride of a "this-here," a manifold is always revealed. Thus, what the look attained by this intuition presents, "contains" manifoldness. This can never "be represented as such a manifold . . . , if the mind does not differentiate time in the sequence of one

---

248. A 98–100.

impression upon another." In distinguishing time, our mind must already be saying constantly and in advance "now and now and now," in order to be able to encounter "now this" and "now that" and "now all this in particular." Only in such a differentiating of the now does it first become possible to "run through" and collectively take up the impressions.

Intuition is just a representation of the manifold—a *repraesentatio singularis*—if, as that which takes things in stride, it takes up and comprehends the offering of the manifold "exactly" and at once. Intuition is in itself "synthetic." This synthesis has the peculiarity that within the horizon of the succession of the sequence of nows, it takes up "exactly" the offer of the impression of each look (image).[31] It is an immediate forming-from [*Ab-bilden*] in the sense already clarified.

But we also necessarily have a pure, apprehending synthesis, because without it there is no way we could have the representation of time, i.e., this pure intuition. The pure, apprehending synthesis does not first take place within the horizon of time, but instead it first forms precisely the like of the now and the sequence of nows. Pure intuition is "original receptivity," i.e., a taking-in-stride of what it, as taking-in-stride, lets come forth from out of itself. Its "offering" is one which "produces" [*"erzeugendes"*]; what the pure intuiting offering (forming as giving a look) produces (forming as creating) is the immediate look of the now as such, i.e., always the look of the actual present as such.

Empirical intuition is directly concerned with the being which is present in the now. The pure apprehending synthesis, however, is concerned with the now, i.e., with the present itself, so that indeed this intuiting concern with . . . in itself forms that with which it is concerned. The pure synthesis as apprehension, as that which offers the "present in general," is time-forming. Accordingly, the pure synthesis of apprehension in itself has a temporal character.

Now, however, Kant expressly says: "It is thus an active faculty in us for the synthesis of this manifold which we call imagination, and its immediate action on perceptions I call apprehension."[249]

Synthesis in the mode of apprehension springs forth from the power of imagination; hence the pure apprehending synthesis must be spoken of as a mode of the transcendental power of imagination. But now if this synthesis is time-forming, the transcendental power of imagination has in itself a pure temporal character. To the extent, however, that the pure power of imagination is an "ingredient" of pure intuition and hence to the extent that a synthesis of imagination is already found in intuition, then what Kant initially calls "imagination" [*"Einbildung"*] in what follows cannot be identical with the transcendental power of imagination [*transzendentalen Einbildungskraft*].

---

249. A 120. See also Kant's note.

b) Pure Synthesis as Pure Reproduction[250]

Kant again begins the analysis with a reference to the reproductive synthesis in empirical representing. The "mind" can represent the being, e.g., something previously perceived, even "without the presence of the object." Such making-present however, or as Kant says, such "imagination," presupposes that the mind has the possibility of bringing forth again representationally the being represented earlier in order to represent it in a more actual unity[32] with the being directly perceived from time to time. The bringing-forth-again—reproduction—is, accordingly, a kind of unifying.

This reproducing synthesis, however, can only unify if the mind does not "lose from thought"[251] what is brought-forth-again in it. Hence the not-losing, i.e., the ability to retain, is necessarily found in such synthesis. Beings experienced earlier, however, can only be retained if the mind "differentiates time," and thereby has in view such [temporal distinctions] as *"earlier"* and *"at that time."* The being experienced earlier would constantly be lost completely with each now, if it were not in general retainable. Hence, if empirical synthesis in the mode of reproduction is thereby to become possible, the no-longer-now *as such* must in advance and prior to all experience have been brought forth again and unified with the specific now. This occurs in pure reproduction as a mode of pure synthesis. Nevertheless, if the empirical synthesis of reproduction belongs primarily to the empirical imagination, then pure reproduction is pure synthesis of the pure power of imagination.

And yet, is not the pure power of imagination accepted as essentially productive? How is a reproductive synthesis to belong to it? Pure reproduction—does this not mean productive reproduction, hence a square circle?[33]

But is pure reproduction then a productive reproducing? In fact, it forms the possibility of reproduction in general, namely, due to the fact that it brings the horizon of the earlier into view and holds it open as such in advance.[252] Pure synthesis in the mode of reproduction forms having-been-ness [*Gewesenheit*] as such. But this says: the pure power of imagination, with regard to this

---

250. A 100–102.

251. A 102.

252. On p. A 102 Kant says: ". . . the reproductive synthesis of the power of imagination [belongs] to the transcendental acts of the mind." Now Kant usually calls the nontranscendental power of imagination (i.e., the empirical) the reproductive imagination. If one takes reproductive as "empirical" in this sense, then the previously cited sentence becomes meaningless. Riehl ("Korrekturen zu Kant," *Kantstudien*, vol. V [1901], p. 268) thus proposes writing "productive" instead of "reproductive." This would indeed remove the alleged inconsistency, but at the same time it would also remove in general the sense that Kant wants to express with the sentence, for it should indeed show directly that the productive, i.e., here the pure power of imagination, is purely reproductive in that it makes possible reproduction in general. The insertion of "productive" only makes sense, then, if it does not replace the "reproductive," but if instead it determines it more precisely. Given the entire context, however, that is superfluous. If it is to be improved, then it must read "pure reproductive synthesis."

mode of synthesis, is time-forming. It can be called pure "reproduction" not because it attends to a being which is gone nor because it attends to it as something experienced earlier. Rather, [it can be called pure "imitation"] to the extent that it opens up in general the horizon of the possible attending-to, the having-been-ness, and so it "forms" this "after"[34] as such.

Where, however, does the pure character of synthesis stand with this forming of time in the mode of the "at that time"? The original, forming retaining of the "at-that-time" is in itself the retaining forming of the no-longer-now. This forming is occasionally unified as such with the now. Pure reproduction is essentially unified with the pure synthesis of intuition as that which forms the present. "The synthesis of apprehension is thus inseparably bound up with the synthesis of reproduction,"[253] for every now is now already just-arrived. In order for the synthesis of apprehension to give the current look perfectly in an image, it must be able to retain as such the present manifold which it runs through; and at the same time it must be pure synthesis of reproduction.

But if the synthesis of apprehension as well as that of reproduction is an act of the transcendental power of imagination, then this latter must be grasped as that which functions synthetically and in itself "inseparably" as faculty of "synthesis in general" according to both of these modes. In this original unity of both modes, then, it can also be the origin of time (as unity of present and having-been-ness). If this original unity of both modes of synthesis did not exist, then "the purest and first grounding representations of space and time could not spring forth even once."[254]

But if time is now the threefold-unified whole made up of present, past, and future, and if Kant now adds a third mode to both modes of synthesis which have now been shown to be time-forming, and if finally all representing including thought is to be subject to time, then this third mode of synthesis must "form" the future.

c) Pure Synthesis as Pure Recognition[255]

The analysis of this third synthesis is indeed much more extensive than the first two, and yet at first one searches in vain for what would normally be developed in such "compelling" argumentation. The synthesis of pure recognition is to constitute the third element of pure knowledge, pure thinking. But what has recognition got to do with the future? How in general is pure thinking, the I of pure apperception, to have a temporal character when Kant opposes in the sharpest terms the "I think" in particular and reason in general to all time-relations?

---

253. A 102.
254. A 102.
255. A 103-110.

"Pure reason, as a faculty which is merely intelligible, is not subject to the form of time or, consequently, to the conditions of the succession of time."[256] And immediately following the Schematism chapter, with the introduction to the determination of the highest principle of all synthetic judgments, does not Kant show that the temporal character must continue to be excluded from the "highest principle of all analytical judgments," the Principle of Contradiction, which delimits the essence of mere thinking? The "at the same time" (ἄμα) can have no place in the formula for this basic principle. Otherwise, "the principle would be affected by the condition of time."[257] "Now the Principle of Contradiction, as a merely logical basic principle, must not in any way reduce its claims to time-relations. Therefore, such a formula is completely contrary to the intention of this principle."[258]

Is it surprising, then, that we find nothing in Kant about a temporal character for this third mode of synthesis? And yet, neither empty suppositions and conclusions nor allowing the matter to be decided by what we find initially in reading the discussion of this third synthesis, are of any avail here.

Kant also begins the presentation of the third mode of synthesis with a characterization of empirical recognition, namely, from synthesis as reproduction he establishes: "Without consciousness of the fact that what we are thinking is the same as what we thought an instant before, all reproduction in the series of representations would be in vain."[259] The reproductive synthesis should effect and maintain what it brings forth in unity with the being which is revealed directly in perception.

And yet, when the mind again returns from its going-back into the past, when it returns again to the directly present being in order to set the former in unity with the latter, who then tells it that this being which is now present is the same as that which it previously abandoned, so to speak, with the fulfillment of the visualization?[35] According to its essence, the reproducing synthesis stumbles upon something which it claims is the same being and which will be experienced before, during, and after its fulfillment in the present perception. This perception itself always attends just to what has presence [das Anwesende] as such.

Does not the whole succession of representings break up into individual representations so that the returning synthesis of reproduction must set what it brings along at any time into unity with a being—always other—which is directly at hand? What is the unity of apprehending intuition and reproducing imagination to be if what they want to present as unified and the same is, so to speak, placeless?

---

256. A 551, B 579.
257. A 152, B 191.
258. A 152f., B 192.
259. A 103.

Does this place first come to be created, then, after the achievement of a perception and the recollection connected to it, which recollection wants to set what is remembered in unity with what has presence "in the current state"? Or are these two ways of synthesis already oriented in advance toward the being as something which has presence in sameness?

Apparently [the latter]. For at the ground of both syntheses, and directing them, a unifying (synthesis) of the being with respect to its sameness is already found. This synthesis of the same, i.e., the holding of the being before us as one which is the same, Kant calls—and justly so—the synthesis "in concepts," for the concept is indeed the representing of unity which as selfsame "applies to many." "For this *one* consciousness {representing this unity as conceptual representing} is what unifies the manifold, which is intuited again and again and which is then also reproduced, into one representation."[260]

It has thus been shown: what emerged as the third synthesis in the characterization[a] of the empirical genesis of conceptual development is in fact the first, i.e., the synthesis which in the first place directs the other two characterized above. It pops up in advance of them, so to speak. Kant gives this synthesis of identification a most appropriate name: its unifying is a reconnoitering. It explores in advance and is "watching out for"[261] what must be held before us in advance as the same in order that the apprehending and reproducing syntheses in general can find a closed, circumscribed field of beings within which they can attach to what they bring forth and encounter, so to speak, and take them in stride as beings.

As empirical, however, this exploring, advancing synthesis of identification necessarily presupposes a pure identification. That is to say: just as a pure reproduction forms the possibility of a bringing-forth-again, so correspondingly must pure recognition present the possibility for something like identifying. But if this pure synthesis reconnoiters, then at the same time that says: it does not explore a being which it can hold before itself as selfsame. Rather, it explores the horizon of being-able-to-hold-something-before-us [*Vorhaltbarkeit*] in general. As pure, its exploring is the original forming of this preliminary attaching [*Vorhaften*], i.e., the future. Thus the third mode of synthesis also proves to be one which is essentially time-forming. Insofar as Kant allocates the modes of taking a likeness, reproduction, and prefiguration [*Ab-, Nach- und Vorbildung*] to the empirical imagination, then the forming of the preliminary attaching as such, the pure preparation, is an act of the pure power of the imagination.

---

260. A 103.
261. A 126.

a. If one characterizes the empirical genesis of conceptual development—then this is all right; but this characterization is not Kant's goal.

Although at the outset it appeared hopeless, even absurd, to elucidate the inner formation of the pure concepts as essentially determined by time, now not only has the time-character of the third mode of synthesis been brought to light, but also this mode of pure pre-paration, according to its inner structure, even exhibits a priority over the other two, with which at the same time it essentially belongs together. In this Kantian analysis of pure synthesis in concepts, which is apparently completely aloof from time, when exactly does the most original essence of time, i.e., that it is developed primarily from the future, come to the fore?

Be that as it may, the task of proving the inner time-character of the transcendental power of imagination, which was undecided, has been accomplished. If the transcendental power of imagination, as the pure, forming faculty, in itself forms time—i.e., allows time to spring forth—then we cannot avoid the thesis stated above: the transcendental power of imagination is original time.

The universal character of pure sensibility, i.e., of time, however, now has likewise been revealed. Consequently, the transcendental power of imagination is able to support and form the original unity and wholeness of the specific finitude of the human subject, which has been asserted to be pure, sensible reason.

And yet, do not pure sensibility (time) and pure reason remain simply heterogenous, and does not the concept of a pure, sensible reason remain simply a nonconcept?[36] The objections to the attempt to grasp the selfhood of the self as inherently temporal and not as something which only the empirical grasping of the empirical subject is to recognize as time-determined, appear insurmountable.

But if [the attempt] cannot succeed in showing the self as temporal, does the opposite way perhaps have a chance of success? How does it stand with the proof that time as such has the character of selfhood? Its chances of failure are just as slight as those of the claim, which indeed is undisputed, that time "apart from the subject is nothing."[262] This indeed implies that in the subject, it is everything.

But what does "in the subject" mean here? Time is certainly not at hand "in the subject" as cells are in the brain. The constant reference to the subjectivity of time yields little. Now had Kant himself seen only this negative aspect, that time "apart from the subject is nothing"? Did Kant not show in the Transcendental Deduction and in the chapter on Schematism that time takes part essentially in the innermost essential structure of transcendence? And does not transcendence determine the Being-as-self [*Selbstsein*] of the finite self? Must we not keep this essence of subjectivity in view, even though we only

---

262. A 35, B 51.

want to ask legitimately about the much-discussed "subjective" character of time? If Kant came across time in the "depths" of the essential ground of transcendence, then will what was said in an introductory way about time in the Transcendental Aesthetic be the last word? Or is what was discussed there only an indication of the more original essence of time? In the end, is not the elucidating of the temporal character of the subject first permitted on the basis of the correctly understood subjective character of time?

§34. Time as Pure Self-Affection and the Temporal Character of the Self

In the passage delimiting the essential unity of pure knowledge for the first time (the second stage of the ground-laying), Kant remarks that space and time "must always affect" the concept of representations of objects.[263] What does the initially obscure thesis mean here: time affects a concept, namely, that of the representations of objects?

We begin the interpretation with the clarification of the "concept of the representations of objects." First of all, this expression means the "universal" which characterizes every representing of objects as such, i.e., the letting-stand-against of . . . . This, says the thesis, will necessarily be affected through time. And yet, the discussion of this matter up to now has been just that time, as well as space, form the horizon within which the affections of the senses from time to time strike us and are of concern to us. Now time itself is to affect us. All affection, however, is the self-announcing [Sich-melden] of a being which is already at hand. But time is neither at hand nor is it generally "outside." From whence does it come, then, if it is to be affecting?

Time is only pure intuition to the extent that it prepares the look of succession from out of itself, and it *clutches* this as such *to itself* as the formative taking-in-stride. This pure intuition activates itself with the intuited which was formed in it, i.e., which was formed without the aid of experience. According to its essence, time is pure affection of itself. Furthermore, it is precisely what in general forms something like the "from-out-of-itself-toward-there . . . ,"[37] so that the upon-which[38] looks back and into the previously named toward-there. . . .

As pure self-affection, time is not an acting affection that strikes a self which is at hand. Instead, as pure it forms the essence of something like self-activating. However, if it belongs to the essence of the finite subject to be able to be activated as a self, then time as pure self-affection forms the essential structure of subjectivity.

---

263. A 77, B 102.

Only on the grounds of this selfhood can the finite creature be what it must be: dependent upon taking-things-in-stride.

Now, in the first place, we must clarify what the [following] obscure statement says: time necessarily affects the concept of the representations of objects. The letting-stand-against as such, i.e., as pure turning-one's-attention-to . . . , pure affecting, means: to bring something like an "against-it," the Being-in-opposition, into opposition to it in general; "to it"—to the pure letting-stand-against of . . . , but that means to pure apperception, to the I itself. Time belongs to the inner possibility of this letting-stand-against of. . . . As pure self-affection, it forms in an original way the finite selfhood, so that the self can be something like self-consciousness.

By working out the presuppositions decisive for the intrinsic problematic of the *Critique of Pure Reason*,[264] the finitude of knowledge is drawn to center stage. The finitude of knowledge rests on the finitude of intuiting, i.e., on taking-in-stride. Consequently, pure knowledge, i.e., the knowing of what stands-against in general, the pure concept, is grounded in an intuition which takes [things] in stride. Pure taking-in-stride, however, means: becoming affected in the absence of experience, i.e., self-affecting.

Time as pure self-affection is that finite, pure intuition which bears and makes possible in general the pure concept (the understanding) that stands in essential service to intuition.

The idea of pure self-affection, which as we have now seen determines the innermost essence of transcendence, was thus not introduced by Kant for the first time in the second edition. In that edition it was simply formulated more explicitly, and indeed it appears characteristically [at the beginning] in the Transcendental Aesthetic.[265] To be sure, this passage must remain obscure as long as the interpretation lacks that perspective which should have been secured by means of the preceding presentation of the stages of the ground-laying and their more original setting. But then, from this perspective it is almost "self evident." "Now that which, as representation, can be antecedent to every act of thinking anything, is intuition; and if it contains nothing but relations, it is the form of intuition. Since this form represents nothing except insofar as something is posited in the mind, it can be nothing other than the way the mind, through its own activity (namely, this positing of its representation), consequently comes to be affected through itself, i.e., according to an inner sense of its form."[266]

---

264. See above, §§4 and 5, p. 14ff. [Additional reference to §5 added in GA—tr.]
265. B 67f.
266. Ibid. The proposed change of the phrase "their representation" into "its representation" (*des "ihrer Vorstellung" in "seiner"*) removes precisely what is essential in the text. The "their" is not [intended] to express that the representation is a representation of the mind, but rather that the representing, posited by the mind, re-presents the "pure relations" of the succession of the sequence of nows as such and allows them to come up to the taking-in-stride.

Sense means finite intuition. The form of sense is pure taking-in-stride. Inner sense does not receive "from without," but rather from the self. In pure taking-in-stride, the inner affection must come forth from out of the pure self; i,e., it must be formed in the essence of selfhood as such, and therefore it must constitute this self in the first place. Pure self-affection provides the transcendental, primal structure of the finite self as such. Thus it is absolutely not the case that a mind exists among others which, for it, are also something related to it, and that it practices self-positing. Rather, this 'from-out-of-itself-toward . . . and back-to-itself' first constitutes the mental character of the mind as a finite self.

In this way, however, it is obvious at a glance that time as pure self-affection is not found "in the mind" "along with" pure apperception. Rather, as the ground for the possibility of selfhood, time already lies within pure appercep-tion, and so it first makes the mind into a mind.

The pure, finite self has, in itself, temporal character. However, if the I, pure reason, is essentially temporal, then it is precisely on the basis of this temporal character that the decisive determination which Kant gives of transcendental apperception first becomes understandable.

Time and the "I think" no longer stand incompatibly and incomparably at odds; they are the same. With his laying of the ground for metaphysics, and through the radicalism with which, for the first time, he transcendentally interpreted both time, always for itself, and the "I think," always for itself, Kant brought both of them together in their original sameness—without, to be sure, expressly seeing this as such for himself.

Can we read over it with as little concern as previously, then, when Kant refers to both time and the "I think" with the same essential predicates?

In the Transcendental Deduction, the transcendental essence of the I (i.e., that which makes transcendence possible) is characterized as follows: "The fixed and perduring I (of pure apperception) constitutes the correlate of all of our representations . . . . "[267] And in the chapter on Schematism, wherein the transcendental essence of time comes to light, Kant says of time: "Time does not elapse . . . , time "which is itself unchanging and perduring."[268] And later: "Time . . . perdures and does not change."[269]

Naturally, we could reply, this covering over of the essential predicates for time and the I is not surprising, for Kant only wants to say with this that neither the I nor time is "in tune." To be sure. But does it follow from this that the I is not temporal, or does it come about directly that the I is so "temporal" that it is time itself, and that only as time itself, according to its ownmost essence, does it become possible?

---

267. A 123.
268. A 143, B 183.
269. A 182, B 224f.

What then does it mean to say: the "fixed and perduring" I constitutes the "correlate" of all our representations? First of all, it means this: the fixed and perduring I carries out the letting-stand-against by such a thing, which is not only a relation of there-upon . . . [des Hin-zu-auf . . .], but is a correlation of the back-into . . . [des Zurück-zu-in . . .], and so it forms the Being-in-opposition-to [das Dawider]. But why does Kant say that the "fixed and perduring I" forms this letting-stand-against? Does he want to impress upon us that this forming I always lies at the ground of all mental events and "persists" as something which has been relieved of any change of mental events? Should Kant, who worked out the paralogism of substantiality based on the particular laying of the ground for ontology,[270] have meant by the "fixed and perduring" I something like a mental substance? Or did he merely want to confirm that this I is not temporal, but rather that in a certain sense it is infinite and eternal, although not as substance? But why does this supposed confirmation appear precisely where he delimits the finitude of the I, i.e., its letting-stand-against? For the simple reason that this "fixing and perduring" of the I belongs essentially to this letting-stand-against.

This "fixing" and this "perduring" are no ontic assertions concerning the unchangeability of the I, but are transcendental determinations which mean the following: insofar as the I as such brings before itself in advance something like fixedness and perduring in general, it forms the horizon of selfhood within which what is objective becomes experienceable as the same throughout change. The "fixed" I is so called because as "I think," i.e., as "I place before,"[39] it brings before itself [something] like standing and enduring.[40] As I, it forms the correlate of constancy [Beständigkeit] in general.

This pure supplying of the pure look of the present in general, however, is the essence of time itself as pure intuition. The "fixed and perduring" I goes so far as to mean: the I, in the original forming of time, i.e., as original time, forms the letting-stand-against of . . . and its horizon.

Concerning the timelessness and eternality of the I, not only is nothing decided, but it has not subsequently been questioned within the transcendental problematic in general. The I, however, is "fixed and perduring" in this transcendental sense as long as it is temporal, i.e., [as long as it is] as finite self.

Now, if these same predicates are attributed to time, that does not simply mean: time is not "in time." On the contrary, if time as pure self-affection allows the pure succession of the sequence of nows to spring forth for the first time, then this, which springs forth from it and which, so to speak, comes to be discerned for itself alone in the customary "chronology," essentially cannot be sufficient to determine the full essence of time.

---

270. A 348ff., B 406ff.

Accordingly, if we are to come to a decision regarding the "temporality," or rather the timelessness, of the I, then the original essence of time as self-affection must be taken as our guide. And wherever Kant denies, with full justification, a temporal character to pure reason and to the I of pure apperception, he merely says that reason may not be subject to "temporal form."[41]

In this sense alone, the deletion of the "at the same time" in the formulation of the "Principle of Contradiction" is also justified.[271] Hence, Kant argues on this point: if we grant what is said about the "at the same time" [das "Zugleich"] and hence "time" ["Zeit"] in the "Principle of Contradiction," then the principle would be restricted to empirical, accessible beings "within time." However, this basic principle rules all thought of anything at all. Consequently, the determination of time has no place in it.[b]

And yet—the more certain it is that the "at the same time" is a determination of time, the less it has to mean the "within-time-ness" of beings. Rather, the "at the same time" expresses that temporal character which, as preliminary "recognition" ("pre-paration"), originally belongs to all identification as such. However, this lies solidly at the ground of both the possibility and the impossibility of contradiction.

With his orientation toward the nonoriginal essence of time, Kant must deny the temporal character of the "Principle of Contradiction," for it is illogical to want essentially to determine what time itself is originally with the help of a product derived from it. Precisely because in its innermost essence the self is originally time itself, the I cannot be grasped as "temporal," i.e., as within time. Pure sensibility (time) and pure reason are not just of the same type; rather they belong together in the unity of the same essence, which makes possible the finitude of human subjectivity in its wholeness.

---

271. See above, §33c, p. 128f. A passage from the dissertation of 1770 shows that Kant himself wavers in his judgment concerning the "at the same time": "Tantum vero abest, ut quis unquam temporis conceptum adhuc rationis ope aliunde deducat et explicet, ut potius ipsum principium contradictionis eundem praemittat ac sibi conditionis loco substernat. A enim et non A non *repugnant*, nisi *simul* (h.e. tempore eodem) cogitata de *eodem* . . . De mundi sensibilis atque intelligibilis forma et principiis." (§14,5, *Werke*, ed. Cassirer, vol. II, p. 417.[a]) Here Kant shows the impossibility of the "rational" derivation of time, i.e., of its intuitive character, through a reference to the fact that all "*ratio*," even the grounding principle of thinking in general, presupposes "time." Nevertheless, it indeed remains obscure as to which "temporal" meaning the "*tempore eodem*" has. If it goes so far as to mean "in the same now," then Moses Mendelsohn was justified when he wrote in a letter to Kant (25 December 1770), with reference to the preceding passage: "I believe the stipulation *eodem tempore* to have been unnecessary for the Principle of Contradiction. Insofar as it is the same subject, A and *non* A cannot be predicated of it, even at different times, and nothing further is required of the concept of the impossible than that the same subject have two predicates, A and *non* A. One can also say: *impossibile est, non A praedicatum de subjecto A*." (Kant, *Werke*, vol. IX, p. 93.)

a. In this regard, what is more, see Haering, *Der Duisburg'sche Nachlaß*, 10.[6] (p. 60).

b. See WS 1935/36 [*Die Frage nach dem Ding. Zu Kants Lehre von den transzendentalen Grundsätzen*, GA, vol. 41], p. 175f. [*What Is a Thing?* tr. Barton and Deutsch, p. 172f.]

§35. The Originality of the Previously Laid Ground
and the Problem of Metaphysics

Kant's laying of the ground for metaphysics asks about the grounds for the intrinsic possibility of the essential unity of ontological knowledge. The ground upon which it comes is the transcendental power of imagination. As opposed to the arrangement of two basic sources for the mind (sensibility and understanding), the transcendental power of imagination obtrudes as an intermediate faculty. The more original interpretation of this previously laid ground, however, unveils this intermediate faculty not just as original, unifying center, but rather it unveils this center as the root of both stems.

Thus the way is opened to the original ground for the source of both basic sources.[42] The interpretation of the transcendental power of imagination as root, i.e., the elucidation of how the pure synthesis allows both stems to grow forth from out of it and how it maintains them, leads back from itself to that in which this root is rooted: to original time. As the original, threefold-unifying forming of future, past, and present in general, this is what first makes possible the "faculty" of pure synthesis, i.e., that which it is able to produce, namely, the unification of the three elements of ontological knowledge, in the unity of which transcendence is formed.

The modes of pure synthesis—pure apprehension, pure reproduction, pure recognition—are not therefore three in number because they refer to the three elements of pure knowledge, but rather because, originally unified in themselves, as time-forming, they constitute the ripening of time itself. Only because these modes of pure synthesis are originally unified in the threefold-unifying of time, is there also to be found in them the possibility for the original unification of the three elements of pure knowledge. For that reason, however, the original unifying which is apparently only the mediating, intermediate faculty of the transcendental power of imagination, is in fact none other than original time. This rootedness in time alone enables the transcendental power of imagination in general to be the root of transcendence.

Original time makes possible the transcendental power of imagination, which in itself is essentially spontaneous receptivity and receptive spontaneity. Only in this unity can pure sensibility as spontaneous receptivity and pure apperception as receptive spontaneity belong together and form the unified essence of a finite, pure, sensible reason.

If, however, as occurs in the second edition, the transcendental power of imagination is deleted as a particular grounding faculty and if its function is taken over by the understanding as mere spontaneity, then the possibility of grasping pure sensibility and pure thinking with regard to their unity in a finite, human reason diminishes, as does even the possibility of making it into a problem. However, because the transcendental power of imagination, on the grounds of its indissoluble, original structure, opens up the possibility of the laying of a ground for ontological knowledge, and thereby for metaphysics, then for this reason the first edition remains closer to the innermost thrust of the problematic of a laying of the ground for metaphysics. With reference to this most central question of the whole work, therefore, it [the first edition] deserves a fundamental priority over the second. All reinterpretation [*Umdeutung*] of the pure power of imagination as a function of pure thinking—a re-interpretation which "German Idealism" even accentuated subsequent to the second edition of the *Critique of Pure Reason*—misunderstands its specific essence.

Original time allows the pure formation of transcendence to occur. Based on the previously presented, more original[43] unveiling of the previously laid ground, we now also understand for the first time, retrospectively, the innermost thrust of the five stages of the ground-laying and the meaning which its nucleus—the Transcendental Schematism—has been adjudged as having.

Because transcendence ripens in original time, [instances of] ontological knowledge are "transcendental determinations of time."

It is true that this necessary central function of time is always first shown by Kant in such a way that it is just introduced as the universal form of all representations. However, what remains decisive is the context within which this occurs. The "Preliminary Remark" to the Transcendental Deduction[44] is intended to show the extent to which the three modes of pure synthesis in themselves are originally unified. Indeed, Kant does not succeed in expressly bringing them to light as time-forming and hence as unified in original time. All the same, the fundamental function of time is emphasized precisely here, namely, with the analysis of the second synthesis, that of reproduction in the imagination.

What is it that constitutes the "a priori ground of a necessary synthetic unity" of a possible and indeed representing restoring of the being to specific, direct presence? "What that something is we soon discover when we consider that appearances are not things in themselves, but are rather the mere play of our representations, which in the end emerge from determinations of inner sense."[272]

Now does this mean: for itself the being is nothing and dissolves in a playing of representations? In no way. Kant wants to say: the encountering of the being itself occurs for a finite creature in a representing whose pure representations of objectivity as such have played up to one another [*aufeinander eingespielt*]. This Being-played-up [*Eingespieltsein*] is tantamount to the end, i.e., it is determined in advance in such a way that in general it can be played out in a play-space [*in einem Spiel-Raum abspielen kann*]. This [play-space] is formed through pure determinations of the inner sense. The pure inner sense

---

272. A 101.

is pure self-affection, i.e., original time. The pure schemata as transcendental determinations of time are what form the horizon of transcendence.

Because from the first Kant saw the problem of the inner possibility of the essential unity of ontological knowledge from this perspective and because he held fast to the central function of time, he could forego an explicit discussion of time in the presentation of the unity of transcendence on the two paths of the Transcendental Deduction.

Admittedly, in the second edition Kant appears to rescind this transcendental priority of time in the formation of transcendence as such together with the transcendental power of imagination, i.e., he appears to renounce the nucleus of the laying of the ground for metaphysics, the Transcendental Schematism.

In the second edition, a "General Note on the System of Principles," i.e., [a general note] on the whole of ontological knowledge, was inserted.[273] It begins with the sentence: "It is quite noteworthy that we cannot recognize the possibility of a thing according to the mere category, but must always have an intuition at hand in order to expose with respect to same the objective reality of the pure concept of the understanding." Here, in a few words, we have expressed the essential necessity of the pure sensibilization of the notions, i.e., their presentation in a "pure image." However, the fact that this pure image must be pure intuition as time is not stated.

On the contrary, the next paragraph begins with an explicit reference to the previous sentence: "It is even more noteworthy, however, that in order to understand the possibility of things in conformity with the categories, and so to demonstrate the *objective reality* of the latter, we need not just intuitions, but intuitions that are always *external intuitions*."[274] Here the transcendental function of space comes to the fore. That Kant himself has hereby opened up a new insight is unmistakable. Space also enters into the pure schematism. Nevertheless, the chapter on the Schematism in the second edition has in no way been altered in this sense. Must we not infer, then, that the priority of time has been dropped? This conclusion would not only be rash, it would be a complete misunderstanding of the entire interpretation to this point if we choose to deduce from this passage that time alone is not what originally forms transcendence.

But, one could object, if transcendence is not to be grounded in time alone, Kant is just [being] consistent if, with the delimitation of the priority of time, he eliminates the pure power of imagination. Yet, with this reflection we forget that as pure intuition, pure space is no less rooted transcendentally in the transcendental power of imagination than "time," insofar as this is understood

---

273. B 288ff.
274. B 291.

merely as what is formed in pure intuition as the pure intuited, the pure succession of the sequence of nows. In fact, space in a certain sense is always and necessarily equivalent to time so understood.

However, it is not in this form, but rather as pure self-affection, that time is the more original ground of transcendence. As such, it is also the condition for the possibility of the representing forming, i.e., the making-apparent, of pure space. The rejection of the priority of time in no way follows from the insight into the transcendental function of pure space. Instead, it just develops into the positive problem of showing that, like time, space in a certain sense also belongs to the self as something finite, and that this [self], on the grounds of original time to be sure, is essentially "spatial."

In the second edition, the knowledge that in a certain sense space also belongs to the Transcendental Schematism only makes it clear that this [Schematism] cannot be grasped in its innermost essence as long as time is only grasped as the pure succession of the sequence of nows. It must be understood as pure self-affection; otherwise its function in the schema-formation of every discernibility is lacking.

With that, we encounter a peculiarity, and indeed not an accidental one, pertaining to the whole Kantian [project of] laying the ground for metaphysics. Precisely what was unveiled in the going-back to the ground for the source in fact manifests itself in its essence which forms transcendence. The faculties of the mind which take part, as well as the pure intuition, time, nevertheless are not determined expressly and primarily on the basis of this transcendental function. Instead, they are given during the ground-laying and even at its conclusion, which is still completely within the provisional composition of the first point of departure. The elucidation of the pure schemata as transcendental determinations of time must remain so scanty and opaque because, with the presentation of the Transcendental Schematism, Kant had not prepared a worked-out interpretation of the original essence of time; for time, taken as pure sequence of nows, offers throughout no possible way to the "temporal" interpretation of the notions.[275]

Now, if an interpretation [Interpretation] merely gives back what Kant has expressly said, then from the outset it is not a laying-out [Auslegung], insofar as the task of such a laying-out remains framed as the making visible in its own right of what Kant had brought to light in his ground-laying over and above the explicit formulation.[45] Kant himself, however, was unable to say more about this. But with any philosophical knowledge in general, what is said in uttered propositions must not be decisive. Instead, what must be decisive is what it sets before our eyes as still unsaid, in and through what has been said.

---

275. See above, §22, p. 75f.

Thus the fundamental intention of the present interpretation of the *Critique of Pure Reason* was to make visible in this way the decisive content of this work and thereby to bring out what Kant "had wanted to say." With this procedure, the laying-out creates a maxim of its own which Kant himself would have wanted to know had been applied to the interpretation of philosophical investigations and which he put in the following words at the end of a reply to the critique by the Leibnizian Eberhard: "Thus the *Critique of Pure Reason* may well be the proper *apologia* for Leibniz, even in opposition to his adherents who elevate him with dishonorable words of praise, as it can also be for various older philosophers about whom many writers of the history of philosophy, with all their praise, still let themselves speak nonsense. They do not discover the intentions of these philosophers while they neglect the key to all interpretations [*Auslegungen*] of the pure products of reason on the basis of mere concepts, the critique of reason itself (as the common source for all), and while they cannot see, beyond the etymology of what their predecessors have said, what they had wanted to say."[276]

Certainly, in order to wring from what the words say, what it is they want to say, every interpretation [*Interpretation*] must necessarily use violence. Such violence, however, cannot be roving arbitrariness. The power of an idea which shines forth must drive and guide the laying-out [*Auslegung*]. Only in the power of this idea can an interpretation risk what is always audacious, namely, entrusting itself to the concealed inner passion of a work in order to be able, through this, to place itself within the unsaid and force it into speech. That is one way, however, by which the guiding idea, in its power to illuminate, comes to light.

Kant's laying of the ground for metaphysics leads to the transcendental power of imagination. This is the root of both stems, sensibility and understanding. As such, it makes possible the original unity of ontological synthesis. This root, however, is rooted in original time. The original ground which becomes manifest in the ground-laying is time.

Kant's laying of the ground for metaphysics starts with *Metaphysica Generalis* and thus becomes the question of the possibility of ontology in general.[a] This poses the question concerning the essence of the constitution of the Being of beings, i.e., concerning Being in general.

The laying of the ground for metaphysics grows upon the ground of time. The question concerning Being, the grounding question for a laying of the ground for metaphysics, is the problem of *Being and Time*.

This title contains the guiding idea of the preceding interpretation of the *Critique of Pure Reason* as a laying of the ground for metaphysics. The idea,

---

276. *Über eine Entdeckung*, vol. VI, p. 71.

a. It is nevertheless driven by *Metaphysica Specialis—Theologie*, see p. 145 below.

however, attested to through this interpretation, provides an indication of the problem of a fundamental ontology. This is not to be grasped as something ' supposedly "new," as opposed to the allegedly "old." Rather, it is the expression of the attempt to adopt in an original way what is essential in a laying of the ground for metaphysics, i.e., to aid in the ground-laying through a retrieval [Wiederholung] of its own, more original possibility.

Part Four

The Laying of the Ground for Metaphysics in a Retrieval[1]

By the retrieval of a basic problem, we understand the opening-up of its original, long-concealed possibilities, through the working-out of which it is transformed. In this way it first comes to be preserved in its capacity as a problem. To preserve a problem, however, means to free and keep watch over those inner forces which make it possible, on the basis of its essence, as a problem.

Retrieval of the possible does not just mean the taking-up of what is "customary," "grounded overviews [of which] exist" from which "something can be done." The possible in this sense is always just the all-too-real which everyone manages to manipulate in its prevailing mode of operation. The possible in this sense directly hinders a genuine retrieval, and thereby in general it hinders a relationship to history.

A correctly understood retrieval of the laying of the ground for metaphysics, however, must first have made sure of what constitutes the authentic outcome of the earlier, in this case the Kantian, [ground-laying]. At the same time, the sought-after "result" of the laying of the ground for metaphysics in the *Critique of Pure Reason* and, on that basis, the way in which the findings were determined, must be allowed to test how far the understanding of the possible, which guides all retrieval, reaches, and whether it is a match for what is retrievable.

A. THE LAYING OF THE GROUND FOR METAPHYSICS IN ANTHROPOLOGY

§36. The Previously Laid Ground and the Outcome of the Kantian Laying of the Ground for Metaphysics

In running through the individual stages of the Kantian ground-laying, we saw how it finally hit upon the transcendental power of imagination as the ground for the inner possibility of ontological synthesis, i.e., transcendence. Now, is the establishment of this ground, or rather its more original interpretation as temporality, the result of the Kantian ground-laying? Or does his ground-laying yield something else? Certainly, to establish the aforesaid result there was no need for the effort exerted to exhibit the groundlaying, particularly in its internal workings and in the succession of its steps. The citation of the appropriate quotations regarding the central function of the transcendental power of imagination in the Transcendental Deduction and in the Transcendental Schematism would have been sufficient. But if the outcome does not consist in the knowledge that the transcendental power of imagination constitutes the ground, then what else is the ground-laying to yield?

If the outcome of the ground-laying does not lie in its "result," then we must ask what the ground-laying reveals, in its occurring as such, concerning the problem of a grounding of metaphysics. What occurs in the Kantian ground-laying? Nothing less than this: the grounding of the inner possibility of ontology is brought about as an unveiling of transcendence, i.e., [an unveiling] of the subjectivity of the human subject.

The question as to the essence of metaphysics is the question concerning the unity of the basic faculties of the human "mind." The Kantian ground-laying yields [this conclusion]: the grounding of metaphysics is a questioning with regard to the human being, i.e., anthropology.

And yet, did not the first attempt to grasp the Kantian ground-laying more originally, namely, the going-back to its anthropology, break down?[277] Certainly, insofar as it was shown that Anthropology offers to the interpretation of knowledge and its two sources was brought to light in a more original form precisely through the *Critique of Pure Reason*. But from that, all that now follows is that the Anthropology worked out by Kant is an empirical one and not one which is adequate for the transcendental problematic, i.e., it is not pure. That now makes the demand for an adequate, i.e., a "philosophical anthropology" for the purpose of a laying of the ground for metaphysics, even more pressing.

---

277. See above, §26, p. 89ff.

That the outcome of the Kantian ground-laying lies in the insight into the necessary connectedness of anthropology and metaphysics can even be verified unambiguously through Kant's own assertions. Kant's laying of the ground for metaphysics takes aim at a grounding of "metaphysics in its final purpose,ª" of *Metaphysica Specialis*, to which belong the three disciplines of Cosmology, Psychology, and Theology. As critique of pure reason, this grounding must nevertheless understand these [disciplines] in their innermost essence, if indeed metaphysics is to be grasped in its possibility and its limits as "natural human tendency." The innermost essence of human reason demonstrates itself, however, in those interests which, as human, always move it. "All the interests of my reason (both speculative and practical) are united in the following three questions:

1. *What can I know?*
2. *What should I do?*
3. *What may I hope?*"[278]

These three questions, however, are those associated with the three divisions of authentic metaphysics, as *Metaphysica Specialis*.[b] Human knowledge refers to nature in the widest sense of what is at hand (Cosmology); deeds [*das Tun*] are human actions [*Handeln des Menschen*] and refer to human personality and freedom (Psychology); hope aims at immortality as blessedness, i.e., as the unification with God (Theology).

These three original interests do not determine the human being as a creature of nature, but rather as a "citizen of the world." They constitute the object of Philosophy "in the aims of the world-citizen" ["*in weltbürgerlicher Absicht*"], i.e., they constitute the domain of authentic philosophy. Hence Kant says in the introduction to his lectures on Logic, where he develops the concept of Philosophy in general: "The field of Philosophy, in this context of world citizenship, allows for the following questions to be brought:

1. What can I know?
2. What should I do?
3. What may I hope?
4. What is the human being?"[279]

Here a fourth question appears together with the preceding three. But is not this fourth question concerning the human being attached superficially to the first three, and superfluous as well, if we consider that *Psychologia Rationales*, as a discipline of *Metaphysica Specialis*, already treats human beings?

However, Kant did not simply piece this fourth question onto the first three.

---

278. A 804f., B 832f.
279. *Werke*, vol. VIII, p. 343.

a. Philosophy as *teleologia rationis humanae, Critique of Pure Reason*.
b. wrong! Freedom belongs to Cosmology because it was thought of as "primordial" ["*Ursache*"] — see SS 1930 [*Der Anfang der abendländischen Philosophie*, GA, vol. 35].

Rather, he says: "Basically, we can classify all of these under Anthropology because the first three questions refer to the last."[280]

With this, Kant himself unequivocally expresses the proper outcome of his laying of the ground for metaphysics. The attempt at a retrieval of the ground-laying hereby receives a clear directive with regard to its task. To be sure, Kant speaks only in general of Anthropology. However, according to what we have discussed above, it stands beyond doubt that only a philosophical anthropology can assume the laying of the ground for authentic philosophy, for *Metaphysica Specialis*. Does the retrieval of the Kantian ground-laying not come to pursue as its proper task, therefore, the systematic working-out of a "philosophical anthropology," and hence must it not have determined the idea of the same beforehand?

§37. The Idea of a Philosophical Anthropology

What belongs to a philosophical anthropology? What is anthropology in general, and how does it become one which is philosophical? Anthropology means the science of man [*Menschenkunde*]. It embraces all that is knowable [*erkundbar*] relative to the nature of man as this corporeal, ensouled, spiritual creature. Within the domain of anthropology, however, fall not only man's human qualities which, because they are at hand, are discernible and distinguish this determinate species from animals and plants, but also his latent abilities, the differences according to character, race, and sex. And inasmuch as human beings appear to be not only creatures of nature, but also creatures that act and create, anthropology must also seek to grasp what the human being, as one who acts, can and should "make out of itself." Man's abilities and obligations[2] are based finally and specifically on fundamental attitudes which man as such can always take up and which we call "Worldviews"—the "psychology" of which delimits the whole of the science of man.

What is present in Anthropology, as the somatic, biological, psychological consideration of the human being, all flows together as Characterology, Psychoanalysis, Ethnology, Pedagogical Psychology, Cultural Morphology, and the Typology of World-views. This is not only vast from the standpoint of its content, but above all it is fundamentally heterogenous with respect to the manner of posing questions, claims of grounding, the intent of the presentation and the form of communication, and finally with respect to the guiding presuppositions. Insofar as all these [differences], and ultimately the totality of beings in general, in some way can always refer to humans and, accordingly,

---

280. Ibid., p. 344.

can be ascribed to Anthropology, it [Anthropology] becomes so comprehensive that the idea of it becomes mired in complete indeterminacy.

Today, then, Anthropology is no longer just the name for a discipline, nor has it been such for some time. Instead, the word describes a fundamental tendency of man's contemporary position with respect to himself and to the totality of beings. According to this fundamental position, something is only known and understood if it is given an anthropological explanation. Anthropology seeks not only the truth about human beings, but instead it now demands a decision as to what truth in general can mean.

No time has known so much and such a variety about mankind as is the case today. No time has been able to present its knowledge of mankind so urgently and in so captivating a manner as is the case today. No time has previously been able to offer this knowledge as quickly and easily as today. But also, no time has known less about what man is than today.[3] In no other time has man become as questionable as in ours.[281]

However, is not precisely this breadth of and uncertainty about anthropological questions sufficient to allow a Philosophical Anthropology to arise and, for the effort, sufficient to bestow upon it a particular force? With the idea of a Philosophical Anthropology, has not that discipline been attained upon which the whole of philosophy must concentrate?

Several years ago, Max Scheler had already spoken of this Philosophical Anthropology: "In a certain sense, all the central problems of philosophy can be reduced to the question of what man is and what metaphysical place and situation he occupies within the totality of Being, the world, and God."[282] But Scheler also saw directly and with particular keenness that the variety of determinations regarding the essence of human beings cannot be allowed simply to be packed together in a common definition: "The human being is so broad, motley, and diverse a thing that the definitions all fall a bit short. Man has too many facets."[283] So Scheler's endeavors, which in his last years intensified and ushered in a new fruitfulness, were directed not only at attaining a unified idea of man, but just as much at the working-out of the essential difficulties and complications associated with this task.[284]

But perhaps the basic difficulty of a Philosophical Anthropology does not lie primarily in the task of attaining the systematic unity of the essential determinations of this multifaceted creature. Perhaps instead a difficulty lies in its concept itself—a difficulty which even the richest and most distinct anthropological knowledge can no longer gloss over.

---

281. See Max Scheler, *Die Stellung des Menschen im Kosmos* (1928), p. 13f.

282. See *Zur Idee des Menschen: Abhandlungen und Aufsätze*, vol. 1 (1915), p. 319. In the second and third editions (1927), the volumes appeared under the title *Vom Umsturz der Werte* (*Werke*, vol. III, p. 173).

283. Ibid., p. 324 (*Werke*, vol. III, p. 175).

284. See *Die Stellung des Menschen im Kosmos*.

By what means, then, does an anthropology in general become a philosophical one? Is it simply due to the fact that its knowledge is differentiated in the
degree of its universality from knowledge of the empirical, whereby it remains
permanently questionable as to the point at which the degree of universality
appropriate to empirical knowledge ends and that appropriate to philosophical knowledge begins?

Certainly, an anthropology can be called philosophical insofar as its method
is a philosophical one, perhaps in the sense of an essential consideration of
the human being. This, then, is intended to differentiate between the being
called man [on the one hand] and plants, animals, and the remaining regions
of beings [on the other], and thereby to work out the specific, essential
composition of this determinate region of beings. Philosophical Anthropology
then becomes a regional ontology of human beings, and as such it remains
arranged alongside the other ontologies which, along with it, spread out over
the entire field of beings. Without doubt and, above all, not on the grounds
of the inner structure of its problematic, Philosophical Anthropology thus
understood is not at the center of philosophy.

Anthropology, however, can also be philosophical provided that, as Anthropology, it determines in particular either the goal of philosophy or its point
of departure or both at once. If the goal of Philosophy lies in the working-out
of a world-view, then an Anthropology will have to delimit the "place of man
in the cosmos." And if man is reputed to be that being which is simply the
first given and most certain in the order of grounding an absolutely certain
knowledge, then the building-up of philosophy planned in this way must
bring human subjectivity in as the central starting point. The first task can be
compatible with the second and, as anthropological investigations, both can
make use of the method and the results of a regional ontology of human
beings.

But it is on the basis of precisely these various possibilities for delimiting
the philosophical character of an anthropology that the indeterminateness of
this idea arises. The indeterminateness increases if we keep sight of the variety
of anthropological knowledge which lies at the heart of every Philosophical
Anthropology, at least at the outset.

As natural and self-evident as the idea of a Philosophical Anthropology may
be, for all its ambiguity, and as irresistibly as it increases in value, so too it
becomes increasingly necessary to combat the "anthropologism" in Philosophy.
The idea of a Philosophical Anthropology is not only not sufficiently determined, but also its function in the whole of philosophy remains unclarified
and undecided.

This deficiency, however, has its basis in the inherent limits of the idea of
a Philosophical Anthropology. For it is itself not expressly grounded in the
essence of Philosophy, but is instead fixed with reference to the goal of philosophy, which is initially composed superficially, and its possible point of

departure. Thus the determination of this idea finally ends in the fact that anthropology presents a possible catchment area for the central philosophical problems, a characterization whose superficiality and philosophical question-ableness jump out at us.

But even if anthropology in a certain sense gathers into itself all the central problems of philosophy, why are these able to lead back to the question of what man is? Are they only able to lead back to this question if someone has the inspiration to undertake it, or must they lead back to it? If they must do so, where does the ground for this necessity lie? Perhaps in the fact that the central problems of philosophy come forth from man, perhaps not only in the sense that man poses them, but rather because in their inherent content they refer to him? But to what extent are all central philosophical problems resident in the essence of human beings? In general, then, which are the central problems and where does their center lie? What does philosophizing mean if its problematic has such a center which is resident in the essence of human beings?

As long as these questions are not unpacked and determined with respect to their inner systematics, not even the inherent limits of the idea of a philoso-phical anthropology become discernable. Without discussion of these ques-tions, the basis for the decisiveness regarding the essence, right, and function of a philosophical anthropology within philosophy is lacking.

Again and again we encounter attempts to offer a philosophical anthropo-logy in understandable arguments and to maintain the central position of this discipline without grounding it in the essence of philosophy. Again and again the opponents of anthropology are able to refer back to the fact that human beings do not belong at the center of beings, but that there is a "sea" of beings "alongside" them—a rejection of the central position of philosophical anthro-pology, which is no more philosophical than is affirming it.

Thus, a critical consideration of the idea of a philosophical anthropology yields not only its indeterminateness and its limits, but also makes clear above all that in general the basis and framework for a fundamental question regar-ding its essence are lacking.

Hence, it was also hasty, if only because Kant reduces the three questions of authentic metaphysics to the fourth, what is man, in order to grasp this question as anthropological and to carry the laying of the ground for metaphy-sics over to a philosophical anthropology. Anthropology does not ground metaphysics, therefore, just because it is anthropology.

But[a] was not the proper outcome of the Kantian ground-laying just this coherence of the questions concerning the human essence with the grounding

---

a. Yes [Doch]

of metaphysics? Hence, must not this coherence guide the task of a ground-laying, which is to be retrieved?

However, the critique of the idea of philosophical anthropology shows that it is not sufficient simply to pose the fourth question, what is man. On the contrary, the indeterminacy of this question indicates that in the end, and even now, we have not yet come into possession of the decisive task of the Kantian ground-laying.

§38. The Question Concerning the Human Essence and the Authentic Result of the Kantian Ground-Laying

It becomes increasingly obvious that we are not coming any closer to the proper outcome of the Kantian ground-laying as long as we hold to any definition or to a formulated thesis. We only come closer to Kant's authentic philosophizing if, with even more resolve than previously, we ask not about what Kant says, but instead about what occurs in his ground-laying. The more original interpretation of the *Critique of Pure Reason* carried out above takes aim only at exhibiting this occurrence.

But what has actually resulted from the occurrence of the Kantian ground-laying? Not that the transcendental power of imagination is the previously-laid ground; not that this ground-laying becomes a question of the essence of human reason. Rather, as a result of unveiling the subjectivity of the subject, Kant falls back from the ground which he himself had laid.

Does this falling-back not belong as well to the result? What occurs therein? Perhaps an inconsistency to which Kant should own up? Are the falling-back and the not-going-to-the-end just something negative? By no means. On the contrary, they make it obvious that with his ground-laying, Kant himself undermines the floor upon which he initially placed the *Critique*. The concept of pure reason and the unity of a pure, sensible reason become the problem. Inquiring into the subjectivity of the subject, the "Subjective Deduction," leads us into darkness. Therefore, Kant does not refer to his Anthropology, not just because it is empirical and not pure, but rather because in and through the execution of the ground-laying itself, the manner of questioning regarding human beings becomes questionable.

It is not a matter of searching for the answer to the question, what is man. Rather, it is first of all a matter of asking how, in a laying of the ground for metaphysics in general, we can and must have *asked about* man exclusively.

The questionableness of the questioning about human beings is the problematic which is forced to light in the process of the Kantian laying of the ground for metaphysics. Now it appears for the first time: Kant's falling-back before the ground which he himself unveiled, before the transcendental power of imagination, is—for purposes of the rescue of pure reason, i.e., of holding-fast to the proper foundation—that movement of philosophizing which makes manifest the breaking-open of the foundation and thus makes manifest the abyss of metaphysics.

On the basis of this outcome the original interpretation [*Auslegung*] of the Kantian ground-laying, carried out above, first acquires its justification and the grounding of its necessity. It is not the empty pressing after what is more original, not the wanting-to-know-better, but just the task of freeing the in-nermost drive of the ground-laying, and with it its ownmost problematic which guides all the efforts of the interpretation [*Interpretation*].

If the ground-laying, however, perhaps does not push aside the question 'what is man,' but still does not obtain a clear-cut answer to it, if instead it first makes the question visible in its questionableness, how then does it stand with the fourth of Kant's questions, to which *Metaphysica Specialis*, and with it authentic philosophizing, is to be reduced?

We will thus only be able to pose this fourth question as it should have been posed if we work it out as a question on the basis of the understanding of the outcome of the ground-laying which we have now attained and if we forego a hasty answer.

It is a matter of asking: Why can the three questions—(1) What can I know? (2) What should I do? (3) What may I hope?—be "related to" the fourth? Why "can we . . . assign all of these to Anthropology"? What is common to these three questions, in what respect are they unified so that they indeed can lead back to a fourth? How must this fourth question itself be asked so that it can take up and bear each of the three questions unified within it?

The innermost interest of human reason unites these three questions in itself. In it, an ability, a duty, and an allowing [to hope][4] of human reason stand in question.

Where an ability is questionable and wants to be delimited in terms of its possibilities, it already places itself within a disability [*in einem Nicht-Können*]. An all-powerful entity need not ask: What can I do, i.e., What can I not do? It not only does not have to so ask, but according to its essence it cannot pose this question at all. This disability, however, is no deficiency; it is rather what is untouched in every deficiency and "not." Whosoever asks: What can I do? betrays thereby a finitude. Whosoever comes wholly to be moved by his inner-most interest in this question reveals a finitude in the depths of his essence.

Where a duty is questionable, the questioning creature hovers between "yes" and "no" and worries about what it should not do. A creature that is fundamentally interested in a duty knows itself in a not-yet-having-fulfilled, so that what indeed it should do becomes questionable to it. This not-yet of a fulfilling, which is itself still undetermined, gives us a clue that a creature whose innermost interest is with a duty is fundamentally finite.

Where an allowing [to hope] becomes questionable, it rises up in what has been conceded or in what remains denied to the questioner. What is asked about is what can be placed in the expectation and what cannot. All expecting, however, needs a privation. If this neediness even arises in the innermost interest of human reason, then it attests to that reason as one which is essentially finite.

But human reason does not just disclose finitude in these questions; rather, its innermost interest is with finitude itself. For this reason, it is not a matter of doing away with the ability, duty, and allowing [to hope], in this way to extinguish finitude, but rather the reverse. It is precisely a question of becoming certain of this finitude in order to hold oneself in it.

Accordingly, finitude does not depend simply upon pure human reason, but instead its finitude is perishing [*Verendlichung*], i.e., "Care" about the potentiality-to-be-finite.[5]

From this it follows that: human reason is not finite just because it poses the three questions cited above, but the reverse: it poses these questions because it is finite, indeed it is so finite that in its Being-rational this finitude itself is at issue. Because these three questions ask about this one [problem], finitude, "they let themselves be related" to the fourth: What is a human being?

The three questions, however, do not simply allow themselves to be related to the fourth. Rather, in themselves they are in general no different from it, i.e., according to their essence they must be related to it. However, this relation is then a more essentially necessary one only if the fourth question abandons its intimately given generality and indeterminacy and attains an unequivocality so that in it we can ask about the finitude in human beings.

As such a question, however, it is not legitimately just subordinate to the first three. Rather, it is transformed into the first, which then discharges the remaining three from itself.

But with this outcome, in spite of all the determinacy of the question regarding human beings, and even because of it, the problem contained in this question is honed for the first time. As a question about human beings, it becomes questionable what kind of question this question is, whether in general it can be another anthropological question. Thus the outcome of the Kantian ground-laying now makes it acutely clear for the first time that a more original possibility of retrieval has become visible in it.

The laying of the ground for metaphysics is grounded in the question concerning the finitude in human beings, so that indeed this finitude can now become a problem for the first time. The laying of the ground for metaphysics is a "disentangling" (analytic) of our knowledge, i.e., of finite knowledge, into its elements. Kant calls it a "study of our inner nature."[285] But this study, however, is not just an arbitrary, directionless questioning about human be-

---

285. A 703, B 731.

ings. Rather, "to the philosopher . . . [it] even [becomes] a duty"[286] if the problematic which essentially guides it is grasped with sufficient originality and comprehensiveness and if from that the "inner nature" of "our" self as the finitude in human beings is made into a problem.

"Philosophical Anthropology" may indeed produce such diverse and essential knowledge about human beings, yet for just that reason it can never rightly claim to be a fundamental discipline of philosophy because it is anthropology. On the contrary: it conceals in itself the constant danger that the necessity of developing the question concerning human beings first and foremost as a question, with a view toward a laying of the ground for metaphysics, will remain concealed.

All the same, that and how "Philosophical Anthropology"—apart from the problem of laying the ground for metaphysics—presents a particular kind of task, cannot be discussed here.

B. THE PROBLEM OF FINITUDE IN HUMAN BEINGS AND THE METAPHYSICS OF DASEIN

The present interpretation of the *Critique of Pure Reason* has been undertaken in order to bring to light this fundamental problem of the necessity of the question concerning the finitude in human beings for the purpose of a laying of the ground for metaphysics. Accordingly, finitude also had to be recalled in advance at the start of the interpretation and then constantly during its execution. If in his ground-laying Kant undermines the previously established foundation which underlies it, then that now means: what was singled out at the beginning of the interpretation as Kant's unspoken "presuppositions,"[287] the essence of knowledge and its finitude, have attained the character of decisive problems. Finitude and the peculiarity of the question concerning it first decide from the ground up the inner form of a Transcendental "Analytic" of the subjectivity of the subject.

§39. The Problem of a Possible Determination of Finitude in Human Beings

How are we to ask about finitude in human beings? Is this in general a serious problem? Is not the finitude of human beings evident everywhere and always in a thousand different ways?

---

286. Ibid. [Ellipses added in the 4th edition—tr.]
287. See above, Part 2, p. 13ff.

Thus, in order to designate the finite in human beings it might suffice to cite any of our imperfections. In this way, we gain, at best, evidence for the fact that the human being is a finite creature. However, we learn neither wherein the essence of his finitude exists, nor even how this finitude completely determines the human being from the ground up as the being it is.

Even if we could succeed in adding up the sum of all human imperfections and in "abstracting" what is common to them, we would grasp nothing of the essence of finitude because it remains questionable in advance whether the imperfections of man in general allow his imperfections to be seen immediately, or whether on the contrary they are not remote, factical consequences of the essence of his finitude and hence only become understandable through it. And even if the impossible were possible, even if a Being-created of man [ein Geschaffensein des Menschen] could be rationally proven, then by means of the characterization of man as an *ens creatum* we would only prove once more the fact of his finitude, would not exhibit its essence, and would not determine this essence to be the basic constitution of the Being of man. So it is, then, that it is not at all self-evident how the question of the finitude in man—the most everyday manifestation of his essence—is in general to be fixed. The preceding investigation only yielded this one [point]: the present question concerning finitude in human beings is no random exploring of human qualities. On the contrary, it arises in the course of the task of the laying of the ground for metaphysics. As a fundamental question, it is demanded by this task itself. Consequently, the problematic of the laying of the ground for metaphysics must in itself offer guidance concerning the direction in which the question of the finitude of human beings has to move.

But if the task of the laying of the ground for metaphysics allows for a more original retrieval, then by means of this the essential connectedness of the problem of ground-laying and the question which led from it concerning the finitude in human beings must come to light more clearly and more precisely.

The Kantian laying of the ground for metaphysics began with the grounding of what underlies authentic metaphysics, or *Metaphysica Specialis*—began with the grounding of *Metaphysica Generalis*. This, however—as "ontology"—is already the form which has been consolidated into a discipline, the form of what, in Antiquity and finally with Aristotle, remains established as a[a] problem of the πρώτη φιλοσοφία, of authentic philosophizing. The question concerning the ὄν ἧ ὄν (or the being as such), however, is maintained there in an admittedly obscure connection to the question concerning beings as a whole (θεῖον).

The title "Metaphysics" denotes a conception of the problem in which both basic directions pertaining to the question concerning the being, and at the

---

a. the

same time its possible unity, are questionable. In this connection, we will again learn whether the two directions for the questioning in general, previously cited, [in fact] exhaust the whole of the problematic of a fundamental knowledge of the being.

But if the question concerning the finitude in human beings is to be determined on the basis of a more original retrieval of the laying of the ground for metaphysics, then the Kantian question itself must be turned away from an orientation to the fixed discipline and systematic of Scholastic metaphysics and must be transferred to the free field of the particular problematic. At the same time, therein lies the reason that the Aristotelian way of posing the question likewise cannot be adopted as something finished.

With the τί τὸ ὄν, the question concerning the being has indeed been posed. However, to pose a question[b] does not yet mean to take hold of the problematic which lies within it and to work it out. The extent to which the problem of metaphysics still remains veiled in the question τί τὸ ὄν allows us to recognize in it, first, that nothing whatever has been cut from this question, and, second, how, to the extent that it is to be grasped as a problem, the problem of finitude in human beings is included in it. Still less can we gain a direction for it merely by expressing and echoing the question of how we may ask about the finitude in human beings. Retrieval of the problem of the laying of the ground for *Metaphysica Generalis* thus does not mean echoing the question of what the being as such might be. The retrieval must develop this question, which we call the Question of Being for short, as a problem. This development has to show the extent to which the problem of the finitude in human beings and the investigations it prescribes necessarily belong to the mastering of the Question of Being. Stated basically: the essential connection between Being as such (not the being) and the finitude in human beings must be brought to light.

§40. The Original Working-Out of the Question of Being as the Way to the Problem of Finitude in Human Beings

The fundamental question of the ancient φυσιολόγοι[288] concerning beings in general (concerning the λόγος about the φύσις) was built up—and that is the inner development of metaphysics from its beginning to the time of Aristotle—from the indeterminacy and fullness of its initial universality to the

---

288. See Aristotle, *Physics*, G 4, 203b 15. Moreover, in the *Critique of Pure Reason* (A 845, B 873) Kant speaks of the "Physiology of Pure Reason."

b. See SS 1930 *[Der Anfang der abendländischen Philosophie*, GA, vol. 35].

determinacy of both directions of questioning which, according to Aristotle, constitute authentic philosophizing.

As obscure as their connection also remains, still in one respect it is possible to establish an order of precedence between them. If the question concerning the being as a whole and in its principle divisions already presupposes a certain grasping of what the being is as such, then the question of the ὄν ἠ ὄν must take precedence over the question of the being as a whole. The question of what the being in general and as such is, is the first one in the order of the possible pursuit of a fundamental knowledge of the being as a whole. Whether this priority also falls to it in the ordering of the decisive self-grounding of metaphysics, however, is a question that we can only mention here.

But is not the general question τί τὸ ὄν so indeterminate that in general it is no longer asked, and it denies us any clue as to where and how an answer to it is to be sought?

In the question as to what the being as such might be, we have asked what generally determines the being as a being. We call it the Being of the being, and we call the question concerned with it the Question of Being. It asks about what determines the being as such. This determining should be known in the How of its determining, it should be interpreted, i.e., it should be grasped, as such and such. In order to be able to grasp the essential determinacy of the being through Being, however, the determining itself must be sufficiently comprehensible; *Being as such*, and not the being as such, must first be grasped. Thus in the question τί τὸ ὄν (What is the being?) lies the more original question: *What does Being mean, which is already understood in advance in every question?*

If the question τί τὸ ὄν is already incomprehensible enough, how then can one more original and indeed "more abstract" allow a concrete problematic to spring forth?

In order to verify that such a [concrete problematic] presents itself, however, a reference to something in ancient philosophy which has been accepted as all too self-evident will suffice. We determine and interrogate with reference to its what-Being (τί ἐστιν) the being which is manifest to us in every type of relationship [we have] to it. Philosophy calls this what-Being *essentia* (essence). It makes a being possible in that which it is. Therefore, the designation *possibilitas* (inner possibility) also stands for the thingness of a thing (*realitas*). The appearing (εἶδος) of a being gives the same information [in response] to the question of what it is. The what-Being of the being is therefore called ἰδέα.

To every being the question then arises, or it has always already been answered, whether it—the being with this determinate what-Being—might be, or rather might not be. Hence, we also determine the being according to its "that-Being"[6] (ὅτι ἐστιν), which philosophy is accustomed to expressing terminologically as *existentia* (actuality).

To every being, then, "there is" what-Being and that-Being, *essentia* and *existentia*, possibility and actuality. Does "Being" mean the same thing here [in both expressions]? If not, how is it that the Being in what-Being and that-Being has been split? Is there this all too self-evident difference—*essentia* and *existentia*—which was snatched up, just as there are dogs and also cats, or is there a problem awaiting us here which finally must be posed and which obviously *can* only be posed *if what is asked about becomes, what is Being as such?*

Without a working-out of this question, are we not lacking any horizon for the attempt to "define" the essentiality of the essence and to "explain" the actuality of the actual?

And is not the meaning of Being as true-Being, which plainly comes to light in every "is" of every proposition whether expressed or unexpressed (but not just there), at the same time always intertwined with the previously cited articulation of the Being in what-Being and that-Being, which was obscure with regard to the ground of its possibility and the type of its necessity?[289]

Is not what lies contained in the problem word "Being" already more than sufficient and all too important? Is it permissible any longer to abide by the indeterminacy of the Question of Being, or must we even risk a still more original step toward the working-out of this question?

How is the question "What does Being mean?" to find its answer if it remains obscure as to from whence in general we can come to expect this answer? Must we not first ask: From whence in general do we lay hold of the point of view from which to determine Being as such and thus to win a concept of Being from out of which the possibility and the necessity of the essential articulation of Being becomes understandable? Hence the question of "First Philosophy," namely, "What is the being as such?" must drive us back beyond the question "What is Being as such?" to the still more original question: *From whence in general are we to comprehend the like of Being, with the entire wealth of articulations and references which are included in it?*

Now, if a more intrinsic connection exists between the laying of the ground for metaphysics and the question concerning finitude in human beings, then the more original working-out of the Question of Being now achieved will reveal in a more elementary manner its essential relation to the problem of finitude.

But for the present this is still opaque, particularly since we may not be inclined at all to expect such a relation to the question which has come up. It may be at issue in Kant's previously cited questions: What am I allowed to hope?, etc. Yet, how is the question of Being, particularly in the form in which it has now been developed as the question concerning the possibility of

---

289. See *Vom Wesen des Grundes*, first section.

comprehending Being in general, to have an essential relation to the finitude in human beings? Within the abstract ontology of a metaphysics which derives its orientation from Aristotle, the Question of Being may acquire a certain sense, and so it may claim the right of a special problem which is scholarly and more or less unorthodox. Nevertheless, an essential relation to finitude in human beings is not obvious.

But if up to now we have clarified the original form of the problem of Being in the orientation derived from the Aristotelian question, this is not to say that the origin of this problem also lies there. On the contrary: authentic philosophizing will only then be able to come upon the Question of Being if this question belongs to the innermost essence of Philosophy, which itself is only as a decisive possibility[a] of human Dasein.

If we ask about the possibility of comprehending something like Being, we do not then invent this "Being" and violently force it into [becoming] a problem in order, perhaps, to take up again a question from the philosophical tradition. Rather, what is asked about is the possibility[b] of comprehending what all of us as human beings already and permanently understand. For its part, the Question of Being as a question concerning the possibility of the concept of Being, springs forth from the preconceptual understanding of Being. Thus the question concerning the possibility of the concept of Being is once again driven back a step to the question concerning the essence of the understanding of Being in general. The task of the laying of the ground for metaphysics, grasped in a more original way, is therefore transformed int the elucidation of the inner possibility for the understanding of Being. The working-out of the Question of Being so conceived brings about for the first time the decision as to whether and in what way the problem of Being by itself shows an inner relation to finitude in human beings.

§41. The Understanding of Being and Dasein in Human Beings

That we human beings comport ourselves toward beings is obvious. Faced with the task of representing beings, we can always specify any being: a being which is not like us and which is also not our equal, a being which is like we ourselves are, and a being which is not like us but which nevertheless, as a self, is our equal. The being is known to us—but Being? Are we not seized with vertigo when we [try to] determine such a thing, even if we should comprehend it properly? Is Being then not something like the Nothing [das

---

a. conditional possibility
b. completely revertible, in the sense of the transcendental posing of the question

Nichts]? In fact, no less a person than Hegel said: "Pure Being and pure Nothing are thus the same."[290]

With the question concerning Being as such, we are poised on the brink of complete obscurity. Yet it is worthwhile not to evade this prematurely, but to bring the full peculiarity of the understanding of Being closer to us. For as impenetrable as the obscurity is which shrouds Being and its meaning, still it remains certain that, at all times and in the entire field of the openness of beings, we understand what Being is in order to concern ourselves with the what-Being and the so-Being of beings, in order to experience and dispute the that-Being, in order to decide about the true-Being [*Wahrsein*] of the being, and in order to mistake it. In every expressing of a proposition, e.g., "today is a holiday," we understand the "is," and equally what Being is.

In the cry "Fire" [we understand] the following: "Fire has broken out,[7] help is needed, he who can save himself—who can bring his own Being to safety—should do so!" But at the same time, if we do not express ourselves in particular about the being and if instead we relate to it silently, we understand its characteristics of what-Being, that-Being, and true-Being, which function with one another, although in a veiled way.

With every mood wherein "something is this way or that," our Being-there [*Da-sein*] becomes manifest to us. We thus understand Being, and yet we lack the concept. For all its constancy and breadth, this preconceptual understanding of Being is for the most part completely indeterminate. The specific manner of Being, e.g., of material things, of plants, animals, human beings, numbers, is known to us, but this knowledge is unrecognized for what it is. Furthermore: the Being of the being, which is understood preconceptually in its full breadth, constancy, and indeterminacy, is given as something completely beyond question. Being [*Sein*] as such comes into question so seldom that it appears as if there "is" nothing of the sort.

The understanding of Being, which we have concisely sketched out, remains on the undisturbed and safe level of the purest self-evidentness. And yet, *if the understanding of Being did not occur,*[a] man could never be as the being which he is, and this would be so regardless of the wonderful faculties with which human beings have been equipped. Moreover, man is a being in the midst of beings in such a way that for man the being which he is himself and the being which he is not are always already manifest. We call this mode of the Being of human beings existence.[8] Existence is only possible on the grounds of the understanding of Being.

In man's comportment toward beings which he himself is not, he already finds the being as that from which he is supported, as that on which he has

---

290. *Wissenschaft der Logik*, *Werke*, vol. III, p. 78f.

a. History as destiny of appropriation

depended, as that over which, for all his culture and technology, he can never become master. Depending upon the being which he is not, man is at the same time not master of the being which he himself is.

With the existence of human beings there occurs an irruption into the totality of beings, so that now the being in itself first becomes manifest, i.e., as being, in varying degrees, according to various levels of clarity, in various degrees of certainty. This prerogative, however, of not just being among other beings which are also at hand without these beings becoming manifest as such to themselves, but rather [of being] in the midst of the beings, *of being surrendered to it as such, and itself to have been delivered up as a being*—for this prerogative to exist harbors in itself the need to require the understanding of Being.

The human being could not be the thrown being as a self if in general it *could* not *let* the being as such *be*.[9] In order to allow the being to be what and as it is, however, the existing being[10] must already have projected that it is a being on the strength of what has been encountered. Existence means dependency upon the being as such in the submittance to the being as such which is dependent in this way.

As a mode of Being, existence is in itself finitude,[b] and as such it is only possible on the basis of the understanding of Being. There is and must be something like Being where finitude has come to exist. Thus the understanding of Being which thoroughly dominates human existence, although unknown in its breadth, constancy, indeterminacy, and indisputability, manifests itself as the innermost ground of human finitude.[c] Compared with many other human peculiarities, the understanding of Being does not have the harmless universality of others which frequently occur. Its "universality" is the originality of the innermost ground of the finitude of Dasein. Only because the understanding of Being is the most finitude in what is finite, can it also make possible the so-called "creative" capacities of the finite human creature. And only because it occurs within the ground of finitude, does it have the breadth and constancy, but also the concealedness, previously characterized.

On the grounds of the understanding of Being, man is the there [*das Da*],[11] with the Being of which occurs the opening irruption into the being so that it can show itself as such for a self.[12] *More original than man*[d] *is the finitude of the Dasein in him.*

The working-out of the basic question of *Metaphysica Generalis*, the τί τὸ ὄν, has been thrown back upon the more original idea concerning the inner essence of the understanding of Being, which first and foremost sustains, drives, and directs the explicit questioning concerning the concept of Being.

---

b. Nothingness of the *Nothing* [*Nichtigkeit des Nichtens*]
c. and thus as the *essence* of this "*finitude*"
d. ek-sistent

We strove for the more original apprehension of the basic problem of meta-physics, however, with the intention of making visible the connection between the problem of ground-laying and the question concerning the finitude in human beings. Now it appears: we do not even need first to ask about a relationship between the understanding of Being and the finitude in human beings, that it itself *is* the innermost essence of finitude. With that, however, we have attained the very concept of finitude which is taken as the basis for a problematic of the laying of the ground for metaphysics. If this ground-laying is based on the question of what the human being should be, then the questionable nature of this question at a first level is now removed, i.e., from now on the question concerning the human being has attained determinacy.

If man is only man *on the grounds of the Dasein in him*, then in principle the question as to what is more original than man cannot be anthropological. All anthropology, even Philosophical Anthropology, has already assumed that man is man.

The problem of the laying of the ground for metaphysics is rooted in the question concerning the Dasein in man, i.e., concerning his innermost ground, concerning the understanding of Being as essentially existent finitude. This question about Dasein asks what the essence of the being[e] determined in this way is. Insofar as its essence lies in existence, the question concerning the essence of Dasein is the existential question. Every question concerning the Being of a being, however, and even the question concerning the Being of that being to the constitution of whose Being finitude as the understanding of Being belongs, is metaphysics.

Hence, the laying of the ground for metaphysics is grounded in a meta-physics of Dasein. Is it astonishing, then, that a laying of the ground for metaphysics at the very least must itself be metaphysics, and indeed a preem-inent one?

Kant, in whose philosophizing the problem of the possibility of metaphysics was awake to a degree found in none before or after him, must have under-stood all too little of his innermost intention if this connection did not appear to him. He did speak out in the brightness and tranquility which the comple-tion of the *Critique of Pure Reason* immediately bestowed on him. In 1781, he wrote to his friend and disciple Markus Herz about this work: "This kind of investigation will always remain difficult, for it is equivalent to the Metaphy-sics of Metaphysics . . . ."[291]

This remark decisively puts to rest any attempt to search, even partially, for a "theory of knowledge" in the *Critique of Pure Reason*. At the same time, however, it also obliges any retrieval of a laying of the ground for metaphysics

---

291. *Werke*, vol. IX, p. 198.

e. *Da-sein*, not "being" in the ontic sense

to make up its mind about this "Metaphysics of Metaphysics" to the extent that it is able to place itself on solid footing, safeguarding a possible course for the happening of the ground-laying.

C. THE METAPHYSICS OF DASEIN
AS FUNDAMENTAL ONTOLOGY

No anthropology which understands its own particular questioning and the presuppositions thereof can even claim to develop the problem of a laying of the ground for metaphysics, let alone carry it out. The necessary question for a laying of the ground for metaphysics, namely, that of what man is, is taken over by the metaphysics of Dasein.

The expression is ambiguous in a positive sense. The Metaphysics of Dasein is not just metaphysics about Dasein, but is the metaphysics which occurs necessarily *as Dasein*. But for that reason: it can never become metaphysics "about" Dasein, as for example zoology is about animals. The Metaphysics *of* Dasein is no fixed and ready-for-use "organon" at all. It must always be built up anew amid the transformation of its idea in the working-out of the possibility of metaphysics.

Its fate remains bound to the concealing occurring of metaphysics in Dasein itself, by virtue of which man first numbers or forgets the days and hours, years and centuries [he has devoted] to his endeavors.

The requirements intrinsic to a Metaphysics of Dasein and the difficulty of its determination have been sufficiently demonstrated by the Kantian effort. Its most authentic, correctly understood outcome, however, lies precisely in the unveiling of the connectedness which exists between the question concerning the possibility of ontological synthesis and that of the unveiling of the finitude in human beings, i.e., in the demand for a reflection concerning how a Metaphysics of Dasein is to be concretely realized.

§42. *The Idea of a Fundamental Ontology*

In the posing of its task, in the point of departure, course, and goal of the carrying-through of this task, the laying of the ground for metaphysics must have been guided solely and with constant intensity by the fundamental question of the laying of the ground for metaphysics.[13] This fundamental question is the problem of the inner possibility of the understanding of Being, from out of which all explicit questions concerning Being should be able to grow. The Metaphysics of Dasein, guided by the question of ground-laying, should unveil the constitution of the Being of [*Dasein*] in such a way that this becomes visible as the inner making-possible of the understanding of Being.

The unveiling of the constitution of the Being of Dasein is Ontology. Insofar as the ground for the possibility of metaphysics is found therein—the finitude of Dasein as its fundament—it is called Fundamental Ontology. Locked up in the content of this title is the problem of finitude in human beings, which is decisive for purposes of making the understanding of Being possible.

Fundamental Ontology, however, is only the first level of the Metaphysics of Dasein. What belongs to this [Metaphysics of Dasein] as a whole, and how from time to time it is rooted historically in factical Dasein cannot be discussed here. Now the only task is to clarify the idea of Fundamental Ontology which guided the above interpretation of the *Critique of Pure Reason*. Furthermore, the characterization of Fundamental Ontology should be given only in its distinctive features, in order to show once more the simple sequence of steps by which a previous attempt at the carrying-through of this idea moved.[292]

The constitution of the Being of every being, and that of Dasein in a special sense, only becomes accessible to the understanding insofar as it [the understanding] has the character of projection [*Entwurf*]. Because the understanding—and Fundamental Ontology shows us precisely this—is not just a type of knowing, but on the contrary is primarily a basic moment of existing in general, then the explicit execution of the projecting, and even what is grasped in the ontological, must necessarily be construction.

But construction here does not mean: free-floating thinking-out of something. It is instead a projecting in which the preliminary guidance as well as the taking-off of the projection [*der Absprung des Entwurfs*] must be predetermined and protected. Dasein should be construed in its finitude, namely, with a view toward the intrinsic making-possible of the understanding of Being. Any fundamental-ontological construction asserts its truth in what its projection allows to be seen, i.e., in how it brings Dasein to its manifestness and lets its inner metaphysics be-there [*da-sein*].

The fundamental-ontological construction is distinguished by the fact that it should expose the inner possibility of something which, precisely as what is best known, thoroughly masters all Dasein, but which, nevertheless, is indeterminate and even much too self-evident. This construction can be understood as Dasein's assault upon the primal metaphysical factum in it, an assault which arises from within Dasein itself. This factum consists in the fact that what is most finite in its finitude is indeed known, but nevertheless has not been grasped.

The finitude of Dasein—the understanding of Being—lies *in forgetfulness*.[14]

---

292. See *Being and Time*.

This [forgetfulness] is nothing accidental and temporary, but on the contrary is necessarily and constantly formed. All fundamental-ontological constructions which take aim at the unveiling of the inner possibility of the understanding of Being must, in projecting, wrest the forgetfulness away from what is apprehended in the projection.

The basic fundamental-ontological act[15] of the Metaphysics of Dasein as the laying of the ground for metaphysics is hence a "remembering again."

True remembering, however, must at all times interiorize what is remembered, i.e., let it again come closer and closer in its innermost possibility With regard to the carrying-through of a Fundamental Ontology, this means: it places its main effort on the unique and constant guidance of the Question of Being, which is allowed to become more effective without being impaired, in order to keep the existential analytic of Dasein, which was delivered up by it, on the right path.

§43. The Inception and the Course of Fundamental Ontology[293]

The Dasein in man determines him as that being which, Being in the midst of beings, comports itself to them as such. Further, as this comporting to beings, man is determined in his own Being as essentially other than all remaining beings which are manifest in Dasein.

Now, from the beginning, an analytic of Dasein must see to it that the Dasein in man is first made visible precisely within that mode of human Being which it established, according to its essence, to suppress Dasein and the understanding of Being which pertains to it (i.e., original finitude) in forgetfulness. This decisive mode of the Being of Dasein—seen solely from the standpoint of Fundamental Ontology—we call everydayness. At the same time, the analytic of everydayness has the methodological intention from the first of not allowing the interpretation of the Dasein in human beings to enter the realm of an anthropological-psychological description of man's "experiences" and "faculties." Anthropological-psychological knowledge is not thereby declared to be "false." It is necessary to show, however, that with all its correctness it is not sufficient to hold in view from the start and constantly the problem of Dasein's existence—and that means its finitude—as demanded by the guiding problematic of the Question of Being.

The existential analytic of everydayness does not want to describe how we

---

293. For a concrete understanding of this and the following paragraphs a study of *Being and Time* is imperative. We refrain from taking a position regarding the criticisms that have surfaced to date. That is to be reserved—insofar as the real hodgepodge of "objections" move in general within the dimension of the problem—for a special publication.

use a knife and fork. It should show that and how all association with beings, even where it appears as if there were just beings, already presupposes the transcendence of Dasein—namely, Being-in-the-world. With it, the *projection* of the Being of the being in general, although concealed and for the most part indeterminate, *takes place* so that indeed the Being of this being first of all and for the most part is undivided and yet is manifested understandably in the totality. Nevertheless, the *difference* between Being and beings *as such* remains concealed.[16] The man himself emerges as a being among other beings.

Being-in-the-world, however, is not first and foremost the relationship between subject and object, but is instead that which has already made such a relationship possible in advance insofar as transcendence carries out the projection of the Being of the being. Now this projecting (understanding) is first of all made visible in the existential analytic only within the confines established by its employment. It is not so much a matter of directly pursuing an understanding of the innermost composition of transcendence as it is a matter of elucidating its essential unity with the disposition and thrownness of Dasein.[17]

All projection—and consequently, even all of man's "creative" activity—is *thrown*, i.e., it is determined by the dependency of Dasein on the being already in the totality, a dependency over which Dasein itself does not have control. The thrownness, however, is not restricted to the concealed occurring of the coming-to-Dasein. Rather, it thoroughly masters precisely the Being-there as such. This expresses itself in the happening which has become prominent as falling [*Verfallen*]. This does not refer to the possibly negative occurrences in human life, the cultural importance of which can be estimated, but to a characteristic of the innermost transcendental finitude of Dasein which is unified with the thrown projection.

The progress of the existential ontology which begins with the analysis of everydayness, however, takes aim solely at the working-out of the unity in the transcendental primal structure of the finitude of Dasein in human beings. In transcendence, Dasein shows itself as in need of the understanding of Being. Through this transcendental neediness, properly speaking, "care has been taken" to see that in general something like Being-there can be. It is the innermost finitude that sustains Dasein.

The unity of the transcendental structure of the innermost neediness of the Dasein in human beings has been given the designation "Care" ["*Sorge*"]. There is nothing at all [of consequence] in the word itself; instead, everything is to be found in an understanding of what the analytic of Dasein seeks to bring out with it. But if one then takes the expression "Care"—contrary to and in spite of the still explicit, previously given directive that it has nothing to do with an ontic characterization of man—in the sense of an estimation of "human life" which reflects its world-view and ethics, instead of as an indication of the *structural unity* of the transcendence of Dasein which is finite in itself, then everything becomes confused. From this, the problematic which alone guides the analytic of Dasein then becomes completely invisible.

To be sure, it remains to be considered that precisely the working-out of the innermost essence of finitude, which was demanded for the intended grounding of metaphysics, must itself always be fundamentally finite and can never become absolute. From that, however, only this follows: the renewed consideration of finitude cannot succeed by means of a reciprocal playing-out and equalizing of standpoints which mediates them in order, finally and yet nevertheless, to attain absolute knowledge of finitude, secretly put forth, which is "true in itself." Rather, there remains only the working-out of the problematic of finitude as such. Finitude becomes manifest according to its ownmost essence if it is made accessible through unswerving application, accompanied in turn by the originally grasped, basic question of metaphysics which, to be sure, can *never* be claimed as the *only* one possible.

From this it has already become clear that the Metaphysics of Dasein, as the laying of the ground for metaphysics, has its own truth which so far is essentially still much too veiled. No world-view-oriented position, i.e., one which is always ontically popular, and especially no theological position—which wants to approve or reject—comes as such in any way into the dimension of the problem of a Metaphysics of Dasein. As Kant says, "the critique of reason can never become popular, but it also has no need to be."[294]

Hence, if a critique wants to engage in the transcendental interpretation of "Care" as the transcendental unity of finitude—and who wants to deny this possibility and necessity?—then, first, it must show that the transcendence of Dasein, and, consequently, the understanding of Being, is not the innermost finitude in the human being. Second, it then must show that the grounding of metaphysics does not have this innermost reference to the finitude of Dasein at all, and, finally, it must show that the basic question of the laying of the ground for metaphysics does not lie enclosed in the problem of the inner possibility of the understanding of Being.

Immediately prior to the integral interpretation of transcendence as "Care," the fundamental-onotological analytic of Dasein intentionally seeks to work out "anxiety" as a "decisive basic disposition," in order in this way to give a concrete reference to the fact that the existential analytic was constantly guided by the question of the possibility of the understanding of Being from which it arises. It is not with the intention of [offering] some world-view-derived proclamation of a concrete ideal of existence that anxiety is supposed to be the decisive basic state of attunement. Rather, it derives its decisive character *solely on the basis of the consideration of the problem of Being as such.*

Anxiety is that basic disposition which places us before the Nothing. The

---

294. B xxxiv.

Being of the being, however, is in general only understandable—and herein lies the profoundest finitude of transcendence—if in the ground of its essence Dasein holds itself into the Nothing.[18] This holding-itself-into-the-Nothing is no arbitrary and occasionally attempted "thinking" of the Nothing, but is rather an event[a] which underlies all instances of finding oneself[19] in the midst of beings which already are, and this event is one which must be elucidated according to its inner possibility in a fundamental-ontological analytic of Dasein.

"Anxiety" thus understood, i.e., according to fundamental ontology, completely removes the harmlessness of a categorical structure from "Care." It gives it the peculiar precision necessary for a fundamental existential [Grundexistenzial], and so it determines the finitude in Dasein not as a quality which is at hand, but rather as the constant although mostly concealed shimmering of all that exists.

However, the working out of Care as the transcendental constitution of the ground of Dasein is only the first stage of Fundamental Ontology. For further progress toward the goal, the determinative guidance we receive from the side of the Question of Being must make itself felt with increasing inexorability.

§44. The Goal of Fundamental Ontology

The next, decisive step in the existential analytic is the concrete elucidation of Care as temporality. Because the problematic of the laying of the ground for metaphysics has an inner relation to the finitude in man, it might appear as if the working out of "temporality" stands in the service of a concrete determination of man's finitude as a "temporal" creature. Indeed, the "temporal" commonly passes for the finite.

But the fact that we already apprehend any finite being—not just human beings—as "temporal" in the sense of the common determination of time, a legitimate determination within its limits, must thereupon lead to the fact that the interpretation of Dasein as temporality cannot move within the field of the common experience of what is temporal.

Nor has the interpretation of Dasein as temporality already happened just because contemporary philosophy (Bergson, Dilthey, Simmel) has sought to apprehend "life" in its aliveness [Lebendigkeit] more thoroughly—in a "more lively" ["lebendiger"] manner—because they determined its temporal character.

---

a. the nihilating comportment [das Nichtende Verhalten]; but this is grounded in Gelassenheit [The term "Gelassenheit," so important in Heidegger's later works, means "calmness" or "composure," but specifically the calmness required to free Dasein for thinking and questioning, particularly for the sort of questioning and thinking associated with the question of Being—tr.]

Rather, if the interpretation of Dasein as temporality is the goal of Funda-mental Ontology, then it must be motivated solely by the problem of Being as such. With that, however, the fundamental-ontological sense—i.e., the *only* guiding sense in *Being and Time*—of the *question* concerning time is first opened up.

The fundamental-ontological laying of the ground for metaphysics in *Being and Time* must be understood as retrieval [*Wiederholung*]. The passage from Plato's *Sophist* which opens the study[20] serves not as a decoration, but rather as an indication of the fact that in ancient metaphysics the gigantomachy[21] over the Being of beings had broken out. In this battle, the way in which *Being as such* comes to be understood—however generally and ambiguously the Question of Being may have been posed there—must already be visible. Insofar as the Question of Being as such is being fought for in this gigantoma-chy, however, and is *not yet* worked out in the designated way as the problem of the inner possibility of the understanding of Being, then neither the inter-pretation of Being as such nor even the horizon for the interpretation as such, which is necessary to it, can explicitly come to light. With the retrieval of the problem, it becomes all the more imperative to listen in to the way in which the philosophizing in this first war about Being, so to speak, was spontane-ously expressed in this regard.

To be sure, the present investigation can give no thematic presentation, much less an interpretation, of the basic movements of this gigantomachy. An allusion to the obvious must suffice.

What is the significance of the fact that ancient metaphysics determined the ὄντως ὄν—the being that is being in a way that only a being can be being[22]—as ἀεὶ ὄν? The Being of beings obviously is understood here as permanence and constancy [*Beständigkeit und Ständigkeit*]. What projection is to be found in this understanding of Being? The projection upon time; for even "eternity," perhaps taken as the "*nunc stans*," is only, thoroughly graspable as the "per-manent" "now" on the basis of time.

What is the significance of the fact that the authentic being comes to be understood as αὐσία, παρουσία in a sense which basically means the "estate" ["*Anwesen*"][23] the immediate and always present [*gegenwärtigen*] possession, the "property"?

This projection betrays the fact that: Being means *permanence in presence* [*Anwesenheit*].

In this way, namely, in the spontaneous understanding of Being, do not determinations of time accumulate? Is not the immediate understanding of Being thoroughly developed in an original, but also self-evident *projection of Being upon time*?

Does not all war over Being, then, move in advance within the horizon of time?

Is it then surprising if the ontological interpretation of the what-Being of the being is expressed in the τὸ τί ἧν εἶναι? Is there not contained in this "what always already was," and now, what is more, even in the nature of previousness, the moment of constant presence?

But is it then sufficient simply to explain the "a priori," which in the tradition of ontology passes as the nature of the determination of Being, by simply saying that this "earlier" "naturally" has nothing to do with "time"? Certainly not with the time that the common understanding of time knows. But is this "earlier" positively determined thereby, and is the troublesome character of time thus removed? Does it not recur as an intensified problem?

And is it then only a more or less fortunate habit which originates somewhere and at some time that, with the classification of beings, i.e., with the distinction of a being with regard to its Being, we determine it "by itself" as temporal, nontemporal, or supratemporal?

But where is the *ground* for this spontaneous and self-evident understanding of Being on the basis of time? Have we likewise only attempted to *ask*—in the sense of a problem which has *already been worked out*—why that is so and why it must even occur?

The essence of time as first put forward by Aristotle in the way that has proven decisive for the subsequent history of metaphysics gives *no* answer to this. On the contrary: it can be shown that precisely this analysis of time was guided by an understanding of Being that—concealing itself in its action —understands Being as permanent presence[24] and that accordingly determines the "Being" of time from the "now," i.e., on the basis of the character of time which is always and constantly presencing [*anwesend*], i.e., which strictly speaking *is* in the ancient sense.

Now to be sure, for Aristotle as well time passes for something which occurs in the "soul," in the "mind." However, the determination of the essence of the soul, the mind, spirit, human consciousness, was neither directed primarily and decisively by the problematic of the laying of the ground for metaphysics, nor was time interpreted in the preview of this problematic, nor, finally, was the interpretation of the basic transcendental structure of Dasein as temporality grasped and carried through in the sense of a problem.

On the basis of the philosophizing "remembrance" of the concealing projection of Being upon time as the innermost happening in the understanding of Being for ancient and subsequent metaphysics, a task arises for a retrieval of the grounding question of metaphysics: to carry out the going-back into the finitude in human beings which was demanded by this problematic so that in the *Da-sein* as such, temporality as transcendental primal structure, becomes visible.

On the way to this goal of Fundamental Ontology, i.e., together in the service of the working-out of human finitude, the existential interpretation of conscience, guilt, and death becomes necessary. The transcendental interpretation of historicality on the grounds of temporality should at the same time give a preconception of the mode of Being of that happening which happens in the retrieval of the Question of Being. Metaphysics is not something which was just "created" by human beings in systems and doctrines. Rather, the understanding of Being, its projection and its rejection, *happens* in Dasein as such. "Metaphysics" is the basic happening for the incursion into the being which occurs with the factical existence of something like man in general.

The metaphysics of Dasein, which is to be cultivated in Fundamental Ontology, is not claimed to be a new discipline within the framework of those which are already at hand. Rather, in it is demonstrated the will to the awakening of the insight that philosophizing occurs as the explicit transcendence of Dasein.

If the problematic of the Metaphysics of Dasein comes to be designated as that of "*Being and Time*," it now becomes clear from the clarification of the idea of a Fundamental Ontology that the "and" in this title conceals within itself the central problem. Neither "Being" nor "time" needs to give up its previous meaning, but it is true that a more original interpretation of their justification and their limits must be established.

§45. The Idea of Fundamental Ontology and the Critique of Pure Reason

Kant's laying of the ground for metaphysics, as unprecedented, resolute questioning about the inner possibility of the manifestness of the Being of beings, must come up against time as the basic determination of finite transcendence, if in fact the understanding of Being in Dasein projects Being from itself[a] upon time, so to speak. But at the same time, his laying of the ground for metaphysics must also have been driven back past the common concept of time to the transcendental understanding of it as pure self-affection. This self-affection is essentially unified with pure apperception, and in this unity the totality of a pure sensible reason is made possible.

It is not because time functions as "form of intuition" and was interpreted as such at the point of entry into the *Critique of Pure Reason*, but because the understanding of Being must be projected upon time from out of the ground of the finitude of the Dasein in man,[b] that time, in essential unity with the transcendental power of imagination, attained the central metaphysical function in the *Critique of Pure Reason*.

This [*Critique of Pure Reason*] itself thus rattles the mastery of reason and

---

a. what does this mean?
b. How was the question of space included here? "Spatiality" of *Da-sein* (*Being and Time*).

the understanding. "Logic" is deprived of its preeminence in metaphysics, which was built up from ancient times. Its idea has become questionable.

If the essence of transcendence is grounded in the pure power of imagination, or more originally in temporality, then precisely the idea of the "Transcendental Logic" is something inconceivable, especially if, contrary to Kant's original intention, it is autonomous and is taken absolutely.

Kant must have anticipated something of this collapse of the mastery of Logic in metaphysics if he could say of the grounding character of Being, of "possibility" (what-Being) and "actuality" (which Kant called "Dasein"): "Possibility, existence [Dasein], and necessity can be explained in no other way save through obvious tautology if we intend to gather their definitions solely from the pure understanding."[295]

And yet, in the second edition of the *Critique of Pure Reason*, did Kant not give mastery back to the understanding? And is it not a consequence of this that with Hegel metaphysics became "Logic" more radically than ever before?

What does the struggle against the "thing in itself," which started with German Idealism, mean, other than the growing forgetting of what Kant struggled for: that the inner possibility and necessity of metaphysics, i.e., its essence, are at bottom brought forth and preserved through the more original working-out and increased preservation of the problem of finitude?

What has the outcome of the Kantian effort been if Hegel explains metaphysics as logic thusly: "Logic is consequently to be grasped as the system of pure reason, as the realm of pure thought. This realm is truth, as it is without a veil, in and for itself. One can therefore express it thus: that this content is the presentation of God as He is in His eternal essence before the creation of nature and a finite spirit."[296]

Can there be more compelling proof for how little the metaphysics which belongs to human nature, and hence how little "human nature" itself, is self-evident?

Do we want to understand the present fundamental-ontological interpretation of the *Critique of Pure Reason* in such a way that, by possessing it, we ourselves seem more clever than our great predecessors? Or in the end, is there not also to be found in our own endeavor, if in general we need to compare it, a concealed evading in the face of something which we—and indeed not by accident—no longer see?

Perhaps through the interpretation of the *Critique of Pure Reason* which is

---

295. A 244, B 302.

296. *Wissenschaft der Logik, Einleitung*, WW [presumably Hegel's *Gesamtausgabe* of 1832 ff], vol. III, p. 35f. [Other editions: *Philosophische Bibliothek* (Hamburg: Felix Meiner, 1932; reprinted, 1975), vol. I, p. 31; *Gesammelte Werke*, ed. Friedrich Hogemann and Walter Jaeschke (Hamburg: Felix Meiner, 1978), p. 21, lines 17-21; *Hegel's Science of Logic*, tr. Arnold Miller (New York: Humanities, 1976), p. 50.]

oriented to Fundamental Ontology, the problematic of a laying of the ground for metaphysics was made more precise, even though it stops short of what is decisive. So there remains but one thing to do: to hold the investigation open by means of questions.

By extension, following the Transcendental Analytic, to the interpretation of which our investigation was restricted, is there not a "Transcendental Dialectic"? If at first this also can only be the critical application of the insight into the essence of *Metaphysica Generalis* which was attained with the rejection of the traditional *Metaphysica Specialis*, then is there not also a positive problematic to be found in this characterization of the Transcendental Dialectic, which appears to be only negative?

And what if this [positive problematic] is concentrated in the same question which, although concealed and not worked out, has already guided all the previous problematics of metaphysics, namely, the problem of the finitude of Dasein?

Kant says the "transcendental appearance," to which traditional metaphysics owes its possibility, was more necessary. Must not this transcendental untruth, with regard to its original unity with transcendental truth, come to be positively grounded on the basis of the innermost essence of the finitude in Dasein? Does the nonessence [*Unwesen*] of that appearance belong to this essence of finitude?

But then, does the problem of the "transcendental appearance" not require a liberation from that architectonic into which Kant forced it—in accordance with his orientation to traditional logic—especially if, through the Kantian ground-laying, logic in general as possible ground and guide for the problematic of metaphysics has been shaken?

What is the transcendental essence of truth in general? How, particularly on the grounds of the finitude of Dasein, are this [essence of truth] and the nonessence of untruth, which were originally unified with man's basic neediness as a being who has been thrown into beings, to be compelled to understand something like Being?

Does it make sense, and is there a justification for grasping man on the grounds of his innermost finitude—that he requires "Ontology," i.e., understanding of Being—as "creative" and consequently as "infinite," where indeed there is nothing which even the idea of an infinite creature recoils from as radically as it does from an ontology?

At the same time, however, is it permissible to develop the finitude in Dasein only as a problem, without a "presupposed" infinitude? What in general is the nature of this "presupposing" in Dasein? What does the infinitude which is so "composed" mean?

Will the Question of Being, in all its elementary weight and breadth, free itself again from all this questionableness? Or have we already become so much the fools of the organization, of the hustle and bustle, that we are no longer able to befriend the essential, the simple, and the constant? It is in this friendship (*philia*) alone that the turning to the beings as such takes place, from which the question concerning the concept of Being (*sophia*)—the grounding question of philosophy—arises.

Or do we also first need remembrance for this?

So Aristotle offered the saying:

Καὶ δὴ καὶ τὸ πάλαι τε καὶ νῦν καὶ ἀεὶ ζητούμενον καὶ ἀπορούμενον, τί τό ὄν. . . .

(*Metaphysics* Z1, 1028, b2ff.)[25]

APPENDIX I

Notes on the Kantbook

1. *On the Kantbook*

It was taken (1) as a one-sided interpretation of Kant, (2) as a forerunner for "Being and Time"—both were *confused ways of thinking*.

Discovering "Kant in himself" is to be left to Kant philology. Even if it should emerge that it has actually learned something from the violent Heideggerian interpretation.

But the question is: the *Problem of Metaphysics*, and that *means—the Question of Being*.

To be sure, by itself as "'historical' ['geschichtliche'] introduction" to "Being and Time" in a more limited sense—not "historiological" ["historisch"], rather—"questioning debate" ["*Auseinandersetzung*"].

2. *Kantbook*

an attempt to question what has not been said, instead of writing in a fixed way about what Kant said. What has been said is insufficient, what has not been said is filled with riches.

3.

The distinction between *analytic* and *synthetic* judgments and these ways of judging always exhibited for themselves as characteristics of finitude.

Finite thinking is a tautology, after the fashion of a round circle. What does it mean: that thinking is *finite*?

4. *Critique of Judgment*
Aesthetics

Only considered far enough to be able to see that it is not contradicted.

But now the highest corroboration of the interpretation; see §59, p. 258 [Bernard translation, p. 198—tr.]!!, likewise p. 238 [Bernard translation,

p. 186—tr.]; the intelligible! whererupon taste (reflection—imagination) looks out (into itself).

5.

See Kant's sketch of a "Science of *Ontology* as Immanent Thinking." Letter to Sig. Beck. 20.I.92 (WW [Cassirer] X, p. 115 ff.).

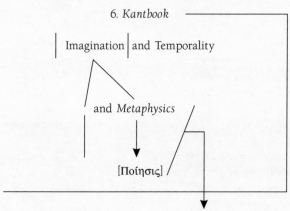

6. *Kantbook*

Imagination and Temporality

and *Metaphysics*

[Ποίησις]

In Terms of the Amphiboly of the Concepts of Reflection, the essential origin of these concepts.

7.

The fourth section is translated into French in *Qu'est-ce que la métaphysique?* by H. Corbin, 1938 [*What is Metaphysics?* tr. D. Krell. In: *Martin Heidegger: Basic Writings* (New York: Harper & Row, 1977), pp. 95–112—tr.].

Effect on Sartre is crucial; from there "Being and Time" is first to be understood.

see my French Forward to this translation.

5 Oct. 45

8. Concepts of Reflection

See B316ff. Disputation with Leibniz—logical dogmatism!
    See Concept in general, empirical Concept, pure concept of the understanding (Category), pure concept of reason (Idea).

"under which subjective conditions . . . can we arrive at concepts"? B316.[1]

If we ask in this way, we stand in the *reflexio* (re-flection [*Über-legung*]), not in the "simple" apprehending (exposition) of *objects*, in order to obtain Concepts from them (setting forth the fundamental difference between sensibility and understanding, see B327).

Reflecting, we pay attention to the relationship of given representations, i.e., Concepts in this case, "to our various sources of knowledge" (see *Modality!*) (*Sensibility* and *Understanding* B316 (Imagination? Reason?)).

Only by means of these reflective glances back to the powers of knowledge "can the relationship of the representations under one another be determined correctly" (relationship of the Concepts, i.e., judgment and its truth (B317)), i.e., only so as to make out in *which powers* they belong together! to which [powers] they owe their specific unity (what kind of synthesis).

The *reflexio*—consequently: question concerning the unity of the manifold of given representations (concepts), more precisely: *according to the forum before* which they would be "*compared*," would be "combined"—*discursus*! and that means at the same time according to the a priori unifying instance!

To which power of the understanding does a given concept belong?

The comparison of representations in general will always be employed in a power of the Understanding. I can only "hold together" this comparison with the power of Knowledge, and discern, distinguish, whether by means of this comparison the representations were thought as belonging to pure Understanding or to Sensuousness—"*Transcendental Reflection*"—*how in the comparison, the comparing in general is thought—whether ontic—or ontological*; whether belonging to Sensuousness or to the pure Understanding, B324, through which what is represented in it, "its object" B325, i.e., the determination of the "*transcendental place [Ortes]*" (ibid). Therefore B319 (see 318): "Transcendental Reflection" "bears on the objects themselves" (is not merely logical comparison [*Komparation*], i.e., straight comparing [*vergleichen*] of the representations as such), rather, as transcendental reflection it is "the Ground for the possibility of objective comparison [*objektiven Komparation*]" B319.[2]

Answer to the question: for which power of Knowledge shall the represented object be? Without this transcendental reflection, "amphiboly" creeps in: "confusing the object of pure understanding with appearance" B326.

By means of Categories, "what constitutes the concept of an object" (B325), what belongs to an object as such, is "presented."

By means of the "four titles" for the concepts of reflection, only "the *comparison [Vergleichung]* of the representations, which precede the concepts of things" have been presented.

More precisely—the formal ontological (!) possibilities for the comparing [*Vergleichens*] are in general not important to the transcendental place of the representations.

This problem is important for Kant because the dogmatic metaphysics of formal logic in the widest sense has been surrendered up (see B326 concerning *Leibniz*!); i.e., the manner of thinking which a priori would judge things, see B319.

9. Matter—Form (see B322ff.)

1) taken as purely formalized—and from the Concept of what is understood—as *what is determinative, determinans*—i.e., as what affirms or negates, created *predicatively* (Baumgarten) and at the same time *transcendentally*, i.e., in connection with the possibility of the knowledge of objects in general. Expressed here as: the determinative—the determinable.

But this is only possible on the grounds of the intentionality-transcendence of existence [*Daseins*]. It is here that the condition for the possibility and formal necessity of this correlation is found.

I may not, however, formally and universally create this out of thin air.

For Kant the answer can already be found here, because Formal Logic—which is not grounded in fundamental ontology, but is only in itself—is the most certain.

See B345: "apperception, and with it thought, precedes all possible determinative ordering of representations." Here the presupposition, which Kant along with Descartes and Leibniz adhered to—the most original a priori is for them the "I think," and it is in this that the priority of Logic is grounded!

That Descartes's presupposition is still active in this way for Kant in a completely different problematic prevents for the most part its original embedding, and therefore one can at the least overlook this presupposition, or simply strike it out.

It is synonymous with the misunderstanding of the problem of transcendence.

2) but at the same time, the predominance of this separation must be destroyed, and it must lead back to the ontic-ontological correlate.

This is motivated by the ancient ontological difference ὕλη-εἶδος, and from this the *productive horizon* [*Herstellungshorizont*] comes forth, i.e., from the completely determined absolutizing of the *concept of Being*. Beings as what is at hand, and knowledge = determinative perception of these [beings].

3) The dominance of the formalization must be broken by means of the evidence that while everything is indeed interpretable, at the same time everything is also constrained by a Schema, which diverts it from the ontological problematic, derived from the original, as well as from the logical problematic.

The pure, taken logico-*transcendentally*, is material to what is primary. Determining presupposes what is determinable. Thus it appears remarkable: with Space and Time, to set the Form as what is primary ahead of the Matter, which makes these determinable, i.e., lets them be encountered, in the first place,

B324. But one may not judge here in a purely intellectual manner according to mere concepts of things themselves. Rather, from appearances one can see that Space and Time precede all data. See B322–23 concerning the use of concepts of matter.

Matter—metaphysically explained—purely accessible, not through predicates that approach it as Object [*Objekt*], = "object" ["Gegenstand"] in another sense, object of perception [Gegenstand der Empfindung], "the authentically empirical in sensuous intuition," *Metaphysical Principles of Natural Science*, Erklärung I, Anmerkung 2.

APPENDIX II

Ernst Cassirer: Philosophy of Symbolic Forms.
Part Two: Mythical Thought. Berlin, 1925

This second volume of Cassirer's major work is dedicated to the memory of Paul Natorp. The title, "Mythical Thought," could be misleading, however, in suggesting that the dominant theme of the investigation is to be found in a separation of the mythical thought process from the purely logical. Instead, precisely the insufficiency of mythical "thinking" as a "process of understanding" is to be brought to light by demonstrating that it is grounded in a specific "form of life" in unity with an accompanying "form of intuition." "Thought" here means nothing less than an "attending and intending" [*"Sinnen und Trachten"*] which, however, is still its own "form of thought" (its own way of interpreting and determining). The intent of the investigation is accordingly to pursue the uncovering of "myth" as an original possibility of human Dasein, which has its own proper truth. With this way of posing the question, Cassirer explicitly takes up Schelling's insight, that "namely everything in it (in 'mythology') is to be understood in the way that it is said, and not as if something else is being thought, or something else is being said" (*Einleitung in die Philosophie der Mythologie*. S. W. 2. Abt. I, 195). Myth, the "destiny of a people" (Schelling), is an "Objective process," to which Dasein itself remains subordinated, and in opposition to which it can become free, but never in such a way that it rejects this process. If Cassirer does indeed hold to this basic insight of Schelling, and sees in myth "not a weakness of spirit," not a mere appearance, but rather a proper "formative force," he nevertheless grasps the task of a *philosophy* of myth in a way that differs from Schelling's speculative metaphysics. An empirical psychological "explanation" of myth is certainly never capable of attaining a *philosophical* understanding. Accordingly, in holding to the "Objectivity" of myth and in rejecting the psychological interpretation, Cassirer attempts a "phenomenology of mythical consciousness." This presents itself as an extension of the transcendental problematic in the neo-Kantian sense: to conceive of the unity of "culture," and not only "nature," as the lawfulness of spirit. The "Objectivity" of myth lies in its properly understood "subjectivity"; myth is its own spiritual "creative principle of world formation" (p. 19) [*The Philosophy of Symbolic Forms*, Part 2: *Mythical Thought*, tr. R. Mannheim (New Haven: Yale University Press, 1955), p. 14. Hereafter cited as *Symbolic Forms*—tr.].

In accord with this starting point that is outlined in the Introduction (pp.

Appendix II was translated by Peter Warnek.

180

1-36) [*Symbolic Forms*, pp. 1-26], Cassirer interprets myth as a "form of thought" (Section I, pp. 39-91) [*Symbolic Forms*, pp. 27-70], as a "form of intuition" (Section II, pp. 95-188) [*Symbolic Forms*, pp. 71-151], as a "form of life" (Section III, pp. 191-285) [*Symbolic Forms*, pp. 153-231]. He brings everything to a close by offering an account of the "dialectic of mythical consciousness" (Section IV, pp. 289-320) [*Symbolic Forms*, pp. 233-261].

The analysis of the mythical *form of thought* begins with a general characterization of the manner in which objects come to stand in opposition to mythical consciousness. The consciousness of the objects of mathematical physics as it is conceived in Cohen's Kant interpretation serves to guide this characterization: the active formation of a passively given "chaos of sensations" into a "cosmos." A basic feature of the mythical consciousness of Objects lies in the fact that a demarcated boundary is *lacking* between what is dreamt of and what is experienced while awake, between what is merely imagined and what is perceived, between image and the object that is formed in the image, between word (meaning) and thing, between what is merely wished for and what is actually possessed, and between what is living and what is dead. Everything remains in *one* uniform level of Being that is immediately present, by which mythical Dasein is dazed. This consciousness of objects is entitled to its own peculiar and sufficient "explanation" and "understanding." The co-presence of something with something else "gives" the explanation: the swallow produces the summer. This bringing-with-itself [*Mitsichbringen*] has the character of magical power (see below). What functions here as producer [*Mitbringer*] is not simply random, it is determined from out of the basic connectedness that orients the magical experience. As arbitrary as these magical "actual connections" may appear, for example, to a theoretical consideration of nature, they nevertheless have their own truth. Mythical thought does not know the analytical division of the actual into causal sequences. The interweaving of the magically real becomes clearly evident in the conception of the relationship between whole and part. The part "is" the whole itself, which means it has the undiminished magical power of the whole. Each "thing" bears in itself its belonging to other things within the whole of magical forces. In mythical thinking what holds is "the law of the concrescence and coincidence of the relational parts" (p. 83) [*Symbolic Forms*, p. 64].

In the second section Cassirer shows the effect this form of thought has on the understanding of space, time and number. A chapter precedes this "mythical doctrine of forms" that is entitled: "*The Basic Opposition*" [*Grundgegensatz*] (pp. 95-106) [*Symbolic Forms*, pp. 73-82]. The characterization of the mythical consciousness of objects already showed how mythical Dasein is captivated by what is present, dazed and overwhelmed. Presence means the overpowering. Herein lies the character of what is extraordinary, incomparable, over and against the everyday. But this is not a *nihil negativum*. It has indeed its own character of Being, namely that of the "common," within the horizon of the overwhelmingly uncommon. This "basic division" between the sacred and the profane is the basic articulation of the actual, to which mythical Dasein "comports" itself, whatever that being in its constitution may be. This character of the Being of the mythical "world" and mythical Dasein itself is the meaning of the *mana-representation* which has continued over the last few centuries to stand out more clearly in mythological research as one, if not even *the* basic category of mythical "thinking." Mana does not designate a determinate circle of Objects. It also cannot be attributed to certain "spiritual" powers. The mana is the most general character of Being, the "how" whereby what is actual suddenly comes over the entirety of human Dasein. The expressions "mana," "wakanda," "orenda," "manitu" are interjections within the immediacy of being overtaken by threatening by beings (p. 98ff., 195f., 228) [*Symbolic Forms*, p. 76ff., 158f., 185] [See also E. Cassirer, *Sprache und Mythos. Studien der Bibliothek Warburg*, 1925, p. 52ff. [*Language and Myth*, tr. Susanne Langer (New York: Dover & Harper, 1946)]. Here there is a still more transparent interpretation of the mana-representation in the context of the problem of language.]

In the original being dazed by what is actual as the mana, mythical Dasein carries out the articulation of the dimensions in which Dasein as such always already moves: the interpretation and "determination" of space, time, and number. The specifically mythical modalization of these "representations" is also characterized by the author in constant contrast to the conceptual interpretation that these phenomena have undergone in modern mathematical-physical knowledge.

The "basic feeling of the sacred" and the "basic division" that is given along with it prefigure both the total comprehension of *space* as well as the way in which individual boundaries are posited within it. The original partitioning of space, in which it is first of all uncovered as such, distinguishes two "regions": a "sacred," extraordinary, appropriately preserved and protected region, and a "common" region that is at all times accessible to everyone. Space is, however, never given prior to this "in itself," in such a way that it can then be mythically "interpreted." Rather, mythical Dasein first of all discovers space as such in this manner. The mythical spatial orientation is thereby guided everywhere by the opposition between day and night, which for its part announces itself primarily mythically, that is, in the specific mana-like power that forces all Dasein into its binding spell. To the extent that spatiality, thus uncovered, co-determines in general a possible habitat for Dasein, space and its corresponding factical division can become a schema for the most manifold traits of Dasein (consider, for example, the complicated classification of the totemistic perceptual sphere). Mythical Dasein procures for itself in this way a uniform overall orientation that can be easily mastered.

Time is still more originally constitutive for mythical Dasein than space. Cassirer grounds the characterization of these connections in the vulgar concept of time and understands by the "temporal" character of myth "being-within-time"—for example, of the gods. The "sacredness" of the mythically actual is determined by its origin. The past as such shows itself as the genuine and last 'why' of all beings. In the periodicity of the seasons, in the rhythm of the phases of life and age, the power of time is made evident. The individual sections of time are "sacred times." The comportment toward them, far from being a mere calculation, is regulated by particular cults and rites (for example, initiation rites). The order of time, as an order of destiny, is a cosmic power and thus makes manifest in its regularity a binding obligation that pervades all human practice. Calendrical regulation and ethical obligation are welded to the power of time. The basic mythical-religious relation to time can then especially accentuate an individual time orientation. The individual modifications of the different feelings of time and the conceptions of time that are prefigured in these make up "one of the most profound differences in the character of individual religions." Cassirer shows (p. 150ff.) [*Symbolic Forms*, p. 119ff.] in broad strokes the typical images of time that are found in the Hebrews, the Persians, the Indians, in Chinese and Egyptian religion, and in Greek philosophy.

Numbering and the relations of number are also understood in mythical Dasein from out of the character of the all of everything which is, from out of the power. Each number has its "individual physiognomy," its own magical power. What is equally numbered presents itself as one and the same essence—without regard to whether there is nevertheless a fundamental difference—according to the principle of concrescence: "all magic is for the most part number magic" (p. 178) [*Symbolic Forms*, p. 144]. Numbered determinateness does not mean ordering in a sequence, but rather belonging to a determinate domain of the uncommon. The number is the mediator that connects the whole of mythical actuality to the unity of a power-full world order. As manifold as the forms of the mythical doctrine of numbers may be, and as different as the ways of mythically emphasizing the distinctiveness of individual numbers (for example, three or seven) may be, certain original prefigurations for the making sacred of individual numbers can nevertheless be indicated on the basis of the particular kind of mythical spatiality and temporality: the number four becomes sacred, for example, because of the regions of the sky. Furthermore, the sacredness of the number seven goes back to the power of time, which is made evident in the phases of the moon, through a division by four of the twenty-eight-day month that presents itself on its own to intuition, as it were. In the distinctive emphasis placed mythically upon the number three, one sees, on the other hand, the originally personal relation between father, mother, and child coming through, just as the dual and trinal forms in language refer back to the relation between I, you, and he. Binding these originally *powerful* relations to numbers is something that remains itself utterly bound to having the character of the mythically efficacious.

From the analysis of the mythical Object-world and its way of being discovered and determined, the inquiry then turns toward "*subjective actuality*" and its unveiling in myth. Cassirer begins this discussion with a fundamental and biting critique of "animism," which still dominates in the most diverse ways the investigations of ethnological research. The world of mythical Dasein cannot simply be interpreted on the basis of the prevailing conceptions of the soul; for then the "subject" as such still remains veiled. To the extent that mythical Dasein is familiar with itself at all, it does not interpret itself solely in relation to a world that is grasped purely in terms of things. Object [*Objekt*] and subject and the relation between them is understood by mythical Dasein within the horizon of what makes itself evident as the the general character of the actual, that is, it is understood in terms of mana. What has to be shown here is precisely how mythical Dasein, which in its "indeterminate life-feeling" remains bound to all beings, enacts a "confrontation" between world and I that is proper to it, rooted in its own specific way of being, i.e., in its "doing." The sphere of the actual that is primarily discovered and delimited in doing, in a peculiar reflecting back upon doing itself, makes doing visible in its different "capabilities." Within the horizon of magical power one's own doing is a magical act. "The first force [*Kraft*] by means of which the human places himself as something proper and independent over and against things is the force of *wish* [*Wunsch*]" (p. 194) [*Symbolic Forms*, p. 157]. "The abundance of divine forms that the human creates for himself not only serves to guide it through the sphere of objective being and events but rather above all through the sphere of its own will and accomplishment and illuminates this sphere from within" (p. 251) [*Symbolic Forms*, p. 203]. The further process of the unveiling of "subjectivity" and its ways of comportment is carried out in the transition from nature-myths to culture-myths, until finally, in the more or less magic-free manipulation of tools, the Being-connected between things becomes manifest on its own terms as independent. The human thereby frees itself from being magically bound to things and in a *retreat from* the world lets that world be encountered "Objectively."

Just as the subject does not discover itself in the emergence and return of things that stand purely over and against it, neither is it the case that a divided I-You relationship, or any such form of community, is primarily constitutive for the unveiling of subjectivity. Totemism, which is improperly posited as the grounding phenomenon of mythical Dasein, cannot be explained sociologically. Instead, all social divisions and the individuals that are given along with them, require, like totemism itself, a "grounding" developed from out of the original way of Being of mythical Dasein and the mana-representation that dominates it. The proper problem of totemism lies in the fact that not only the human as such stands in a certain inextricable relation to the animal or the plant, but that each *particular* group has its own particular totemic animal. Farmers, herdsmen, and hunters each discover themselves in reference to plants and animals in a way that is peculiar to each and that makes itself evident immediately as a magical affiliation. At the same time, however, this reference makes it possible, in a reflecting back, for the pertinent human life spheres to become explicit as such. Totemism is not caused by particular kinds of plants and animals but rather emerges from out of the elementary Dasein-relations of the human to its world.

Only when things are grounded in the mana-representation does it then also become possible to conceive how individual *self-consciousness* takes shape and how the "concept" of the *soul* comes to be articulated. What is later conceptually distinguished as body and soul, or life and death, is indeed also always already actual for mythical Dasein but in the mode of magical power, according to which what is dead also *is*, and a force of the soul makes itself known even when the human met with is not encountered bodily. Only in the unity of magical efficacy can the individual forces of the soul or the individual "souls" appear as split apart and dwell along side one another. Correspondingly the "development" of individual Dasein is also distributed among different subjects, between which determinate transitions take place. In its being threatened by magical powers, mythical Dasein's "own" soul stands as an "alien" power over and against it. Even where the representation of protective spirits is awakened, one's own self is still a power, as it were, which protectively takes up the individual I. Only first at higher levels does the magical daemon become *daimonion* and genius, in such a way that Dasein in the end comes to determine itself not as an alien power but rather from out of that for which it is freely *capable*, from itself and for itself as an ethical subject.

If the power and uncommonness of the divine primarily and thoroughly dominates mythical Dasein, then the basic comportment to actuality can never be a mere intuition but is rather in like manner an actualizing that takes on the form of *cult* and *rite*. All mythical narration is always only a derivative report of sacred dealings. In these sacred dealings, in contrast, mythical Dasein presents itself immediately. The earlier the cult takes shape, the more *sacrifice* assumes a central position. Sacrifice is indeed a renunciation, but at the same time it is still a dealing that is *enacted by oneself* which prepares the way for a certain release from the exclusive power of magical forces. Therein, however, the free power of Dasein is exposed and at the same time the cleft between the human and the divine widens, so as to demand at a higher level a renewed overcoming.

In this way, myth becomes visible as a unified autonomous formative power. Mythic shapes display an inner dialectic in which earlier forms are expanded and transformed but not simply rejected. The mythical "process" carries itself out in Dasein itself without reflection. When this process has run through its possibilities, it itself comes up against its own overcoming. Cassirer seeks to show this dialectic in the different positions that myth assumes toward its own world-image (p. 290) [*Symbolic Forms*, p. 235].

This brief account has to forego even a slight treatment of the rich ethnological and religious historical material that grounds Cassirer's interpretation of myth and that he works into the individual analyses with his unique talent for perspicacious and apt presentation. In making available to the author its extensive and rare collections, as well as and especially the use of its entire facilities, the Warburg Library in Hamburg provided exceptional assistance in the work (Foreword, p. xiii) [*Symbolic Forms*, p. xviii]. Among the analyses of mythical phenomena, especially noteworthy are those dealing with the function of the tool in the unveiling of Object-world, and those dealing with sacrifice (p. 273ff.) [*Symbolic Forms*, p. 221ff.].

Our approach to the philosophy of myth outlined here must pursue three points. First, it must be asked: What does this interpretation achieve for the grounding and guiding of the positive sciences of mythical Dasein (ethnology and the history of religion)? Then it becomes necessary to examine the foundations and methodological principles that support the philosophical analysis of the essence of myth. And finally, the basic question arises concerning the constitutive function of myth in human Dasein and in the all of beings as such.

With regard to the first question, Cassirer's work proves itself to be a fruitful success. It brings the problematic of the positive research into myth to a fundamentally higher level by carrying out in a variety of ways the demonstration that myth can never be "explained" by having recourse to determinate spheres of Objects within the mythical world. The critique that is directed in this way against the naturalistic, totemistic, animistic, and sociological attempts at explanation is thoroughly unambiguous and devastating. This critique, for its part, is grounded in the anticipatory determination of myth as one functional form [*Funktionsform*] of spirit, having its own laws. If this conception of myth can prevail in empirical research, then secure guidance has been gained both for the initial appropriation and interpretation of newly discovered material as well as for the elaboration and exploration of already established results.

Yet if this interpretation of myth is to be judged not only with regard to what it achieves as a guide in the positive sciences but also with regard to its *own philosophical* content, then the following questions arise: is the predetermination of myth as a functional form of creative consciousness adequately grounded on its own terms? Where are the foundations for such an admittedly unavoidable grounding to be found? Are the foundations themselves sufficiently secured and elaborated? Cassirer's *grounding* of his guiding predetermination of myth as a creative force [*bildender Kraft*] of spirit ("symbolic form") is essentially an *appeal* to Kant's "Copernican revolution," according to which all "actuality" is to be considered as a formation of productive consciousness.

To begin with, there are good reasons to doubt whether the interpretation carried out by Cassirer and, in general, by neo-Kantian epistemology, of what

Kant means by the "Copernican revolution" gets at the kernel of the transcendental problematic as an ontological problematic in its essential possibilities. But leaving that aside: can the critique of pure reason simply be "extended" to a "critique of culture"? Is it in fact so certain or is it not rather completely in question as to whether in the first place the foundations for Kant's ownmost transcendental interpretation of "nature" have been explicitly elaborated and grounded? How do things stand with regard to the overall unavoidable ontological elaboration of the constitution and way of Being of what is named, vaguely enough, sometimes "consciousness," sometimes "life," sometimes "spirit," sometimes "reason"? To be sure, *before* it becomes a question of the possible use of Kant in the sense of "extending" his problem, it is first of all necessary to clarify the basic and problematic demands harbored in the assumption that myth is a functional form of "spirit." Only from here can it be decided whether and to what extent an appropriation of the questions or schemata posed by Kant is intrinsically possible and justified.

The interpretation of the essence of myth as a possibility of human Dasein remains random and directionless as long as it cannot be grounded in a radical ontology of Dasein in light of the problem of Being in general. The basic problems that arise here cannot be discussed in this context. Let it suffice if we can bring to light, through an immanent critique of Cassirer's interpretation of myth, several of the main problems in their unavoidability, so as thereby to provide a *philosophical* refinement and clarification of the task posed by Cassirer. Cassirer himself stressed (Foreword, p. xiii) that his investigation was to be "merely a first beginning."

The preoccupation with the neo-Kantian problem of consciousness is of such little help that it actually prevents gaining a grasp on the central problem. This is already evident in the arrangement of the work. Instead of taking up the interpretation of mythical Dasein in terms of a central characterization of the constitution of the Being of this being, Cassirer begins with an analysis of the mythical consciousness of objects, the form of its thought and the form of its intuition. Cassirer does indeed see clearly that the forms of thought and intuition must be traced back to the mythical "form of life" as the "spiritually primordial" (p. 89ff.) [*Symbolic Forms*, p. 69ff.]. But the *explicit and systematic* elucidation of the origin of the forms of thought and intuition from out of the "form of life" is nevertheless not carried through. That these original connections do not come to light, and that indeed the problem itself of the possible inner link between the forms of life, of thought, and of intuition is not even posed, demonstrates the indefiniteness of the systematic place of *mana-representation* to which Cassirer inevitably returns in his treatment of all essential mythical phenomena. The mana-representation is not dealt with among the forms of thought, and yet it is also not developed as a form of intuition. It is thematically discussed in the transition from the form of thought to the form of intuition under the title "The Basic Opposition." This is more an expression of a predicament than it is the presentation of the structural determination of this "representation" from out of the whole structure of mythical Dasein as such. At the same time, however, the mana-representation is repeatedly designated as the "fundamental form of thought." And Cassirer's analysis of the mana-representation does indeed have a certain importance over and against the conventional interpretation, to the extent that he does not grasp the mana as a being among other beings but instead sees in it the "how" of everything that is mythically actual, namely, the Being of these beings. Only then, however, does the central problem emerge, insofar as it must be asked: is this fundamental "representation" simply present at hand in mythical Dasein, or does it belong to the ontological constitution of mythical Dasein? And if this latter, as what? In the mana-representation, what becomes evident is nothing other than the *understanding of Being* that belongs to every Dasein as such. This undergoes specific transformations according to each basic way of Dasein's Being—in this case, the mythical—and it illuminates in advance thought and intuition. This insight, however, leads to the further question: *which* is the basic way of Being of mythical "life," such that within this life precisely the mana-representation can function as the leading and illuminating understanding of Being? The possible answer to this question presupposes, to be sure, an anticipatory elaboration of the basic ontological constitution of Dasein as such. If this basic constitution lies in the "care" that is to be understood *ontologically* [cf. *Sein und Zeit. Jahrb. f. Philos. u. phänomenolog. Forschung* vol. VIII (1927), pp. 180-230], then it becomes clear that mythical Dasein is primarily determined through "thrownness." We can give here only a preliminary indication of the manner in which a grounded articulation moves from "thrownness" to the ontological structure of mythical Dasein.

In "thrownness" there is a being-delivered-over of Dasein to the world, so that this being-in-the-world is overwhelmed by that to which it is delivered over. Overpoweringness as such is capable on the whole of announcing itself only *for* a being that is delivered over to something. In this being referred to the overpowering, Dasein is dazed *by* it and is capable therefore of experiencing itself only as belonging to and affiliated with this actuality itself. In thrownness any and all uncovered beings have, accordingly, the Being-character of overpoweringness (mana). If the ontological interpretation were to push forward to the specific "temporality" that grounds thrownness, then it could be made ontologically understandable *why* and *how* what is actual as mana always makes itself evident in a specific "instantaneousness." In thrownness there is a proper being driven here and there that is open from out of itself for what is always in each case the suddenly extraordinary. The specific "categories" of mythical thought must then be "deduced" by following the guiding thread of the mana-representation.

Another phenomenon in this indissociable group emerges from out of the question concerning mythical Dasein's basic comportment and its comportment to itself. The "first force" (power) in which mythical Dasein's own Being becomes manifest to it, according to Cassirer is the force of the *wish* (p. 194) [*Symbolic Forms*, p. 157]. But *why* is it the first? We must make visible how this wishing is also rooted in thrownness and demonstrate how the (mere) wish, on the basis of a peculiar non-survey [*Nichtüberschauen*] of its many possibilities, can have the force of this efficacy. Only when wishing itself is understood in advance as bound to mana can it make itself evident as such an "effecting." But when wishing is supposed to constitute the "confrontation" between world and I, then it must be noted that these kinds of comportment of mythical Dasein are always only ways according to which the *transcendence* of Dasein toward its world is *unveiled* but not first produced. The "confrontation" is *grounded* in the transcendence of Dasein. And mythical Dasein can thereby identify *itself with* Objects only because it comports itself to its world as a being-in-the-world. But how this properly understood transcendence can belong to Dasein has to be shown. Beginning with a chaos of "sensations" that are "formed" is not only insufficient for the philosophical problem of transcendence but already covers over the original phenomenon of transcendence as the condition for the possibility of any "passivity." Hence, a basic confusion also arises in Cassirer's talk of "impressions": sometimes what is meant is the pure sensation-like affection, sometimes, however, the being dazed by the actual itself, understood as bound to mana. To be sure, the mana is *not grasped as a way of Being* in mythical Dasein itself, but rather it is grasped as what is itself bound to mana, that is, it is represented as a being. For this reason the ontic interpretations of mana are also not completely unjustified.

Cassirer, in characterizing the formative power of myth, often speaks of mythical *phantasy*. But this fundamental capability remains completely unclarifed. Is it a form of thought or a form of intuition? Or both? Or even neither of the two? Here an orientation guided by the phenomenon of the transcendental power of imagination, and its ontological function within the *Critique of Pure Reason* and the *Critique of Judgment*, an orientation that admittedly would lie far from neo-Kantianism, could have at least made it clear that an interpretation of the mythical understanding of Being is much more labyrinthine and abysmal than is suggested by Cassirer's presentation.

Finally, we must still indicate the *methodological* maxims which serve as the guidelines in Cassirer's attempt at interpreting the phenomena of Dasein: "The basic rule which governs all development, namely, that spirit achieves true and complete inwardness only in expressing itself" (p. 242; see 193, 229, 246, 267) [*Symbolic Forms*, p. 196; see pp. 156, 185, 199-200, 217]. A grounding is also needed here that would account for why this basic rule prevails. And there is need for an answer to the basic question: which is the constitution of the Being of human Dasein as such, such that it comes to its own self only by way of this detour through the world? What do selfhood [*Selbstheit*] and independence [*Selbständigkeit*] mean?

And yet, in all this the fundamental philosophical problem of myth is not yet reached: in what way does myth in general belong to Dasein as such? In what respect is myth an essential phenomenon within a universal interpretation of Being as such and its modifications? Whether a "philosophy of symbolic forms" attains a solution, or only the elaboration of these questions, is something that here can be left undeveloped. Access to these questions is first acquired not only when *all* "symbolic forms" are presented, but rather above all when also the basic concepts of this system are thoroughly elaborated and brought back to their ultimate foundations. [See now the admittedly still general and too free-floating discussions by Cassirer in his lecture, "The Problem of Symbol and Its Place in a System of Philosophy." *Zeitschrift für Ästhetik und allgemeine Kunstwissenschaften*, XXI (1927), pp. 295ff.]

The critical questions that have been raised here cannot detract from the importance of Cassirer's work, which lies precisely in its having placed myth as a systematic problem, for the first time since Schelling, once again within the sphere of philosophical inquiry. The inquiry will remain a valuable starting point for a renewed philosophy of myth, even if it is not joined to a "philosophy of symbolic forms." To be sure, it will have this value only if we grasp in a manner that is more resolute than heretofore that even such a rich presentation of the phenomena of spirit, running as it does against the dominant consciousness, is never at all philosophy itself, whose need first erupts when its few elementary and basic problems, having remained unconquered since antiquity, are newly taken up.

Davos Lectures

KANT'S *CRITIQUE OF PURE REASON* AND THE TASK OF A LAYING OF THE GROUND FOR METAPHYSICS

These lectures are to demonstrate the thesis: Kant's *Critique of Pure Reason* is a, or rather the first, express ground-laying for metaphysics.

(Negatively, and in opposition to the traditional interpretation of neo-Kantianism, that means: it is no theory of mathematical, natural-scientific knowledge—it is not a theory of knowledge at all.)

Through the elucidation of this laying of the ground for metaphysics, it should become clear at the same time that and how the question of the essence of human beings is essentially within a "metaphysics of metaphysics."

The main emphasis of the explanations thus lies in proving the intrinsic thrust of the problematic of the ground-laying, the major steps, and their necessity.

Accordingly, the division of the whole is threefold:

1. The laying of the ground for metaphysics in the point of departure,
2. The laying of the ground for metaphysics in the carrying-through,
3. The laying of the ground for metaphysics in its originality.

As to 1. Kant's point of departure in traditional metaphysics determines the form of the problem. If *Metaphysica Specialis* constitutes the knowledge of the supersensible (the totality of world, soul [immortality], God),[3] the "proper metaphysics" (Kant), then the question of its possibility generally runs as follows: How is knowledge of beings in general possible? If the previous understanding of the constitution of the Being of beings belongs to the possibility of the knowledge of beings, then the question concerning the possibility of ontic knowledge is thrown back onto the question of the possibility of *ontological* [knowledge], i.e., the laying of the ground for *Metaphysica Specialis* is focused on the laying of the ground for *Metaphysica Generalis* (ontology).

It is then shown how this question concerning the possibility of ontology assumes the form of the problem of a "Critique of Pure Reason."

As to 2. To understand the carrying-through of the ground-laying, it is crucial to make clear that and how the purely *human*, i.e., *finite* reason, alone delimits the sphere of the problematic in advance. To this end, it is necessary to emphasize the essence of finite knowledge in general and the basic character of finitude as such. From this, the insight into the metaphysical—not the psychological and sensualistic—concept of sensibility as finite intuition arises for the first time. Because the intuition of human beings is finite, it requires thinking, which as such is finite through and through. (The idea of an infinite thinking is an absurdity.)

Finite knowledge consists of "two basic sources of the mind" (sensibility and understanding) or of "two stems" which "perhaps" "spring forth from a common, but to us unknown, root."

The elucidation of the possibility of ontological knowledge (synthetic a priori knowledge) becomes the question of the essence of a "pure" (experience-free) synthesis of pure intuition and pure thought.

The major stages of the carrying-through of the ground-laying, therefore, are the following:

a. The emphasizing of the *elements* of the essence of pure knowledge: i.e., of pure intuition (space, time) and pure thinking (Transcendental Aesthetic and Analytic of the Concepts).
b. Characterization of the *essential unity* of these elements in pure synthesis (§10 of the 2d ed.).
c. Elucidation of the *inner possibility* of this essential unit, i.e., of pure synthesis (Transcendental Deduction).
d. Unveiling of the *grounds* for the possibility of the essence of ontological knowledge (chapter on Schematism).

As to 3. The ground-laying in its originality.

Outcome of the former: the ground for the possibility of a priori synthetic knowledge is the transcendental power of imagination. In the course of the ground-laying, Kant introduced a *third* basic source of the mind, contrary to the operative point of departure.

This does not lie "between" both of the previously cited stems, but rather is their root.

This [root] is indicated by the fact that pure sensibility and pure understanding lead back to the power of imagination—not only this, but to theoretical and practical reason in their separateness and their unity.

The point of departure in reason has thus been broken asunder.

With that Kant himself, through his radicalism, was brought to the brink of a position from which he had to shrink back.

It implies: destruction of the former foundation of Western metaphysics (spirit, *logos*, reason).

It demands a radical, renewed unveiling of the grounds for the possibility of metaphysics as natural disposition of human beings, i.e., a metaphysics of Dasein directed at the possibility of metaphysics as such, which must pose the question concerning the essence of human beings in a way which is *prior to* all philosophical anthropology and cultural philosophy.

APPENDIX IV

DAVOS DISPUTATION BETWEEN ERNST CASSIRER
AND MARTIN HEIDEGGER

Cassirer: What does Heidegger understand by neo-Kantianism? Who is the opponent to whom Heidegger has addressed himself? I believe that there is hardly a single concept which has been paraphrased with so little clarity as that of neo-Kantianism. What does Heidegger have in mind when he employs his own phenomenological critique in place of the neo-Kantian one? Neo-Kantianism is the whipping boy of the newer philosophy. To me, there is an absence of existing neo-Kantians. I would be thankful for some clarification as to where it is here that the difference properly lies. I believe that absolutely no essential difference arises. The term "neo-Kantianism" must be determined functionally rather than substantially. It is not a matter of the kind of philosophy as dogmatic doctrinal system; rather, it is a matter of a direction taken in question-posing. As I had not expected to find it in him, I must confess that I have found a neo-Kantian here in Heidegger.

Heidegger: For the present, if I should name names, then I say: Cohen, Windelband, Rickert, Erdmann, Riehl. We can only understand what is common to neo-Kantianism on the basis of its origin. The genesis [of neo-Kantianism] lies in the predicament of philosophy concerning the question of what properly remains of it in the whole of knowledge. Since about 1850 it has been the case that both the human and the natural sciences have taken possession of the totality of what is knowable, so that the question arises: what still remains of Philosophy if the totality of beings has been divided up under the sciences? It remains just knowledge of science, not of beings. And it is from this perspective that the retrogression to Kant is then determined. Consequently, Kant was seen as a theoretician of the mathematico-physical theory of knowledge. Theory of knowledge is the aspect according to which Kant came to be seen. In a certain sense, Husserl himself fell into the clutches of neo-Kantianism between 1900 and 1910.

I understand by neo-Kantianism that conception of the *Critique of Pure Reason* which explains, with reference to natural science, the part of pure reason that leads up to the Transcendental Dialectic as theory of knowledge.

For me, what matters is to show that what came to be extracted here as theory of science was nonessential for Kant. Kant did not want to give any sort of theory of natural science, but rather wanted to point out the problematic of metaphysics, which is to say, the problematic of ontology. What matters to me is to work this core content of the positive element of the *Critique of Pure Reason* into ontology in a positive way. On the grounds of my interpretation of the Dialectic as ontology, I believe I am able to show that the problem of appearance in the Transcendental Logic, which for Kant is only negative in the form in which it first appears there, is [actually] a positive problem, and that the following is in question: is appearance just a matter of fact which we state, or must the entire problem of reason be apprehended in such a way that we grasp from the beginning how appearance necessarily belongs to the nature of human beings.

Cassirer: One only understands Cohen correctly if one understands him historically, not merely as epistemologist.[4] I do not conceive of my own development as a defection from Cohen. Naturally, in the course of my work much else has emerged, and, indeed, above all I recognized the position of mathematical natural science. However, this can only serve as a paradigm and not as the whole of the problem. And the same goes for Natorp. Now to Heidegger's basic systematic problem.

On one point we agree, in that for me as well the productive power of imagination appears in fact to have a central meaning for Kant. From there I was led through my work on the symbolic. One cannot unravel this [the symbolic] without referring it to the faculty of the productive power of imagination. The power of imagination is the connection of all thought to the intuition. Kant calls the power of imagination *Synthesis Speciosa*. Synthesis is the basic power [*Grundkraft*] of pure thinking. For Kant, however, it [pure thinking] does not depend simply on synthesis, but depends instead primarily upon the synthesis which serves the species. But this problem of the species leads into the core of the concept of image, the concept of symbol.

If we keep the whole of Kant's work in view, severe problems surface. One of these is the problem of freedom. For me, that was always really Kant's main problem. How is freedom possible? Kant says that this question does not allow being conceived in this way. We conceive only of the inconceivability of freedom. In opposition to this, then, I might now set the Kantian ethics [*Ethik*]: the Categorical Imperative must exist in such a condition that the law set up is not valid by chance just for human beings, but for all rational entities [*Vernunftwesen*] in general. Here suddenly is this remarkable transition. The restrictedness to a determinate sphere suddenly falls away. The ethical [*das Sittliche*] as such leads beyond the world of appearances. Yet this is so decisively metaphysical that a breakthrough now follows. It is a matter of the transition to the *mundus intelligibilis*. That holds for the ethical [*Ethische*], and in the ethical a point is reached which is no longer relative to the finitude of the knowing creature. Rather, an Absolute has now been set in place. This cannot be illuminated historically. One could speak of a step that Kant had not allowed to be consummated, but we cannot deny the fact that the problem of freedom has been posed in this way, that it broke through the original sphere.

And this ties in with Heidegger's arguments. The extraordinary significance of the Schematism cannot be overestimated. The greatest misunderstandings in the interpretation of Kant creep in at this point. In the ethical [*Ethischen*], however, he forbids the Schematism. There he says: our concepts of freedom, etc. are insights (not bits of knowledge) which no longer permit schematizing. There is a Schematism of theoretical knowledge, but not of practical reason. There is perhaps something else, namely, what Kant calls the Typic of Practical Reason, and he makes a distinction between Schematism and Typic. It is necessary to understand that one cannot penetrate this if one does not give up the Schematism here. For Kant, the Schematism is also the *terminus a quo*, but not the *terminus ad quem*. New problems arise in the *Critique of Practical Reason*, and Kant indeed always adheres to this point of departure in the Schematism, but it is also expanded upon. Kant fled from Heidegger's problem, but he expanded upon this sphere.

Summary: This expansion was therefore necessary because there is a problem at its core: Heidegger has emphasized that our power of knowledge is finite. It is relative and it is fixed. But then the question arises: how does such a finite creature in general come to have knowledge, to have reason, to have truth?

And now to the pertinent question. At one point Heidegger poses the problem of truth and says: there can be no truths in themselves, nor can there be any external truths at all. Rather, insofar as they occur in general, truths are relative to Dasein. And now it follows: A finite creature cannot in general possess eternal truths. For human beings there are no eternal and necessary truths, and here the whole problem again erupts. For Kant, the problem was precisely: Without prejudice to the finitude which Kant himself exhibited, how, nevertheless, can there be necessary and universal truths? How are synthetic, a priori judgments possible—judgments which are not simply finite in their content, but which are necessarily universal? It is therefore because of this problem that Kant exemplifies mathematics: Finite knowledge places itself in a relationship to truth which does not develop anew an "only." Heidegger said that Kant gave no proof for the possibility of mathematics. I believe that the question was well posed in the *Prolegomena*, but it is not and it cannot be the only question. But this pure theoretical question must first be clarified: How does this finite creature come to a determination of objects which as such are not bound to finitude?

Now my question is the following: Does Heidegger want to renounce this entire Objectivity, this form of absoluteness which Kant advocated in the ethical and the theoretical, as well as in the *Critique of Judgment*? Does he want to withdraw completely to the finite creature or, if not, where for him is the breakthrough to this sphere? I ask this question because I really do not yet know. The fixing of the point of transit, then, lies first with Heidegger. I believe, however, that Heidegger cannot be capable of abiding by it, nor can he want to. He must first pose these questions himself, and then, I believe, whole new problems emerge.

Heidegger: First of all, to the question of the mathematical natural sciences. One can say that Nature, as a region of beings, was for Kant not just any such region. For Kant, nature never signifies: object of mathematical natural science. Rather, the being of Nature is a being in the sense of what is at hand. In the Doctrine of Principles, what Kant really wanted to give is not a categorical, structural doctrine of the object of mathematical natural science. What he wanted was a theory of beings in general. (Heidegger verified this.) Kant sought a theory of Being in general, without assuming Objects which were given, without assuming a determinate region of beings (either psychic or physical). He sought a general ontology which exists prior to an Ontology of Nature as object of Natural Science and prior to an Ontology of Nature as object of Psychology. What I want to point out is that the Analytic is not just an Ontology of Nature as object of natural science, but is rather a general Ontology, a critical, well-established *Metaphysica Generalis*. Kant himself says: the problematic of the *Prolegomena*, where he consequently illustrates how natural science is possible, etc., is not the central motive. Rather, the central motive is the question concerning the possibility of *Metaphysica Generalis*, or rather the carrying-out of same.

But now to the other problem, that of the power of imagination. Cassirer wants to show that finitude becomes transcendent in the ethical writings. —In the Categorical Imperative we have something which goes beyond the finite creature. But precisely the concept of the Imperative as such shows the inner reference to a finite creature. Also, this going-beyond to something higher is always just a going-beyond to the finite creature, to one which is created (angel). This transcendence too still remains within the [sphere of] creatureliness [*Geschöpflichkeit*] and finitude. This inner relation, which lies within the Imperative itself, and the finitude of ethics, emerges from a passage in which Kant speaks of human reason as self-supporting, i.e., of a reason which stands purely on its own and which cannot escape into something eternal or absolute, but which also cannot escape into the world of things. This Being-among-them is the essence of Practical Reason. I believe that we proceed mistakenly in the interpretation of Kantian ethics if we first orient ourselves to that to which ethical action conforms and if we see too little of the inner function of the law itself for Dasein. We cannot discuss the problem of the finitude of the ethical creature if we do not pose the question: what does law mean here, and how is the lawfulness itself constitutive for Dasein and for the personality? It is not to be denied that something which goes beyond sensibility lies before the law. But the question is: How is the inner structure of Dasein itself, is it finite or infinite?

In this question of the going-beyond of finitude, we find a wholly central problem. I have said that it is a separate question to ask about the possibility of finitude in general, for one can formally argue simply: As soon as I make assertions about the finite and as soon as I want to determine the finite as finite, I must already have an idea of infinitude. For the moment this does not say much—and yet it says enough for a central problem to exist here. From the fact that now this character of infinitude comes to light precisely in what we have emphasized as the constituent of finitude, I want to make it clear that I would say: Kant describes the power of imagination of the Schematism as *exhibito originaria*. But this originality is an *exhibito*, an *exhibito* of the presentation of the free self-giving in which lies a dependency upon a taking-in-stride. So in a certain sense this originality is indeed there as creative faculty. As a finite creature, the human being has a certain infinitude in the ontological. But the human being is never infinite and absolute in the creating of the being itself; rather, it is infinite in the sense of the understanding of Being. But as Kant says, provided that the ontological understanding of Being is only possible within the inner experience of beings, this infinitude of the ontological is bound essentially to ontic experience so that we must say the reverse: this infinitude which breaks out in the power of imagination is precisely the strongest argument for finitude, for ontology is an index of finitude. God does not have it. And the fact that the human being has the *exhibito* is the strongest argument for its finitude, for ontology requires only a finite creature.

Then Cassirer's counter-question with reference to the concept of truth is elevated in importance. For Kant, ontological knowledge is what is universally necessary, what all factical experiences anticipate, and in connection with this I might point out that in other passages Kant says that what makes experience possible, the inner possibility of ontological knowledge, is accidental.—Truth itself is unified with the structure of transcendence on the most intimate level in order for Dasein to be a being open to others and to itself. We are a being which holds itself in the unconcealedness of beings. To hold oneself in this way in the openness of beings is what I describe as Being-in-truth, and I go further and say: On the grounds of the finitude of the Being-in-truth of human beings, there exists at the same time a Being-in-untruth. Untruth belongs to the innermost core of the structure of Dasein. And I believe here to have found for the first time the root upon which Kant's metaphysical "appearance" is metaphysically grounded.

Now to Cassirer's question concerning universally valid eternal truths. If I say: truth is relative to Dasein, this is no ontic assertion of the sort in which

I say: the true is always only what the individual human being thinks. Rather, this statement is a metaphysical one: in general, truth can only be as truth, and as truth it only has a sense in general if Dasein exists. If Dasein does not exist, there is no truth, and then there is nothing at all. But with the existence of something like Dasein, truth first comes in Dasein itself. Now, however, is the question: How does it stand with the validity of the eternality of truth? With respect to the problem of validity, this question always orients us toward the previously expressed statement, and from there we first come back to what is of value. And from there, we find worth or the like. I believe that the problem must be unraveled in another way. Truth is relative to Dasein. That is not to say that there would be no possibility for everyone to make the being evident as it is. But I would say that this transsubjectivity of truth, this breaking-out of the truth concerning the particulars themselves, as Being-in-truth, already means to be at the mercy of the being itself, to be placed into possibility to shape itself. What is redeemable here as objective knowledge has, according to the respective, factical, individual existence, a truth-content which, as content, says something about the being. The peculiar validity of which he spoke is poorly interpreted if we say: In contrast to the flow of experience there is a permanence, the eternal, the sense, and concept. I pose the counter-question: What, then, does the eternal actually mean here? From where, then, do we know of this eternity? Is this eternity not just permanence in the sense of the ἀεί[5] of time? Is this eternality not just that which is possible on the grounds of an inner transcendence of time itself? My whole interpretation of temporality has the metaphysical intention of asking: Are all these headings from transcendental metaphysics, namely a priori, ἀεὶ ὄν, οὐσία[6] — are they accidental, or from where do they come? If they speak of the eternal, how are they to be understood? They are only to be understood and are only possible owing to the fact that an inner transcendence lies within the essence of time; that time is not just what makes transcendence possible, but that time itself has in itself a horizonal character; that in future, recollected behavior I always have at the same time a horizon with respect to the present, futurity, and pastness in general; that a transcendental, ontological determination of time is found here, within which something like the permanence of the substance is constituted for the first time. —My whole interpretation of temporality is to be understood from this point of view. And in order to emphasize this inner structure of temporality and in order to show that time is not just a setting in which experiences play themselves out to make manifest this innermost character of temporality in Dasein itself, the effort made in my book is required. Every page in this book was written solely with a view to the fact that since antiquity the problem of Being was interpreted on the basis of time in a wholly incomprehensible sense and that time always announced the subject. With a view to the connection of this question to time, with a view to the question concerning Being in general, it is first a matter of bringing out the temporality of Dasein, not in the sense that is now worked out with any theory, but rather in the sense that, in a wholly determined problematic, the question concerning human Dasein will be posed. — This whole problematic in *Being and Time*, which treats Dasein in man, is no philosophical anthropology. For that it is much too narrow, much too preliminary. I believe that there is a problem here of a kind which hitherto has not been brought up as such, a problem which has been determined by means of the question: If the possibility of the understanding of Being is itself to be possible, and with it the possibility of the transcendence of man, and with it the possibility of the formative comporting toward beings and of the historical happening in the world history of man, and if this possibility has been grounded in an understanding of Being, and if this ontological understanding has been oriented in some sense with respect to time, then the task is: To bring out the temporality of Dasein with reference to the possibility of the understanding of Being. And it is with respect to this that all problems are oriented. In one direction, the analysis of death has the function of bringing out the radical futurity of Dasein, but not of producing an altogether final and metaphysical thesis concerning the essence of death. The analysis of anxiety does not have as its sole function the making-visible of a central phenomenon in man, but instead it has the function of preparing for the question: On the grounds of which metaphysical sense of Dasein itself is it possible that the human being in general can have been placed before something like the Nothing? In answer to this question, the analysis of anxiety was provided so that the possibility of something like the Nothing is thought of only as an idea which has also been grounded in this determination of the disposition of anxiety. It is only possible for me to understand Being if I understand the Nothing or anxiety. Being is incomprehensible if the Nothing is incomprehensible. And only in the unity of the understanding of Being and Nothing does the question of the origin [*Ursprung*] spring up [*springt . . . auf*] from the why. Why can man ask about the why, and why must he ask? These central problems of Being, the Nothing, and the why are the most elementary and the most concrete of problems. They are those to which the whole analytic of Dasein has been oriented. And I believe that from this initial grasping we have already seen that the whole supposition under which the critique of *Being and Time* stands, the proper kernel of intent, has not been encountered. On the other hand, as we have also already seen, I can very well concede that if in some measure we take this analytic of Dasein in *Being and Time* collectively as an investigation of the human being and then pose the question of how, on the grounds of this understanding of man, the understanding of a formation of culture and a cultural sphere is to be possible — that if we pose this question in this way, then it is an absolute impossibility to say something about what is under consideration here. All these questions are inadequate with respect to my central problem. At the same time, I pose a further methodological question: How, then, must such a metaphysics of Dasein, which has the ground for its determination in the problem of winning the foundation for the problem of the possibility of metaphysics, be put forth? Is a determinate world-view not taken as a basis for it? I would misunderstand myself if I said that I gave a philosophy free of points of view. And here a problem is expressed: that of the relationship between philosophy and world-view. Philosophy does not have the task of giving world-view, although, again, world-view is the presupposition of philosophizing. And the world-view which the philosopher gives is not a direct one in the sense of a doctrine or in the sense of an influencing. Rather, the world-view which the philosopher gives rests in the fact that in the philosophizing, it succeeds in making the transcendence of Dasein itself radical, i.e., it succeeds in making the inner possibility of this finite creature comport itself with respect to beings as a whole. To turn it another way: Cassirer says: We do not grasp freedom, but only the ungraspability of freedom. Freedom does not allow itself to be grasped. The question: How is freedom possible? is absurd. From this, however, it does not follow that to a certain extent a problem of the irrational remains here. Rather, because freedom is not an object of theoretical apprehending but is instead an object of philosophizing, this can mean nothing other than the fact that freedom only is and can only be in the setting-free. The sole, adequate relation to freedom in man is the self-freeing of freedom in man.

In order to get into this dimension of philosophizing, which is not a matter for a learned discussion but is rather a matter about which the individual philosopher knows nothing, and which is a task to which the philosopher has submitted himself—this setting-free of the Dasein in man must be the sole and central [thing] which philosophy as philosophizing can perform. And in this sense, I would believe that for Cassirer there is a wholly other *terminus ad quem* in the sense of a cultural philosophy. Further, I believe that for Cassirer this question of cultural philosophy first gets its metaphysical function in the happening of the history of humankind, if it is not to remain and to be a mere presentation of the various regions. Rather, at the same time within its inner dynamic, it is so deeply rooted that it becomes visible in the metaphysics of Dasein itself as basic happening, and so deeply rooted that it does so expressly and from the first, not after the fact.

Questions for Cassirer:
1. What path does man have to infinitude? And what is the manner in which man can participate in infinity?
2. Is infinitude to be attained as privative determination of finitude, or is infinitude a region in its own right?
3. To what extent does philosophy have as its task to be allowed to become free from anxiety? Or does it not have as its task to surrender man, even radically, to anxiety?

Cassirer: As for the first: In no way other than through the medium of form. This is the function of form, that while man changes the form of his Dasein, i.e., while he now must transpose everything in him which is lived experience into some objective shape in which he is objectified in such a way, to be sure, that he does not thereby become radically free from the finitude of the point of departure (for this is still connected to his particular finitude). Rather, while it arises from finitude, it leads finitude out into something new. And that is immanent infinitude. Man cannot make the leap from his own proper finitude into a realistic infinitude. He can and must have, however, the metabasis which leads him from the immediacy of his existence into the region of pure form. And he possesses his infinity solely in this form. "From out of the chalice of this spiritual realm, infinity flows to him." The spiritual realm is not a metaphysical spiritual realm; the true spiritual realm is just the spiritual world created from himself. That he could create it is the seal of his infinitude.

As to the second. It is not just a privative determination, but is instead a stranger sphere, although it is not one obtained in a purely negative way in addition to the finite. In infinitude, it is not just an opposition to finitude which is constituted but, in a certain sense, it is just the totality, the fulfillment of finitude itself. But this fulfillment of finitude exactly constitutes infinitude. Goethe: "If you want to step into infinitude, just go in all directions into the finite." As finitude is fulfilled, i.e., as it goes in all directions, it steps out into infinitude. This is the opposite of privation, it is the perfect filling-out of finitude itself.

As to the third. That is quite a radical question, to which one can answer only with a kind of confession. Philosophy had to allow man to become sufficiently free, to the extent that man can just become free. While it does that, I believe, it frees man—to be sure, in a certain radical sense—from anxiety as mere disposition. I believe, even according to Heidegger's explanations earlier today, that freedom can properly be found only along the path of progressive freeing, which indeed is also an infinite process for him. I believe that he can agree with this interpretation. Granted, I see that the most difficult problem is found here. I would like the sense, the goal, in fact the freeing, to be taken in this sense: "Anxiety throws the earthly from you." That is the position of idealism with which I have always been acquainted.

Pos[7]: Philological remark: Both men speak a completely different language. For us, it is a matter of extracting something common from these two languages. An attempt at translation was already made by Cassirer in his "Space for Action" ["*Aktionsraum*"]. We must hear the acknowledgment of this translation from Heidegger. The translational possibility extends to the point at which something emerges which does not allow translation. Those are the terms which demarcate what is characteristic of one of a group of languages. In both of these languages, I have attempted to gather several of these terms which I doubt would allow for translation into the other language. I nominate Heidegger's expressions: *Dasein*, Being, the ontic. On the other hand, I nominate Cassirer's expressions: the functional in spirit and the transformation of original space into another one.[8] Should it be found that there is no translation for these terms from both sides, then these would be the terms with which to differentiate the spirit of Cassirer's philosophy from Heidegger's.

Heidegger: In the first lecture, Cassirer used the expressions *terminus a quo* and *terminus ad quem*. One could say that for Cassirer the *terminus ad quem* is the whole of a philosophy of culture in the sense of an elucidation of the wholeness of the forms of the shaping consciousness. For Cassirer, the *terminus a quo* is utterly problematical. My position is the reverse: The *terminus a quo* is my central problematic, the one I develop. The question is: Is the *terminus ad quem* as clear for me? For me, this occurs not in the whole of a Philosophy of Culture, but rather in the question: τί τὸ ὄν, or rather: what in general is called Being? For me, it was from this question that the problematic of a Metaphysics of Dasein arose in order to win a foundation for the basic problem of metaphysics. Or, in order to come once more to the core of the interpretation of Kant: My intention was not to bring up something new in contrast to an epistemological interpretation and to bring honor to the power of imagination. Rather, it should be clear that the inner problematic of the *Critique of Pure Reason*, i.e., the question concerning the possibility of Ontology, is relegated to a radical bursting-open of the concept in the traditional sense, which was the end result for Kant. In attempting to lay the ground for Metaphysics, Kant was pressed in a way that makes the proper foundation into an abyss [*Abgrund*].[9] If Kant says: The three basic questions are allowed to lead back to the fourth: What is man?, then this question in its character as question has become questionable. I attempted to show that it is not at all self-evident to start from a concept of *logos*, but instead that the question of the possibility of metaphysics demands a metaphysics of Dasein itself as possibility of the fundament of a question of metaphysics. In this way, the question of what man is must be answered not so much in the sense of an anthropological system, but instead it must first be properly clarified with regard to the perspective from within which it wants to be posed.

And here I come back to the concepts *terminus a quo* and *terminus ad quem*. Is this just a heuristic questioning, or does it lie in the essence of Philosophy itself that it has a *terminus a quo* which must be made into a problem and that it has a *terminus ad quem* which correlates to the *terminus a quo*? This problematic does not yet appear to me to have been coined clearly in Cassirer's philosophy up to now. Cassirer's point is to emphasize the various forms of the shaping in order, with a view to these shapings, subsequently to point out a certain dimension of the shaping powers themselves. Now, one could say: this dimension, then, is fundamentally the same as that which I call Dasein.

But that would be erroneous. The difference is clearest in the concept of Freedom. I spoke of a freeing in the sense that the freeing of the inner transcendence of Dasein is the fundamental character of philosophizing itself. In so doing, the authentic sense of this freeing is not to be found in becoming free to a certain extent for the forming images of consciousness and for the realm of form. Rather, it is to be found in becoming free for the finitude of Dasein. Just to come into the thrownness of Dasein is to come into the conflict which lies within the essence of freedom. I did not give freedom to myself, although it is through Being-free that I can first be I myself. But now, not I myself in the sense of an indifferent ground for explanation, but rather: Dasein is the authentic basic occurrence in which the existing of man, and with it every problematic of existence itself, becomes essential.

Based on this, I believe we can answer the question by Pos concerning translation. I believe that what I describe by Dasein does not allow translation into a concept of Cassirer's. Should one say consciousness, that is precisely what I rejected. What I call Dasein is essentially codetermined—not just through what we describe as spirit, and not just through what we call living. Rather, what it depends on is the original unity and the immanent structure of the relatedness of a human being which to a certain extent has been fettered in a body and which, in the fetteredness in the body, stands in a particular condition of being bound up with beings. In the midst of this it finds itself, not in the sense of a spirit which looks down on it, but rather in the sense that Dasein, thrown into the midst of beings, as free, carries out an incursion into the being which is always spiritual and, in the ultimate sense, accidental. [It is] so accidental that the highest form of the existence of Dasein is only allowed to lead back to very few and rare glimpses of Dasein's duration between living and death. [It is] so accidental that man exists only in very few glimpses of the pinnacle of his own possibility, but otherwise moves in the midst of his beings.

The question concerning the type of Being of what is set into his Philosophy of Symbolic Form, the central question concerning the inner constitution of Being, is what the Metaphysics of Dasein determines—and it does not determine it with the intention of a previously given systematic of the cultural jurisdiction and of the philosophical disciplines. In the entirety of my philosophical efforts, I left completely undecided the traditional shape and division of the philosophical disciplines, because I believe that the orientation to these is the greatest misfortune in the sense that we no longer come back to the inner problematic of philosophy. To an equal degree, neither Plato nor Aristotle could have known of such a division of philosophy. A division of this sort was the concern of the schools, i.e., of a philosophy that has lost the inner problematic of its questioning; and it requires exertion to break through these disciplines. What is more, that is why if we pass through the disciplines of aesthetics, etc., we again come back to the specific metaphysical mode of

Being of the region concerned. Art is not just a form of consciousness which shapes itself; rather, art itself has a metaphysical sense within the basic occurrence of Dasein itself.

I have intentionally singled out these differences. It is not suitable to the task at hand if we come up against a process of leveling. Rather, because it is only in and through the rigor of what has been brought forth that the problem gains clarity, I would like once more to place our entire discussion in terms of Kant's *Critique of Pure Reason* and to fix once more the question of what man is as the central question. At the same time, however, [I would like to fix it] as the question which we pose not in some isolated ethical sense, but instead so that both positions become clear on the basis of the problematic, so that the question of man is only essential for the philosophers in the way in which the philosopher simply disregards himself, so that the question may not be posed anthropocentrically. On the contrary, it must be shown that: because man is the creature who is transcendent, i.e., who is open to beings in totality and to himself, that through this eccentric character man at the same time also stands within the totality of beings in general—and that only in this way do the question and the idea of a Philosophical Anthropology make sense. The question concerning the essence of human beings is not to be understood in the sense that we study human beings empirically as given objects, nor is it to be understood in such a way that I project an anthropology of man. Rather, the question concerning the essence of human beings only makes sense and is only justifiable insofar as it derives its motivation from philosophy's central problematic itself, which leads man back beyond himself and into the totality of beings in order to make manifest to him there, with all his freedom, the nothingness of his Dasein. This nothingness is not the occasion for pessimism and melancholy. Instead, it is the occasion for understanding that authentic activity takes place only where there is opposition and that philosophy has the task of throwing man back, so to speak, into the hardness of his fate from the shallow aspect of a man who merely uses the work of the spirit.

Cassirer: I, too, am opposed to leveling. What we both want to, and must, strive for, and also what we can achieve, is that anyone, for all that he remains with his own position, would see not only himself but the other as well. That this must be possible appears to me to lie in the idea of philosophical knowledge in general, in an idea which Heidegger too will appreciate. I do not want to make the attempt to break Heidegger from his position, to force him into another direction of seeing. Instead, I want only to make his position understandable to me.

I believe that where the disagreement lies has already become clearer. It is not fruitful, however, to highlight this disagreement again and again. We maintain a position where little is to be accomplished through arguments which are merely logical. Nobody can be compelled to take up this position, and no such purely logical compulsion can force someone to begin with the position which appears to me to be the essential one. Hence we have been condemned here to a relativity. "What one chooses for a philosophy depends upon what sort of human being one is." But we may not persevere in this relativity, which would be central for empirical men. And what Heidegger finally said was very important.

Like mine, his position cannot be anthropocentric, and if it does not want to be such, then I ask where the common core of our disagreement lies. That it cannot be in the empirical is clear. We must search again for the common center, precisely in the disagreement. And I say, we do not need to search. For we have this center and, what is more, this is so because there is a common, objective human world in which the differences between individuals have in no way now been superseded, but with the stipulation that the bridge here from individual to individual has now been knocked down. This occurs repeatedly for me in the primal phenomenon of language. Each of us speaks his own language, and it is unthinkable that the language of one of us is carried over into the language of the other. And yet, we understand ourselves through the medium of language. Hence, there is something like *the* language. And hence there is something like a unity which is higher than the infinitude of the various ways of speaking. Therein lies what is for me the decisive point. And it is for that reason that I start from the Objectivity of the symbolic form, because here the inconceivable has been done. Language is the clearest example. We assert here that we tread on a common ground. We assert this first of all as a postulate. And in spite of all deceptions, we will not become confused about this claim. This is what I would like to call the world of the objective [objektiven] spirit. From Dasein is spun the thread which, through the medium of such an objective spirit, again ties us together with another Dasein. And I believe that there is no other way from Dasein to Dasein than through this world of forms. There is this factum. Should this not be so, then I would not know how there could be something like a self-understanding. Knowing is also just a basic instance of this assertion: that an objective statement can be formulated about a matter and that it has the character of necessity which no longer takes notice of the subjectivity of the individual.

Heidegger rightly said that the basic question of his metaphysics is the same one which Plato and Aristotle defined: what is the being?[10] And he further said that Kant had again referred to this question which is basic to all metaphysics. This I concede without further ado. But here an essential difference appears to me to exist, namely, with respect to what Kant called the Copernican Turn.[11] Indeed, the question of Being appears to me in no way to have been done away with by this turn. That would be a completely false interpretation. But as a result of this turn, the question of Being now comes to have an extremely complicated shape, as it had had in antiquity. Wherein does the turn

occur? "Previously it was accepted that knowledge must conform to the object
. . . But for once, we now attempt the reverse question. How would it be if it
were not our knowledge that must conform to the object, but if instead it were
the object that must conform to knowledge?" That means that this question
regarding the determinacy of the object is preceded by a question concerning
the constitution of the Being of objectivity in general. And what is applicable
to this objectivity in general now must also apply to every object within this
structure of Being. What is new in this [Copernican] turn appears to me to lie
in the fact that now there is no longer one single such structure of Being, but
that instead we have completely different ones. Every new structure of Being
has its new a priori presuppositions. Kant shows that he was bound to the
conditions for the possibility of experience. Kant shows how every kind of new
form now also refers to a new world of the objective, how the aesthetic object
is not bound to the empirical object, how it has its own a priori categories,
how art also builds up a world, but also how these laws are different from the
laws of the physical. For this reason, a completely new multiplicity enters into
the problem of the object in general. And for this reason, the new Kantian
metaphysics comes into being precisely from out of ancient, dogmatic metaphysics. Being in ancient metaphysics was substance, what forms a ground.[12]
Being in the new metaphysics is, in my language, no longer the Being of a
substance, but rather the Being which starts from a variety of functional determinations and meanings. And the essential point which distinguishes my position from Heidegger's appears to me to lie here.

I stand by the Kantian posing of the question of the transcendental as Cohen
repeatedly formulated it. He saw what is essential to the Transcendental
Method in that this method began with a factum, only[13] it had this general
definition: to begin with a factum in order to ask about the possibility of this
factum, further narrowed down, while mathematical natural science again and
again makes it out to be what is properly questionable. Kant does not stand
within this reduction. But I ask about the possibility of the language of the
factum. How does it come about, how is this, about which we are able to
come to an understanding, thinkable from Dasein to Dasein in this medium?
How is it possible that now and in general we can see a work of art as an
objective determination, as an Objective being, as this significant [thing] in
its wholeness?

This question must be settled. Perhaps from here on, not all of the questions
of Philosophy are to be settled. Perhaps from here on we cannot approach
vast areas. But it is necessary that we pose this question in the first place. And
I believe that if we have posed this question, we have made access to the
question which Heidegger poses free for the first time.

Heidegger: Cassirer's last question in Kant's confrontation with the ancients
gives me another opportunity to characterize the total work. I say that Plato's

question must be retrieved. This cannot mean that we retreat to the Greeks' answer. It turns out that Being itself has been dispersed in a multiplicity and that a central problem exists therein, namely, to attain the foundation in order to understand the inner multiplicity of the ways of Being based on the idea of Being. For my part, I am anxious to establish this sense of Being in general as central. Accordingly, the only trouble for my investigations has been judged to be [the need] to attain the horizon for the question concerning Being, its structure and multiplicity.

Mere mediating will never amount to anything productive. It is the essence of philosophy as a finite concern of human beings that it has been confined within the finitude of human beings as something which is not a creative human achievement. Because philosophy opens out onto the totality and what is highest in man, finitude must appear in philosophy in a completely radical way.

What it comes down to is that you take one thing with you from our debate: do not orient yourselves to the variety of positions of philosophizing human beings, and do not occupy yourselves with Cassirer and Heidegger. Rather, the point is that you have come far enough to have felt that we are on the way toward once again getting down to business with the central question of metaphysics. And on top of that, I would like to point out to you that in small measure what you have seen here is the difference between philosophizing human beings in the unity of the problematic, which on a large scale expresses something completely different, and that it is precisely this freeing of itself from the difference of positions and standpoints which is essential in the debate with the history of philosophy, that it is the first step in the history of philosophy; [it is essential to see] precisely how the differentiation of standpoints is the root of the philosophical endeavor.[14]

APPENDIX V

On Odebrecht's and Cassirer's Critiques of the Kantbook

Basic Question: The Essence and Grounding of the
Finitude of Human Knowledge; the Problem of Finitude in General

1. *The Finitude of Knowing*
(Cassirer, Odebrecht)
(On Their Critiques of My Kant Interpretation)

1) What ought we to find, or do we want to find, from the comparison of our knowing with the absolute? Simply to explain what is meant by the finitude of *our* knowing, wherein its finitude can be seen.

Absolute knowing is merely a constructed idea (see p. 17), that is, it comes from our knowing, in which the specifically finite has been separated and its essence has been freed. The actual knowledge of the actual Being-at-hand of absolute knowledge—which is to say, the *being* of *God himself*—is not needed here. Moreover, we have proven its *finitude* in the first place precisely by only bringing it to the construction of the leading idea.

2) In absolutely no way is finite knowing "deduced" by me from absolute intuition, as *Odebrecht* claims (*Blätter für Deutsche Philosophie*, V, 1, 1931) when he says "the intuitional character of thinking [can be said to] follow necessarily from the broad concept of *intuitus originarius*."

Furthermore: in absolutely no way does this follow from anywhere through deduction, but rather it manifests itself to us in the fundamental experience of the dependency upon what is given. Everything remains as it was for the ancients, even if we conceive of *designating* this as *finite* knowing (to be sure, the finite must then necessarily be explained *differently*, as "earthly"—the perspective and level of this interpretation). Thus it *must* have been composed and named together with and in reference to *Kant's design* (see Phenomena and Noumena! *Kant and the Problem of Metaphysics*, p. 23f.!; see *Kant and the Problem of Metaphysics*: finitude—*elucidated*, wherein it consists with reference to our knowing, with a view toward same).

Thrownness (*Geworfenheit*), the ground for the finitude of knowing (see *Kant and the Problem of Metaphysics*, p. 19), at first grasped as dependency upon beings other than ourselves. Finitude is primarily not that of knowing;

rather, that is but an essential consequence of throwness. And it is precisely therein that the necessity of *thinking* as in service to intuition is grounded, assuming that *interpretation and determinacy* is necessary to the experience of beings (if it was shown to be necessary for *finite* intuiting *qua* primary, finite knowledge, then at the same time the appointment [*Dienststellung*] and the serving [*Dienen*] are shown to be intrinsic to the understanding (see *Kant and the Problem of Metaphysics*, p. 19f.)).

"Thinking" is the index of finitude, i.e., dependency upon intuition, which itself is dependency upon what is given—throwness springs forth. This springing-forth, or grounding, means essential relationships. *Thinking is not reduced to intuiting* (Odebrecht), *but is maintained as representing*, and to understand the representing from something in general, [is to understand] that *for it* finite intuition is necessarily required if it is to be knowledge.

"*Knowing is primarily intuiting*" (*Kant and the Problem of Metaphysics*, p. 15, see notes there), i.e., the *grounding character in knowing is intuiting*. For finite knowing, however, this character as foundational in a primordial sense is indeed necessary, but—precisely because [the knowing] is finite—it is *not sufficient*.

The formal and apophantic-veritative essences of *judgment*, then, are shown from the subordinate character of thinking.

The understanding is *essential* for *finite* knowing, i.e., it itself surpasses intuition, namely in its character of finitude.

2. On Cassirer's Critique

A basic question in *two* respects. Essence of knowledge:

1) that knowledge is "*primarily*" (see text) intuition (not knowledge = intuition), but infinite: "only" intuition (finitude as construction).

"Primarily" refers to "secondarily"—and the latter is not *unimportant*, but rather is essentially just as necessary, but in the structure of the *subordinance* [*Dienststellung*]; that this subordinant [*Dienende*]—as *finite*—*mistakes* precisely itself, which still is no proof for infinitude, but rather the reverse. Kant himself did not develop *this* Phenomenon.

2) From all of this, then, knowledge is a) neither intuition nor thinking "by *itself*," b) but also not: intuition *as well as* thinking, both together, but rather c) the *third*, but *this* as also the more originary, the power of imagination and "time"; but with this we still have a *problem*!

3. Cassirer

What should we make of the teaching as to the spontaneity of the understanding, where for me it is precisely the power of the imagination which has been brought to center stage.

But Cassirer says nothing about the fact that this emphasis on the understanding is indeed ambiguous, that the Marburg [School] undertook something quite different—only understanding and only logic and intuition are simply a disagreeable residue that *should not be part of* the infinite process. *Space and Time as Concepts of the Understanding*!!

I never assert that the Understanding simply brings out something after the fact which is, as it were, superfluous! (Schleppe).

And what Cassirer wants with the torchbearer is thus only an image and says absolutely nothing concerning the essence of the *relation* of thinking to intuition; but that is precisely what is concealed as a problem in the phenomenon of the *Power of Imagination*.

4. *On Cassirer*
Essence of the Understanding and Finitude

The understanding serves as *torchbearer*, serving in any case, and what does *bearing a torch* mean—to illuminate!

It is essentially not what gives the light [*Licht*], but rather what needs the clearing [*Lichtung*]; as understanding, it is simply *to determine*. It *only* illuminates as *schematic Understanding*; from itself, in fact, it is not even able to *serve*.

Cassirer sticks to the letter and overlooks precisely the problematic of pure understanding and logic.

5. *"Finitude"* (Cassirer)

To be sure—a problem, but the decisive question is in fact: why? and how!

To philosophize only in this way concerning finitude, because at one time or another it emerges in the moment as a kind of hangover, but this is certainly no *philosophical* motivation.

It looks like Cassirer had the central theme and yet *completely* passed it by!

6. *Cassirer* (Universal)

Cassirer adheres to his wonderful principle—compliance with Intention ("finitude"? Yes and no!): Question of Being and question concerning man, so that even this becomes problematic—thus the whole problem of consciousness is in motion; *Marburg* [*School*]: Intuition and Thinking, even *the third*!

No! Neither this problem nor the entire interpretation of this question has been understood and assessed. In its place: objections from various sides that have awkward or fallacious aspects but that are all *in part* correct. Cassirer completely misunderstands that what is decisive for interpretation is the working-out of a problem, and indeed that this problem must first be made visible, and that this comes about through recollection of Kant. *In this way* an interpretation was demanded. This determines the historical objectivity. A *Kant in-itself*—which presumably "does not concern" us, or is indeterminate in all respects (Ebbinghaus)—is a fundamental misunderstanding.

But Cassirer also works with the hidden idea of a correct interpretation of this sort.

7. On Cassirer

Agreed: not to cover the entire scope of the problematic (17). Also the intention was never this: to interpret just a part, but instead from one [part], even from the *grounding problem*, [the intention is] to reveal in Kant the "problem of metaphysics," and precisely on the basis of the "part," which was prevented by its customary interpretation as simply "theory of knowledge."

In *this part*, the perspective should be pursued in the direction of the *problem of metaphysics*, which even *Kant fundamentally changed*—the *basis* and location for this change.

8. On Cassirer

Intention: clarification of the common endeavor!

Question: Why cannot Cassirer stick to the ground I picked (p. 3)?

1) Is the *problem of metaphysics* to be unfolded and grounded in a different way?

2) Is Kant not factically moving along this same ground?

3) Or is only *the extent to which* he *consciously* or *primarily* did this debatable?

With respect to 3), I confess without further elaboration, that my interpretation is violent and excessive, but particularly with regard to the assumptions from 1) and 2)!!

The intention pertains to Kant—*and* the *problem* of metaphysics!

9.

The popular quotation of the well-known letter to M. Herz indeed requires that we finally for once question its correctness. It is too seldom noticed that after Kant said he believed he would be ready "within about three months," in fact he required almost ten years.

There must indeed have been something else that broke down in the interim. In the letter, the problem is still all too traditional, although already critically oriented toward the question concerning the possibility of pure abstract knowledge, as if it simply existed for-itself. Although he noticed sensuality, finitude was certainly not properly central.

10. *Cassirer*

The merely anthropological and the law of sensual content, appearance and the thing-in-itself. Instead of Being and Time, *Being and Duty*.

But: Idea—itself *Schema*! (analogue). Law—*intrinsically represented*.

11.

Being in the modality of ought-to-be [*Sollseins*]

12.

The practical reality of freedom. This is [something] intelligible but even theoretically it is *not* comprehensible.

Finite rational essence—affected by sensuousness. *This as such* is not merely anthropological, but is instead the *whole essence*. Precisely *this separation*—sense-content and the merely "psychological"—is to be overcome.

APPENDIX VI

On the History of the Philosophical Chair since 1866

The time frame of this account coincides with the establishing, strengthening, working-out and reorganization of philosophical research at Marburg University, which already has its fixed and unequivocal place in the history of Philosophy as the "*Marburg School*."

By the middle of the 19th century, the breakdown of the Hegelian school led to a general decline of philosophy. Within the confines of the contemporary, towering positive sciences (history and the natural sciences), philosophy altogether lost its prestige. Where it was well kept up, it took place in the midst of an ignorance and perversion of its proper essence. It was able to obtain validity before the predominant scientific consciousness by means of an assimilation of itself, which ran counter to itself, with the positive sciences as *natural-scientific* "philosophy" (psychology), that is, as philosophical *history*.

The uplifting renewal of scientific philosophy underway since the [18]60s undertook, even if in a groping way, to win back an understanding of the original philosophical problematic. The concern with the object, the manner of treatment, and the systematic unity of philosophy received decisive impetus and made fundamental advances through the research conducted at Marburg University. First of all, this [research] sought to secure once again the scientific essence of Philosophy by means of a new appropriation of Kant's "critical" work. In fact, during the 60s, through the work of Ed. Zeller (Professor of Philosophy in Marburg, 1849–62), Otto Liebmann, Herm. Helmholtz and Fr. A. Lange (Ordinarius in Philosophy at Marburg, 1873–75), the call was loudly sounded: back to *Kant*! First, in his work *Kant's Theory of Experience* (1871), H. Cohen had placed the re-appropriation of Kant that was already underway upon a scientifically decisive ground, and in so doing he influenced the subsequent playing-out of "Neo-Kantianism" in both a positive and a negative way. During this same time, two works appeared, W. Dilthey's *Leben Schleiermachers I* (1870) and Fr. Brentano's *Psychologie vom empirischen Standpunkt I* (1874), in which tendencies other than a renewal of Kant were maintained. They became, however, the point of departure for Dilthey's *Lebensphilosophie*, which was oriented with respect to the problem of Dasein's historicality, and provided the impetus for the development of *phenomenological* research, which was grounded in [the work of] E. Husserl. In both instances, which today have systematically begun to be fused, the way was paved for the overcoming

Kant and the Problem of Metaphysics [305-306]

of Neo-Kantianism, indeed to such an extent that they encouraged the strengthening and reorganization of the "Marburg School."

In his major philosophical work *Geschichte des Materialismus* (1865), Fr. A. Lange had assigned a fundamental philosophical meaning to Kant's critical idealism, to the extent that in [Kant's critical idealism], Materialism as "the simplest, *regulative* world view" must be overcome. Lange immediately knew the importance of Cohen's work, based on an understanding of Kant he had laboriously worked out for himself, and he did not hesitate to insert a renewed examination into his own Kant interpretation. Lange arranged for Cohen's habilitation in Marburg (November 1873). After Weißenborn's death the following year, Cohen was the sole candidate to be nominated for Ordinarius. In fact, he did not get this appointment; but as of Easter 1875 he was appointed Extraordinarius Professor, and upon Lange's death (November 1875) he assumed [Lange's] Professorship, which he would hold until 1912. Following his appointment to Emeritus status, Cohen relocated to Berlin where, in addition to writing actively, he held lectures and classes at the Jewish theological academy there until his death (April 1918).

Cohen looked for the center of the Kantian problematic in the original synthetic unity of transcendental apperception. He saw the problem of the constitution of reality in general as contained in the question concerning the origin of the objectivity of the objects of mathematico-physical knowledge in the coherent execution of pure thinking. With the task of a transcendental-logical grounding of the scientific knowledge of nature understood in this way, philosophy should maintain an original complex of problems that is fundamentally inaccessible to the exact sciences. The boundary between theoretical knowledge on the one hand, and the moral-practical and artistic-formative conduct of the subject on the other, presses for a correspondingly far-reaching interpretation of Kant, which Cohen presented in his works *Kants Begründung der Ethik* (1877) and *Kants Begründung der Ästhetik* (1889).

Within this threefold, transcendental laying of the ground for the "world of objects" lies the question of the *systematic unity* of the entire transcendental grounding itself. In his text *Das Prinzip der Infinitesimalmethode und seine Geschichte* (1883), Cohen developed the first and, for his future work, decisive discussion of the idea of system. In the subtitle, it is described as "A Chapter on the Laying of the Ground for the Critique of Knowledge." The change of the expression "Critique of Reason" to "Critique of Knowledge" expresses one of Cohen's principle convictions, which later dominated his own attempts at constructing a system: knowledge is science, or more precisely, mathematical natural science. Accordingly, critical Idealism becomes "scientific" first and foremost by taking "the fact [*Tatsache*] of *science*" to be the object of the transcendental grounding. "In science alone are things given and palpably at hand [*vorhanden*] for philosophical questions." "The knowing consciousness . . . only has in the fact [*Tatsache*] of scientific knowledge that reality to which a philosophical investigation can refer." As a consequence of this narrow fastening together of transcendental philosophy with the scientific fact [Faktum], it also came to pass that ethical and aesthetic objects as *scientifically known* became a problem. In fact, Cohen postulated jurisprudence [Rechtswissenschaft] as the alleged science for ethics, while in aesthetics he was oriented directly toward the works of art and not, as the idea of system would have it, toward the science *of* the works. The systematic of the basic concepts of logic, ethics, and aesthetics, oriented in such a manner, gets worked out in Cohen's three-part system (*Logik der reinen Erkenntnis*, 1902; *Ethik des reinen Wollens*, 1904; *Ästhetik des reinen Gefühls*, 1912). While so far Cohen had dissolved the philosophical problem of religion into that of ethics, in his text *Der Begriff der Religion im System der Philosophie* (1915) he sought to determine the unique meaning of the phenomenon of religion.

Although Cohen never published a great work in the history of philosophy other than his works of Kant interpretation, nonetheless from the beginning his systematic work was nourished and guided through constant engagement with the Pre-Socratics, Plato and Nicholas Cusanus, Descartes and Leibniz.

Cohen's long-time co-worker and friend, Paul Natorp, carried out a more concrete, thorough, and insightful examination of ancient and modern philosophy by means of a systematic understanding of the problems. In the autumn of 1881, Natorp habilitated at Marburg University; in 1885 he became a lecturer at the university; in 1893, as successor to J. Bergmann (see below), he became Ordinarius Professor of Philosophy. In 1922 he became Emeritus, in spite of the fact that he was still active with lectures and classes. Natorp died shortly after his 70th birthday in August 1924. Because Natorp's philosophical work initially took place scrupulously in the same spirit as Cohen's, he could later see the essential gaps and one-sided aspects of the system more clearly, and he could bring it to a more originally grounded, independent level of development. Natorp's earliest investigations were concerned with the loosening up of ancient philosophy through the history of [philosophical] problems. The work *Forschungen zur Geschichte des Erkenntnisproblems im Altertum* (1884) had a strong influence on science. The work *Platos Ideenlehre. Eine Einführung in den Idealismus* (1903) indeed met with fierce opposition. Regardless of the tenability of individual interpretations, it performed the urgent task of clarifying that the history of Philosophy cannot dispense with a systematic understanding of the problem as a hermeneutical presupposition of its work. In a treatise that is too seldom considered, called *Über Thema und Disposition der aristotelischen Metaphysik* (*Philos. Monatshefte*, vol. XXIV, 1888), Natorp anticipated results and problems in which the present age first became more accessible.

The transcendental laying-of-the-ground for logical, ethical and aesthetic conduct has its "highest point" in the subject. Thus the ground-laying itself first comes to the ground through a thematic consideration of consciousness in the sense of a nonempirical Transcendental Psychology. Natorp communicated his first experiments in this direction in his *Einleitung in die Psychologie nach kritischer Methode* (1888). During the following two decades, in the course of his debate with the more spirited, well-formed, fundamental conception of psychology (Dilthey and Husserl), the importance of which psychology itself can only grasp today, Natorp pushed forward to a radical formulation of the problem. The new position was in evidence in the re-casting of the earlier *Einleitung*, which appeared in 1912 as *Allgemeine Psychologie nach kritischer Methode I*. In this work, as was the case with all of his philosophical work, Natorp increasingly aimed for a *systematic unfolding* of the systematic unity of philosophy. In order to overcome a superficial and after-the-fact condensation of the transcendental philosophical disciplines, which had always fundamentally remained standing for Cohen, it was above all a matter of breaking away from the leveling, which Cohen forced, of all possible ways of comportment of Spirit to the sciences *of* these ways of comportment. With the elimination of the methodical priority of the sciences, theoretical comportment draws "alongside" the "atheoretical," i.e., the moral, the artistic, and the religious. The idea of logic was freed from the confines of a laying of the grounds for the sciences, that is, from a "theorizing," and along with the "practical" and the "poetic," it was *pre*-classified as universal doctrine of categories. The freer posing of philosophical questions concerning the originality of the individual areas of spiritual life, prepared for in this way, resulted in a more open interpretation of spiritual history. At the same time, it made possible the positive evaluation of the fundamental meaning of a phenomenological categorical analysis of "subjective" and "objective" spirit. Natorp's own *Vorlesungen über praktische Philosophie*, which were still being readied for publication and which first appeared after his death (1925), offered a concrete glimpse into the new and comprehensively systematic tendencies in his thought.

From the Philosophical Seminar that was established in 1900 a series of valuable investigations have emerged which, since 1906, have been assembled in *Philosophische Arbeiten*, edited by H. Cohen and P. Natorp.

The continuation and re-casting of the "Marburg School" is manifest today in the work of Ernst Cassirer (Ordinarius Professor in Hamburg) and Nicolai Hartmann (habilitated in Marburg in 1909, *außerordentlicher* Professor 1920, Ordinarius Professor as Natorp's successor 1922, since Autumn of 1925 in Cologne). While A. Görland (Professor in Hamburg) and W. Kinkel (Professor in Gießen) for the most part held to the position established by Cohen, for years Cassirer strove to lay out a universal "Philosophy of Culture" on the basis of Neo-Kantian questioning. His *Philosophy of Symbolic Forms* (Part 1, *Language*, 1923; Part 2, *Mythical Thinking*, 1925) attempted to lay out the comportment and shaping of spirit, guided by the idea of the "expression" of a systematic interpretation. Cassirer converges with Natorp's efforts in a particular way, which has its importance more in the universal categorial founding of the system, and not in the concrete interpretation of the individual "symbols" of spirit.

Hartmann's investigations (*Grundzüge einer Metaphysik der Erkenntnis*, 1921, and *Ethik*, 1926) move in the direction of a fundamental change in the problematic of the "school." The understanding of the *ontological* problem, which was newly awakened and guided by phenomenological research and the theory of the object, and which since Antiquity has determined the great tradition of scientific philosophy, led Hartmann to attempt to twist not only epistemological questioning, but rather philosophical questioning in general, out of the narrow confines of the idealistic-critical horizon. In so doing, he nevertheless held fast to the traditional standing of the philosophical disciplines and the prevailing perspectives on problems that they held. As a consequence of this systematic reformation of the "Marburg School," a new understanding is awakened for the history of universal and special ontology. Through his investigation into the ontological antecedents of Kantian philosophy, H. Heimsoeth (habilitated in Marburg, 1912, since autumn of 1923 Ordinarius Professor in Königsberg) advanced in an essential way the knowledge of the development of metaphysics.

Outside of the "school," Julius Bergmann, as Ordinarius in Philosophy from 1874–93, exhibited an urgency and independence in his teaching. As of October 1, 1893, he resigned and relinquished the stipend earned from his lecturing obligations, but he still remained in full possession of his rights as a faculty member until his death in 1904. Bergmann was a student of Lotze and Trendelenburg. His work in the area of the logic of metaphysics (*Allgemeine Logik*, 1879; *Sein und Erkennen*, 1880; *Die Grundprobleme der Logik*, 1882; *Untersuchungen über Hauptpunkte der Philosophie*, 1900) left an impression just as unobtrusive as it was strong. Bergmann established the journal *Philosophischen Monatshefte* in 1868, which was the leading technical journal during the final decade of the last century and which was merged with the "*Archiv für Geschichte der Philosophie*" in 1894.

In 1908, those who managed to attain Extraordinarius in Philosophy were P. Menzer (in Marburg since 1906, called to Halle in 1908 as Ordinarius); H. Schwarz (1908–10, after being Ordinarius in Greifswald); G. Misch (1911–17, after being Ordinarius in Göttingen); M. Wundt (1918–20, after being Ordinarius in Jena); N. Hartmann (1920–22).

REFERENCES FOR APPENDICES

"Besprechung: Ernst Cassirer, *Philosophie der symbolischen Formen*. 2. Teil: *Das mythische Denken*." Berlin: Bruno Cassirer Verlag, 1925 [Appendix II in this volume—tr.]. Appeared in: *Deutsche Literaturzeitung* (Berlin), new series 5 (1928), no. 21, 1000-1012. [This review appeared previously in English in the volume *The Piety of Thinking* (Bloomington: Indiana University Press, 1976—tr.]

"Davoser Vorträge: Kants *Kritik der reinen Vernunft* und die Aufgabe einer Grundlegung der Metaphysik" [Appendix III in this volume—tr.]. Appeared in *Davoser Revue*, IV (1929), no. 7, pp. 194-196.

"Zur Geschichte des philosophischen Lehrstuhles seit 1866" [Appendix VI in this volume—tr.]. Appeared in *Die Philipps-Universität zu Marburg 1527-1927* (Marburg: N. G. Elwert'sche Verlagsbuchhandlung [G. Braun], 1927), pp. 681-687.

EDITOR'S AFTERWORD

This third volume of [Heidegger's] Collected Works contains the text of the expanded fourth edition of the book "Kant and the Problem of Metaphysics," which was published in 1973. This expanded fourth edition was overseen by Martin Heidegger himself and was accomplished through the inclusion of an Appendix. This volume, the appendix to which has again been expanded to now include four [additional] texts, appears simultaneously as a separate, augmented fifth edition.

The first edition from 1929 was published by Friedrich Cohen Press of Bonn, which had been under the management of Vittorio Klostermann since 1928. When this publisher was closed following a period of financial difficulty, a reprinting of the first edition was published by the Gerhard Schulte-Bulmke Press of Frankfurt am Main. Since the publication of the second edition in 1951, the Kantbook, as Heidegger himself called it, has been published by the Vittorio Klostermann Press, which in 1929 had overseen the publishing of the first edition.

In editing this volume, the editor consulted the manuscript of "Kant and the Problem of Metaphysics." A comparison of the printed text of the fourth edition, which had been newly typeset after the publication of the third edition, and a comparison of the second edition with the first, showed that with the resetting of the second edition in 1951, apart from a few spelling or notational mistakes that had simply been corrected without comment, four serious errors had been allowed to creep in as well. On page 28 the word "vorstelliger" replaces "vorstellig"; on page 159 "Selbst" replaces "Seins"; on page 185 the omitted phrase "daß dieses jetzt anwesende Seiende dasselbe sei, wie das" has been put back; on page 197 "ursprünglicheren" replaces "ursprünglichen."

As was the case with volumes 1, 2, 4, 5, 9, and 12 of the first section [of Heidegger's Collected Works] that have been published to date, so too this volume 3 contains Heidegger's marginalia from his personal copy of the first edition. His personal copies of the later editions do not have any marginalia. The placement of the marginalia results from Heidegger's own reference marks. In print, they are designated in footnotes with superscripted small letters, in a sequence that begins again with each numbered section. The majority of the longer or shorter marginal notes were written in ink, with the rest done in pencil. Several of the longer marginalia were written by Heidegger on inserted slips of paper with a page or section reference. Many of the marginalia date from the time when the reviews of the Kantbook by Ernst Cassirer (1931) and Rudolf Odebrecht (1931/32) appeared. Most of these marginalia have an immanent explanatory character; only a few of them make note of the later level of consideration pertaining to the history of Being. Several entries are also merely small stylistic improvements.

*

The Appendix to the fourth edition of 1973, which contained two texts, has here been expanded to include four additional pieces. It now begins with the new *Notes on the Kantbook* which Heidegger had inserted in his personal copy of the first edition. The note which was reproduced in facsimile form and transcribed as part of the foreword to the fourth edition [and which is found on page xii of the Gesamtausgabe edition—tr.] belongs to this same piece. An analysis of both the writing and content show it to date from the 1930s or 1940s.

The second piece is Heidegger's *Review of Ernst Cassirer's Philosophy of Symbolic Forms*, Part 2: *Mythical Thinking* (1925), which has not appeared in print since it was first published in the *Deutsche Literaturzeitung* in 1928. The published text was proofread against the manuscript found in Heidegger's surviving papers—a careful clean copy. A reprint of this piece is among the insertions in Heidegger's personal copy of the Kantbook.

The third place belongs to the summary, first published in the fourth edition and overseen by Heidegger himself, of his 1929 course at the second Davos Hochschule (March 17–April 6, 1929). This course consisted of three lectures on *Kant's Critique of Pure Reason and the Task of a Laying of the Ground for Metaphysics* and is reprinted anew here. There is no manuscript of this summary or of the three lectures themselves in Heidegger's surviving papers. The division of the three lectures mentioned in the summary shows that it arises from the division of the first three of the four total sections of the Kantbook. In the three Davos lectures, Heidegger carried forward the train of thought from the first three sections of the Kantbook, which appeared at the end of that same year. During the proofreading of the fourth edition of 1973, he informed the editor of the present volume that following his return from Davos, he immediately began working out the manuscript for the Kantbook and that after three weeks of uninterrupted work he had set it down in writing.

The next piece, which appeared previously in the fourth edition, is a summary of the Davos lectures, the account of the *Davos Disputation between Ernst Cassirer and Martin Heidegger*. This disputation occurred in connection with a course of lectures held by Heidegger and Cassirer. Otto Friedrich Bollnow and Joachim Ritter, who were participants in the lecture course at the Davos Hochschule, prepared the summary. Because Heidegger did not have his own typewritten copy on hand during the time that the fourth edition was being prepared, Professor Otto Friedrich Bollnow graciously furnished his own copy for use as the book was being typeset. Since that time, however, Heidegger's own copy has been located among his surviving papers. As a result of a new comparison of the typewritten text with the text as printed in the fourth edition, a few omissions have now been replaced.

Among the insertions in Heidegger's personal copy of the first edition of the Kantbook is also an envelope bearing the handwritten inscription "Odebrecht's and Cassirer's Critique of the Kantbook. Basic question: Essence and grounding of the *finitude* of *human* knowledge — *Problem of finitude in general.*" The handwritten notes on the two reviews of the Kantbook (which appeared in 1931/32) contained in this envelope have been published in the Appendix [V in the present volume] under the title "On Odebrecht's and Cassirer's Critiques of the Kantbook." The *separata* of both reviews have also been inserted in [Heidegger's] personal copy. Some of them have been heavily worked through and supplied with numbered marginal notes, the content of which nevertheless continues to advance Heidegger's critical response to both reviews. They are also arranged with numbers which, however, are consistent with the marginal notes from [Heidegger's] personal copy of the Kantbook as printed in this volume. Ernst Cassirer's review, entitled "Kant and the Problem of Metaphysics: Remarks on Martin Heidegger's Kant Interpretation" appeared in *Kantstudien* XXXVI, number 1/2 (1931), pp. 1–26. Rudolf Odebrecht's book review was published in *Blätter für deutsche Philosophie* V(1) (1931–32), pp. 132–35.

The Appendices conclude with a reprinting of the text "On the History of the Chair in Philosophy since 1866," which Heidegger had published in 1927 in the *Festschrift* "Die Philipps-Universität zu Marburg 1527–1927." Because Heidegger presented in this text the origin, development, effect, and re-constitution of the neo-Kantianism of the "Marburg School," to which Ernst Cassirer also belonged, he decided that within the context of a Collected Edition of his writings, it should be included in the Appendix to the Kantbook.

****

The transcription of the marginal notations and the various other pieces published for the first time in the Appendix was collated with Dr. Hermann Heidegger and Dr. Hartmut Tietjen. For this help in safeguarding lexical and textual continuity, I offer my sincere and heartfelt thanks.

Dr. Hans-Helmuth Gander helped me do the proofreading with proven circumspection and care, for which I also sincerely thank him.

Freiburg i. Br., May 1990

F.-W. von Herrmann

The page numbers from the lecture manuscripts, to which Heidegger occasionally refers in his marginal notes, were replaced by the editor with the corresponding page numbers from the published versions that have appeared in the Gesamtausgabe in the interim. Likewise, references in Heidegger's notations to editions, years, and page numbers of the work *Vom Wesen des Grundes* have been brought up to date.

TRANSLATOR'S NOTES

Prefaces

1. This lecture course has been published as volume 25 of Heidegger's *Gesamtausgabe* under the title *Phänomenologische Interpretation von Kants Kritik der Reinen Vernunft*, ed. I. Gland (Frankfurt a. M., 1977).
2. *wenngleich sie bedingende Fragestellung untergelegt wurde.*
3. See translator's note 1 to the preface to the fourth edition for more on this lecture course.
4. Heidegger's initial plan for *Being and Time* called for an Introduction, followed by two main parts ("Part One" and "Part Two"). Each of these two parts, in turn, was to consist of three divisions. The published version as we know it consists of just the Introduction and the first two divisions of Part One. The third division of Part One and all three divisions of Part Two were never published, although Heidegger's attempts to work through the problems he planned to treat in these missing sections can be seen in some of his lectures immediately before and after *Being and Time* appeared. Heidegger's occasional references to the "first half" of *Being and Time*, then, refer to the first half of his total plan for the book, or for the whole of what we know as *Being and Time* plus the missing third division of Part One. It was not until the seventh edition of that book (1953) that Heidegger stopped referring to the published part as the "first half."
5. Part Two was to consist of a division devoted to each of the following: Kant's Schematism and doctrine of time; Descartes's *Cogito sum*; and Aristotle's treatises on time (See *Sein und Zeit*, pp. 39–40). Although Heidegger suggests here that Part Two was written, it never appeared.
6. This essay appears in the anthology *Wegmarken, Gesamtausgabe*, vol. 9 (Frankfurt, 1976).
7. The first essay appears in English as "Kant's Thesis about Being," trans. T. Klein and W. Pohl, *Southwestern Journal of Philosophy*, 4, 1973, pp. 7–33. The second work appears as *What Is a Thing?*, trans. W. B. Barton and V. Deutsch (South Bend, 1967).

Part One

1. *Seienden als Seienden.*
2. *Gegenstand.* Kant makes an important distinction between *Gegenstand* and *Objekt*, which Heidegger preserves and which is almost impossible to carry over into English. For Kant, a *Gegenstand* is a thing in space and time that is encounterable by the senses, while an *Objekt* is an object of thought—Space and Time are themselves *Objekt*. To preserve this distinction, *Gegenstand* and *Objekt* will be rendered as object and Object respectively. If either word appears at the beginning of a sentence, the German word will be given in brackets or in a note. The reader should also note that it is only a perceivable object, a *Gegenstand*, which can "stand in opposition to" (*entgegenstehen*) a being. Heidegger makes a great deal of this word play at various points throughout the book, and the etymological connection to *Gegenstand* should be kept in mind.
3. *des "Allgemeinen" am Seienden.*
4. *Erkenntnistheorie*, often translated as "epistemology." I have rendered this term literally wherever it occurs in the text.

Part Two

1. Translating *vorstelliger* (more representable) as found in GA and in the second edition. The fourth edition reads *vorstellig*, which was translated as "representable" in the previous edition of this translation.
2. Literally, "representation by means of common signs or marks."
3. This quotation from Kant was cited as "'representation (concept) of a representation' (intuition)" in the second edition, thus giving the false impression that the word "concept" (*Begriff*) is part of Kant's text rather than an insertion by Heidegger. This oversight was corrected in the fourth and GA editions when *Begriff* (concept) was placed within brackets, which I have rendered as braces.
4. *die wahr- (offenbar-) machende, veritative Synthesis.*
5. *einer "ursprünglichen [entspringenlassenden] Anschauung."* The expression *ursprünglichen Anschauung* (original intuition) is Kant's. In the second edition the term *entspringenlassenden* was in parentheses, thus giving the false impression that it too is Kant's term. This misunderstanding was corrected in the fourth and GA editions when the term was enclosed in brackets, which I have rendered as braces.
6. A more literal translation might be "the peculiar setting-in-front-of of thinking reveals itself," but I have used "re-presenting" for the sake of consistency.

In this paragraph Heidegger is clearly playing with several words that share the root *stellen*, but it is impossible to render all of them into good English.

7. *als Entstehendes im Entstehenlassen, d.h. als Ent-stand offenbar.*

8. See translator's note 2 to Part One above.

9. To make the distinction between *Entstand* (standing-forth) and *Gegenstand* (object) clearer, we could render the latter more literally as "standing-against," in the sense that a perceivable object stands out against the human being as something radically other.

10. In this paragraph Heidegger is playing the two words *Quellgrund* (ground for the source) and *Grundquellen* (basic sources) off each other in a way that is lost in translation. What is at issue here is Heidegger's attempt to get beneath what Kant took to be the basic sources of human knowledge and to establish the ground for those sources. This should not be seen as simple wordplay, however. Heidegger's point seems to be to show graphically how a hitherto unseen problematic (i.e., the problem of the ground of human knowledge) can be found nested or concealed within the very terminology of conventionally accepted metaphysics. Thus, by playing with that terminology he wants to expose a radical, hitherto unexplored problematic within the very fabric of conventional metaphysics, i.e., within the very language of that metaphysics.

11. *die Anzeige des Quellgrundes der Grundquellen der endlichen Erkenntnis.* Alternative translation: The indications concerning the ground for the basic sources of finite knowledge . . . . While less awkward, this version obscures the word *Quellgrund* and hence the radical nature of the ground being discussed here.

12. *Innerzeitigkeit.* See *Sein und Zeit*, §§80–81.

13. The distinction here and in the next paragraph between *Wasgehalt* and *Inhalt*, both of which can be translated as "content," is, in effect, the distinction between content in the sense of the *capacity* of something (*Inhalt*) and content in the sense of that which determines *what* something is (*Wasgehalt*). In Kant's terminology, *Inhalt* is a priori while *Wasgehalt* is empirical.

14. For more on this distinction see my comment to Heidegger's footnote 33.

15. *Die veritative Synthesis ist dann das, was sich nicht nur in diese Fugen, die Elemente zusammenfügend, einfügt, sondern diese Fugen allererst "fügt."*

16. *Kant . . . die allgemeinen Kenntnisse über das Denken überhaupt . . . beiziehen muß.* Following previous conventions for translating verbs with the prefix *bei-*, I have translated the unusual verb *beiziehen* as "to draw-[something]-along-with-it." In this passage it suggests that Kant must draw this universal knowledge of thinking in general into his problematic along with his primary orientation toward the element of thought.

17. The term rendered "to stand in opposition to" is *entgegenstehen*. It normally means "to be in marked contrast," but is here being rendered literally because of the importance of the notion of "standing-against" in the following discus-

sions. Its etymological connection to the term *Gegenstand* (perceivable object) should also be kept in mind—an object is something which stands out against a thinking I as something other.

18. *einer entgegenstehenlassenden Zuwendung-zu.*

19. *Objekt.* See translator's note 2 to Part One above.

20. *Das Gegenständliche der Gegenstände* might be rendered "That which stands against in objects . . . " in light of the dynamic opposition of Being which Heidegger is suggesting constitutes objectivity in a fundamental way. Thus, he is exploiting a double meaning in terms like *Gegenstand, Widerstand,* and *Gegenstehenlassen* that does not always come through in translation.

21. *die zergliedernde Enthüllung,* literally the unveiling which takes to pieces or dissects.

22. *"ich vermag,"* literally "I have the power." There is, thus, an etymological connection to the reference to apperception as a power (*Vermögen*) that follows.

23. *vor-stellen.* This might also be rendered "pre-present."

24. *vor-stellen,* might also be rendered "re-present," but here it seems to suggest the idea of presenting in advance.

25. The words enclosed in braces in this passage were added by Heidegger for emphasis. But, there are several different versions of this crucial passage:

Erdmann: *"das Mannigfaltige der Anschauung einerseits, mit der Bedingung. . . ."*

Riehl: *"das Mannigfaltige der Anschauung und der Zeit einerseits und mit der Bedingung. . . ."*

Schmidt: *"das Mannigfaltige der Anschauung einerseits, und mit der Bedingung. . . ."*

Heidegger: *"das Mannigfaltige der Anschauung einerseits [in Verbindung], und [dieses] mit der Bedingung. . . ."*

Kemp Smith follows Erdmann: "the manifold of intuition on the one side, into connection with the condition. . . ."

I have rendered Heidegger's version as closely as possible in my translation. Contrary to Heidegger's suggestion, Erdmann and Riehl do not render the passage in the same way and merely delete an "and." In fact, Riehl does not delete the "and" at all.

26. *begründete Befugnis,* which might also be rendered somewhat awkwardly as "grounding authority."

27. *Wasgehalt.* See translator's note 13 to Part Two above.

28. *des Seienden als eines Gegenstandes (Objektes)?* See translator's note 2 to Part One on this distinction.

29. *Anblick.* This word refers to the overall look that something has.

30. *von der Einbildungskraft ("Imagination").*

31. *abbildender Anblick eines Vorhandenen (Abbild).*

32. *bzw. nachbildender Anblick . . . oder aber vorbildender Anblick.*

33. *ein Nachbild* (*Photographie*). Heidegger is distinguishing between *Nachbild* ("copy," literally "after-image") and *Abbild* ("likeness," literally "image from").
34. *das So-wie . . . ein Haus aussehen kann.* The construction *so . . . wie* would normally occur in an expression like *So groß wie ein Haus*, or "As large as a house." Heidegger's point is that in our experience of "house," it always appears *as* a particular house, but not necessarily as any *one specific* house.
35. *Dieses Wie des empirischen Aussehenkönnens.*
36. *Zusammenhang.* The term refers to the whole interconnected complex of possible meanings associated with a term like "house," as discussed in the previous paragraph.
37. *bildet sich schon die Bildmöglichkeit.*
38. This term would normally be rendered "re-presenting," but in light of the context and his discussion of *Vorblick* (premonition), it is clear that Heidegger wants to emphasize how this happens in advance of experience. This way of translating *Vor-stellung* was suggested to me in another context by Joseph Fell.
39. *wenn anders das, was im reinen Gegenstehenlassen entgegensteht, als ein Dawider soll vernehmlich sein können.*
40. Heidegger gives this subheading as it is found in the first edition of the *Critique:* "*Grundsatz der Beharrlichkeit.*" In the second edition, Kant modifies it to read "*Grundsatz der Beharrlichkeit der Substanz*" (translated by Kemp Smith as "Principle of Permanence of Substance"). I have translated Heidegger's text as he wrote it.
41. In his fourth edition, as well as in the new GA and fifth editions, Heidegger mistakenly cites p. A 143 (he cited it correctly in earlier editions), and Kemp Smith's translation also has the page number A 144 marked incorrectly. The Schmidt edition of the *Kritik* in German (Meiner, 1956) has the correct pagination, as verified against a copy of the actual first edition (courtesy of Dr. F. Hogemann at the Hegel-Archiv in Bochum, West Germany).
42. *im Dasein*" (*d.h. Vorhandensein*). Heidegger has added *Vorhandensein* to clarify *Dasein*, but the term Kant himself uses here is *Substanz*. Kant's phrasing reads "*im Dasein, d.i. die Substanz.*"
43. *das rein sich Gebende.*
44. *Einhalt,* or "check" in the sense of checking or slowing one's progress.
45. *das "Dawider" der Gegenständlichkeit.*
46. The second edition of Heidegger's book contained several pagination errors throughout the following outline, but all were corrected in the fourth edition. All references given here have been verified against the Schmidt edition (Meiner Verlag, 1976).
47. This is mistakenly cited as A 154, B 186 in the fourth edition, although it was given correctly in the second edition.
48. Reading "*bloß mit Vorstellungen gespielt*" *hat* (Heidegger's fourth edition) rather than "*bloß mit Vorstellungen spielen*" *kann* (second edition).
49. Schmidt and Heidegger read "*Es ist nur ein Inbegriff . . .* ," although Kemp

Smith translates a variant by Mellin which reads "*Es gibt nur ein Inbegriff. . . .*" Kemp Smith's translation of this sentence thus begins "There is only one. . . ."
50. *Diese "Möglichkeit," die das "möglicherweise" allererst ermöglicht, ist die possibilitas.*
51. Following the fourth edition where Heidegger does not include the words "Definitions of the real are taken" as part of the quotation (they were included in the second edition). Similarly with the word "serve" in the next sentence.
52. In the sense of with what is it in accordance.
53. *Grundsatz*, literally a "grounding proposition," although it is commonly translated as "principle." See, however, the next sentence in which Heidegger distinguishes between *Grundsatz* and *Prinzip*.
54. The contrast here is between standing forth (*Entstand*) and standing against or standing in opposition to (*Gegenstand*).
55. Reading *unseren Begriff* with Andickes, Kemp-Smith, and Heidegger's second edition. Schmidt's edition of the *Critique* and Heidegger's fourth edition have *unsere Begriffe* (our concepts).

Part Three

1. *den Quellgrund der "Grundquellen der Erkenntnis."*
2. *das Sichdenken, Ausdenken, Erdenken, sich Gedanken machen, Einfälle haben und dergleichen.*
3. *die "Bildungskraft,"* as opposed to power of imagination (*die Einbildungskraft*), formative power (*die bildende Kraft*), to form (*bilden*), and image or form (*das Bild*).
4. *das Vermögen des Witzes: Witz* can be meant either in the sense of "keeping your wits about you" or in the sense of "being witty"; presumably, Kant has the former in mind.
5. "*Gegenwart eines Gegenstandes.*" In this paragraph, Heidegger uses both the word *Anwesenheit* (presence) and *Gegenwart*, which usually means the present as opposed to the past and future. In this phrase, however, *Gegenwart* seems to suggest something more like the presence now, or the present presence, of something.
6. *darstellend*, which means pictorial, in the sense of pictorial art, or descriptive. It is also related to the words *darstellen*, translated throughout as the verb "to present," and *Darstellung* (presentation).
7. "*vermag.*" This is a form of the verb *vermögen* (to have the ability to do something), which is obviously related to the noun *Vermögen*, rendered here as "faculty." This connection is lost in translation.
8. "*Grundvermögen.*" This could also be rendered "basic faculty"; see note 7 above.

9. Heidegger actually edited Kant's words somewhat. Kant writes: *"einer blinden, obgleich unentbehrlichen Funktion der Seele"* ("a blind although indispensable function of the soul"), p. A 78, B 103.

10. Although Heidegger gives no page reference, these two short quotes apparently come from p. A 155, B 194. The full sentence reads: "Herein, therefore, exists the possibility for synthetic judgments, and therein are contained all three of the sources of representations a priori." The "herein" refers to inner sense, the power of imagination, and the unity of apperception.

11. *Angeborensein.* This word has the same peculiar form as *Vorhandensein* (Being-at-hand), and, accordingly, it might be rendered literally as "Being-innate."

12. *die von sich aus Anblicke (Bilder) bildend gibt.*

13. *muß . . . die Einheit erblicken.*

14. As the root of "synthesis" and "synopsis," "syn" means "togetherness."

15. *reine Imagination.* Here Heidegger employs a third term for imagination rather than his usual *Einbildungskraft* (power of imagination) or *Einbildung* (imagination).

16. *Dieses sein Angewiesensein ist das Verstandsein des Verstandes.*

17. *Vorstellen.* This word would normally be translated as "representing," except for the obvious reference to the peculiar term *Vor-stellen* in the preceding paragraph.

18. *In solcher Weise "begleitet" das "ich stelle vor" alles Vorstellen.*

19. *als bindende in ihrer Verbindlichkeit.*

20. *im Entgegenstehen des gegenständlichen Horizontes.*

21. *"erschlossen."* See *Sein und Zeit*, §16, p. 75; also *Being and Time*, translator's note 1, pp. 105–6. In this section of *SZ*, Heidegger discusses how something at hand in our surroundings is always already there, or in the "there," before anyone has expressly ascertained it. Such a thing, he says, remains inaccessible (*unzugänglich*) *to* circumspection, but at the same time it is already disclosed (*erschlossen*) *for* circumspection. He then likens his technical term *erschliessen* to the term *aufschliessen*, meaning literally "to lay open," and he contrasts both of these with the notion of "obtaining something mediately through an inference." Similarly in the case of the present passage: to disclose the origin of practical reason, what is required is not argumentation, but expressly unveiling the essence of the practical self.

22. *eine Weise des Selbstbewußtseins darstellen.*

23. *nach der sittlichen Tat.*

24. "Selbst" replaces "Sein" in the fifth and GA editions.

25. The etymological connection between *unterwerfen* (to submit, literally to throw under) and *entwerfen* (to project, literally to throw from) is lost in translation. At the root of both words is the verb *werfen*, to throw.

26. For the importance of the *Objekt/Gegenstand* distinction see translator's note 2 to Part One above.

27. Italics added in fourth edition.

28. *sein Soeben und Sogleich.*

29. *diesen . . . Charakter des Bildens im Einbilden der Einbildungskraft.*

30. *am anwesenden (gegenwärtigen) Gegenstand.* The double sense of presence suggested here is the sense in which the object (*Gegenstand*) is present before us (*anwesenden*) at the present time (*im Gegenwart*).

31. *dem Angebot der Eindrücke je einen Anblick (Bild).*

32. *in seiender Einheit.* The term *seiender* is an adjectival form of the verb *sein*, to be, so it has the sense here of a "new" unity which is in a more immediate sense—a unity with more existence, in a sense, because it is now rather than in the past.

33. *ein hölzernes Eisen*; literally an iron which is wooden.

34. *dieses "Nach" als solches "bildet."* The play on the etymology of the word *Nachbildung* (reproduction), literally forming something after the model of something else, does not come across in the translation.

35. The phrase "that this being . . . the same as that which" was added in the GA edition.

36. *ein Unbegriff.* A more colloquial translation might read "remain simply incomprehensible?"

37. *das "von-sich-aus-hin-zu-auf."*

38. *das Worauf-zu.*

39. *"ich stelle vor."* The connection between *stelle vor* and the verb to represent (*vorstellen*) is lost in translation.

40. *Stand und Bestand.* Both terms are related to the verb *stehen* and its various forms, which I have translated as "fixed" or "to fix," as in to fix something in place or to fix something a certain way.

41. *der Zeitform.* This term has the colloquial meaning "tense," as in the tense of a verb.

42. *der Weg zum ursprünglichen Quellgrund der beiden Grundquellen.*

43. Reading *ursprünglicheren* as in the GA edition, rather than *ursprünglichen* as in previous editions.

44. A 98ff.

45. Heidegger is contrasting two terms in this sentence, *Interpretation* and *Auslegung*, both of which would normally be translated as "interpretation." The difference is that while *Interpretation* is concerned merely with what is stated explicitly, *Auslegung* is concerned with bringing out what has remained unsaid in any explicit sense, what has been concealed in the course of the history of metaphysics. Thus, for example, it is only *Auslegung* and never *Interpretation* that could bring to light something like the Question of Being (the *Seinsfrage*) in *Being and Time*. These concepts receive considerable treatment in *Being and Time*. The notion of what remains unsaid in traditional metaphysical texts becomes increasingly important in the later works by Heidegger, particularly in many essays on poetry and language. As an example, consider his discus-

sion of Parmenides in Part II of *Was heißt Denken?* (*What Is Called Thinking?*). This same idea is also behind such key Heideggerian notions as *Wiederholung* (retrieval) and *Destruktion* (destruction, as in destruction of the history of metaphysics).

Part Four

1. *Wiederholung* is often translated as "repetition." Its literal sense, however, implies going back to get something again—something we had once but left behind. The "something" Heidegger is searching for is the unsaid, ultimately the *Seinsfrage*. In this context no mere replay of the same theme is called for, since in a mere replay of the Western tradition the unsaid would again be concealed. Heidegger's *Wiederholung* is a retrieval which serves as the basis for a re-thinking.

2. The etymological connection between the last two auxiliary verbs in the preceding sentence, "can and should" (*kann und soll*), and the two nouns that begin this sentence, "abilities and obligations" (*Sein Können und Sollen*), is lost in translation.

3. What is at issue in this paragraph, which does not come across completely in translation, is the distinction between knowledge *about* human beings (in which our time is rich) and knowledge of the *Being* of human beings (in which our time is impoverished). In effect, this is the distinction between ontic and ontological knowledge from *Sein und Zeit*. See §4, esp. pp. 12–15.

4. *ein Können, Sollen, und Dürfen*. Although lost somewhat in translation, these are the verbs from the three questions ("can," "should," "may") respectively, but now in noun form.

5. Cf. *Sein und Zeit*, §40ff. for a more complete discussion of "Care" (*Sorge*).

6. "*Daß-seins*."

7. *Feuer ist ausgebrochen*. The "is" (*ist*), the auxiliary verb in the past tense of this German verb, does not carry over into English.

8. *Existenz*, one of the *existentialia* of Dasein. See *Being and Time*.

9. The words *seinlassen könnte* are emphasized by being printed in spaced type. For more on the concepts of thrownness, falling, and projection see *Sein und Zeit*, esp. §38.

10. *das existierende Seiende*, namely, *Dasein*; see note 8 above.

11. *Da* as in *Da-sein*, which is sometimes translated "there-Being" or "Being-there" to emphasize the peculiar character of Dasein's existence as always Being-out-there-ahead-of-itself. See *Being and Time*.

12. *für ein Selbst*. Presumably the "self" to which Heidegger is referring, and to which the being in question can show itself, is Dasein in its world.

13. *der Grundfrage der Grundlegung der Metaphysik*.

14. *Vergessenheit*. For more on this important notion see *Being and Time*, §§68–71, 79–80.

15. *der fundamentalontologische Grundakt*.

16. This difference between Being and beings is usually called the Ontological Difference and features prominently throughout Heidegger's work. See, for example, the introduction to *Being and Time*.

17. *der Befindlichkeit und Geworfenheit des Daseins*. The two terms "disposition" (*Befindlichkeit*) and "thrownness" (*Geworfenheit*) again play a central role in *Being and Time*, as does the term "falling" (*Verfallen*) used later in this paragraph. For an overview of these important terms see *Being and Time*, §§28, 29, and 38.

18. *sich in das Nichts hineinhält*. See *Sein und Zeit*, §§40, 46–53. See also the essay "Was ist Metaphysik" ("What Is Metaphysics").

19. *Sichbefinden*, translated here as "to find oneself," is closely related to *Befindlichkeit*, usually rendered as "disposition." While lost in translation, the connection can be seen in the nature of Dasein's disposition with respect to beings in the world, since Dasein "finds itself" always already attuned to beings in this way or that.

20. The passage, at 244a, is spoken by the Stranger to Theatetus and reads: "For obviously you have long been aware of what you actually mean when you use the expression 'being'. We, however, who once believed we understood it, have now become perplexed." This translation, which is based on Heidegger's rendering of the Greek into German in *Sein und Zeit* (p. 1), differs somewhat from the way Cornford translates it. The main difference is the rendering of the word ὄν, the present participle of the verb "to be." Heidegger translates it into the German participle *seiend*, as do I with the English "being"; Cornford opts for "reality" [in *Plato: The Collected Dialogues*, ed. E. Hamilton and H. Cairns (Princeton, 1973), p. 987].

21. *Gigantomachie*, from Greek mythology, refers to the war of the Giants against Zeus. It has come to mean any war between gigantic powers. In this case the "Giants" are Plato and Aristotle.

22. *das Seiende, das so seiend ist, wie Seiendes nur seiend sein kann*.

23. The term *Anwesen* becomes important for Heidegger in the years immediately after the writing of this book, when it refers to the way a thing comes to presence or the way it comes to be present before us. Here the more colloquial sense seems to be appropriate, namely, the sense of an estate, a designation for the ensemble of property which is what we have to show for ourselves, as well as what persists and survives our passing.

24. Reading *beständige Anwesenheit* from the second edition, rather than *Anwesenkeit* from the fourth edition.

25. "And indeed the question which was raised of old and is raised now and always, and is always the subject of doubt, viz. what being is. . . ." From *The Basic Writings of Aristotle*, ed. R. McKeon, tr. W. D. Ross (New York, 1941).

Appendices

1. Heidegger has paraphrased Kant's words slightly.

2. In his English translation of *CPR*, Kemp Smith ignores the distinction between *Vergleichung* and *Komparation* (he translates both as "comparison"). Kant in fact does distinguish between the two terms, and it is this distinction that Heidegger emphasizes here.

3. The word in brackets appears in brackets in the German and presumably was added by Heidegger.

4. *Erkenntnistheoretiker*, literally theoretician of knowledge.

5. ἀεὶ can be translated as "forever" or "always."

6. Being which always is, presence.

7. Pos is apparently the Dutch scholar H. J. Pos, one of the participants in the Davos course. I am indebted to Prof. O. Pöggeler for his help with this identification.

8. The German terms of Heidegger are: *das Dasein, das Sein, das Ontische*. The German terms of Cassirer are: *das Funktionale im Geist, die Umwandlung des ursprünglichen Raumes in einen anderen*.

9. The words "relegated to a radical . . . Kant was pressed" were added by the editor in the GA edition.

10. *Was ist das Seiende?*

11. *die kopernikanische Wendung*. At B xxii, Kant actually uses somewhat stronger terms when he refers to *"eine gänzliche Revolution"* (a complete revolution), after the examples of the geometricians and natural scientists.

12. *eine Zugrundeliegende*.

13. The fourth edition reads "and now" instead of "only."

14. "that it is the first step . . . of philosophy" was added by the editor in the GA edition.